THE
Great
Lakes

AT TEN MILES AN HOUR

~~~~~~

THE
Great
Lakes

AT TEN MILES AN HOUR

ONE CYCLIST'S JOURNEY
ALONG THE SHORES OF THE INLAND SEAS

Thomas Shevory

UNIVERSITY OF MINNESOTA PRESS
Minneapolis · London

Published by the University of Minnesota Press
111 Third Avenue South, Suite 290
Minneapolis, MN 55401-2520
http://www.upress.umn.edu

A Cataloging-in-Publication record for this book is available from the Library of Congress.
ISBN 978-1-5179-0345-9 (pb)

Design by Chris Long/Mighty Media, Inc.

Printed in the United States of America on acid-free paper

The University of Minnesota is an equal-opportunity educator and employer.

22 21 20 19 18 17   10 9 8 7 6 5 4 3 2 1

I began to feel that myself plus the bicycle equaled myself plus the world, upon whose spinning wheel we must all learn to ride, or fall into the sluiceways of oblivion and despair.

—Francis E. Willard, 1895

Contents

Introduction

An Unexpected Idea

Oddly enough the genesis of this book, and the journey that it recounts, was sparked while I was sitting in my apartment in the capital city Ulan Bator, after nearly a year of teaching at the National University of Mongolia. It had been an exciting, exhausting, and productive year. The courses that I had taught had gone well, and I had established positive connections with my colleagues and a number of students. Although I hadn't mastered the Mongolian language, I'd made some inroads, and I had learned more than I ever would have imagined about the history and culture of central Asia. If you're like me, you never can tell what's kicking around in the back of your head until something reveals itself, unexpected, like a bolt out of the blue. And I was, somewhat improbably given my location, hit with an absolute compulsion to ride a bicycle around each of the Great Lakes.

Perhaps it didn't come completely from nowhere. Mongolia gets quite cold in the winter. Temperatures hover around minus ten degrees Fahrenheit for much of December, January, and February. At night it's not unusual, given Mongolia's very dry climate, for the temperature to drop to minus forty, the point at which Fahrenheit and Celsius temperatures are the same. As a result, I found means for temporary relief. Over my winter break, with the hope of getting some respite from the cold, I decided to bicycle from Chiang Mai, in northern Thailand, to the beaches in the south. Winter is Thailand's dry season, so the ride to Bangkok, through forests in the north and rice fields in the south, was warm and lovely, with spicy food, world-class archeological sites, and friendly people. Unfortunately, things took a turn for the worse as I was riding around Bangkok, as the bike that I had rented started to disintegrate underneath me. So, in spite of the fact that I returned to Mongolia earlier than anticipated and I never actually saw a beach, I didn't feel as though I had much to complain about.

Back in the cold Mongolian sunshine, I hatched a plan to cycle the coast of Vietnam in the summer before returning home to upstate New York. I completed this trip in June and July 2009. But even as I was contemplating it, I was wondering whether all the international travel was diverting me from treasures that might exist in my own backyard. Years previously, I had attended a lecture by a well-known environmentalist who had just published a well-regarded book on ecological protection in the United States. The genesis of her idea, she said, grew from an experience that she had in Ethiopia, where she had been studying human impacts on the Wari River. One day, a local person, whom she had gotten to know reasonably well, asked her if there were polluted rivers where she had lived in United States. When she answered affirmatively, the man asked her why she had traveled all the way to Ethiopia when her own river needed attention and protection. The remark hit her so deeply that she returned to her home in Illinois and began to study the impacts of chemical contamination on the Illinois River, its wildlife, and the people that lived in its watershed.

For a long time, especially when traveling abroad, I've had that story circulating somewhere in the back of my brain, and it was hitting me with particular force while sitting in my apartment in Mongolia on a cold, clear winter day. I have, of course, bicycled in the United States. But at some point, perhaps feeling it to be a little bit mundane and wanting to test my limits and maybe my courage, I started to explore more exotic places: Belize, Mexico, Iceland. Now it was occurring to me that I had been neglecting my own (metaphorical) river.

While I have done some traveling and lived abroad, I am actually pretty firmly rooted. I grew up in western New York, where my family has lived for generations, and I've spent most of my adult life living in central New York. But living in a place doesn't necessarily mean knowing a place, as in *really* knowing a place.

Until recently, for example, I knew virtually nothing about the geological substructures that define the physical features of the upstate New York region. It's easy for an American to view a place like Mongolia as a foreign territory and thus worthy of exploration and understanding. It may be more difficult to see your home turf as interesting in quite the same way. Familiarity may breed a certain contempt, and that contempt may be a form of blindness, a blindness to what is extraordinary in that which you take for granted. While sitting in my apartment in Mongolia, it occurred to me that one of the great natural wonders on planet Earth, the Great Lakes, was very close at hand—at least it would be when I returned home.

Of course, I'd had encounters with the lakes. I grew up twenty-five miles from Lake Erie and had traveled along its southern shore many times with my family, as a kid, on excursions to Buffalo. I've been to Chicago, Cleveland, Detroit, Milwaukee, Rochester, and Toronto, all of which are importantly defined by their relationship to one of the lakes. When I was in college, I hitchhiked out West, across the north shore of Lake Superior, and was amazed by its pristine beauty. And I'd previously cycled long sections of the Ontario shoreline.

The Great Lakes, in other words, were not unknown territory to me before I began these trips, but they still held a certain mystery. Some part of me was, it seemed, prodding some other part of me to establish a deeper connection, as it dawned on me that cycling along the shores of the lakes could be as fantastic an adventure as running the coast of Vietnam or the highlands of central Mexico. That idea, or emotional pull, was the genesis of the trips that I write about in this book. In the end, my hunch turned out to be right, and my hope is that I have captured here some sense of the geological, historical, and cultural wonder that is the Great Lakes region.

Bicycles have always been a part of my life. Growing up in the small city of Jamestown, New York, in the 1960s, owning a bicycle was a must. It was a primary means of transportation for me and most of my friends. For me, a bicycle was simply a practical necessity and a vehicle for escape. Bicycles were my main mode of transportation for most of my young adult life. I didn't own a reliable car until I was thirty years old, and mostly didn't feel the need for one.

My interest in bicycle touring began in summer 1989, when I received a phone call from Brenda, a former girlfriend. I was living in central New York, and she was in Iowa. She was encouraging me to meet up with her on the Iowa RAGBRAI: the *Des Moines Register*'s Annual Great Bicycle Ride Across Iowa. The ride had been started by one of the paper's columnists, Donald Kaul. The first time he went with a few friends, but word got out, and the event caught fire. To me, it seemed like a great opportunity to explore a state with which I had some familiarity and to ride a bicycle for a much longer distance than I'd ever attempted before. When I arrived, I joined fifteen thousand others. In the end, I didn't see much of Brenda, but I had a blast, and I was hooked.

About seventy-five miles from the Illinois border, I turned south to ride to the farmhouse of two old friends who lived near Iowa City, with the hope that one of them would drive me back to my car, which I'd left in the western part of the state. I found myself riding out on the highway alone in what seemed to be the middle of nowhere. Of course, I'd ridden on highways before but never so far from home and so completely removed from any support structure. It seemed somehow to be liberating, exhilarating, and even slightly forbidden. But there was nothing surreptitious about it. Cars, trucks, and even an occasional state trooper passed by me without paying much attention. The farther I traveled, the more confident and happy I felt. Here I was out on a highway, completely free to go wherever I decided to go at my own pace. I could, I realized, do this anywhere.

The next year, I hopped on my old Fuji, loaded up with a tent, a sleeping bag, and a few clothes, and rode from my home in Ithaca to the Canadian border at the northern edge of New York. About ten miles outside of town, clouds darkened, and a storm streaked through, packing a small tornado. I sheltered as best I could under a counter of an abandoned ice cream stand. I was pelted with hail and completely soaked. It was a little frightening but also fun. Riding a bicycle out in the world can make you vulnerable, but that turns out to be one of its key attractions. The weather was warm and sunny for the rest of the ride, which took me along the southeastern edge of Lake Ontario, my first encounter with one of the Great Lakes on a bicycle. Once I reached my goal to the north, I turned around and rode back. By the end of the trip, I'd traveled several hundred miles.

The next year I had accumulated enough frequent flyer miles from a major airline to procure a domestic ticket to practically anywhere in the United States. I would use it to take my bicycle to the farthest city that I could find on the map where that particular airline traveled. That turned out to be Portland, Oregon. I took my bike to the Tompkins County Airport, pulled the seat out, removed the pedals, turned the handlebars, and gave it to the service attendant. She wheeled it off to the baggage area. No box. No charge. I carried the pedals and other gear, along with my helmet, onto the plane. When I arrived in Portland, I was directed to a large roll-up door that was the drop-off point for oversized luggage. After a short wait, the door opened up, and there was my bike. It seemed magical.

It took me only a few minutes to put the bike together, which I did near the front of the terminal entrance. I noticed right away that I drew attention. People wanted to know where I was from and where I was going. They seemed to get a kick out my putting my bike together, first putting the seat back on and then the pedals. The security guard gave me directions for the best ride out of town, to avoid traffic and the city's somewhat sketchy red-light district. I rode off through Portland on marked bicycle paths (which I had never encountered before) and then out along the Columbia River. Astoria is at the confluence of the river and the Pacific Ocean. It was cool and windy and wild. I was completely enthralled. I turned south and rode along the coast. Oregon's coast is spectacular, but it is also quite hilly, if not downright mountainous. I enjoyed the challenge of riding this kind of terrain. Also, I discovered there were quite a few other people riding the same path. One woman I cycled with for a while told me she'd bicycled around Africa. A guy from Canada said he'd circumnavigated the United States on a bicycle and met the woman he married on the trip. He showed me a guidebook that someone had written for cyclists riding the coast. It gave mile-by-mile descriptions of the route. The author had ridden from the southern to northern U.S. borders. His first words of advice were to travel north to south to avoid the headwind. The very idea that someone had written a book about doing this I found to be slightly mind-boggling.

I met two younger guys from Holland. They had been to Idaho, put their bikes on a bus, and brought them to Oregon for another leg of their U.S. tour. I had originally planned to ride to southern Oregon and then ride back north, perhaps through the interior. But the Dutch guys explained to me that I could have my bike shipped home from a bicycle shop for around forty dollars. If I did that, I could ride farther south. In fact, they suggested that I ride to San Francisco. The rock singer Sammy Hagar had a bicycle shop on the northern edge of the city, and it would be an ideal place from which to ship my bike. Their enthusiasm was contagious. After all, we were talking about San Francisco and *Sammy Hagar*. Unfortunately, I never made it that far, because I couldn't get my frequent flyer ticket changed, and my time ran out. So I never got to meet Sammy Hagar, but I did make it to northern California, cycled through a stand of redwoods, sat in a park in Eureka watching guys play hacky sack, and felt like I'd entered a new world that I had been waiting to discover my entire life.

In 1995, I spent a year teaching in Moldova, a former republic of the USSR. Moldova was very isolated, and it had experienced a nearly complete economic collapse after declaring independence from the Soviet Union. There were no tourists and very few foreign nationals. But the Soros Foundation was quite active and sponsored a Friday afternoon English language club featuring different events. At one of them, a couple who ran the local Peace Corps gave a slide show consisting of dozens of photos they had taken while riding bicycles around the world for five years in the 1980s. The audience, mostly university students, was awestruck not just by the beautiful photos but the great stories that accompanied them. I was as well. The event reinforced my belief in the adventurous promises of bicycle touring.

For a period of time during my marriage, touring diminished to some extent—not that I am complaining. The two of us completed a trip to the Canadian Maritime Provinces, which was wonderful, but other things tended to occupy our time, such as her attending law school and starting a new career. But when we amicably split up, I turned back to bicycle touring to help fill the void I was experiencing. I traveled to Canada, Belize, and Iceland and biked the Baja Peninsula and central Mexico, all experiences that it seems in retrospect were somehow pushing me toward the Great Lakes.

The Great Lakes

Cycling across the Unites States, coast to coast, is fairly common practice and one with great appeal. Someday I would like to do it myself. But while working, I've never had the five or six weeks necessary to complete the trip. (That's how long it would probably take me, anyway.) One practical appeal of the Great Lakes in my case is that they can be attacked one at a time in bite-sized chunks of two- to three-week tours. And while a rider may not experience the dramatic vistas of the Rockies, Great Lakes terrain is surprisingly varied, from the flat ancient lake beds of Michigan's thumb to the rugged forested outcroppings of Lake Superior's north shore. The shorelines include cities as vibrant as Chicago, Toronto, and Duluth and as economically challenged as Toledo, Detroit, and Rochester. Having grown up in western New York, I had some basic knowledge of Great Lakes geography, but with Lake Erie being about twenty-five miles away, the lakes seemed slightly beyond my horizon, close enough to be accessible but distant enough to feel remote.

The historical importance of the Great Lakes region cannot be overstated. That history stretches back thousands of years. The first inhabitants of the region are thought to have arrived ten thousand years ago. They established flourishing communities, with tight social bonds and complex cultural systems, grounded in hunting, gathering, and agriculture. It is, of course, impossible to know how they might have evolved if left alone, but they weren't. And the lakes helped to facilitate European displacement and conquest. They provided easy access to western parts of North America by trappers, explorers, and colonizers, first the French and then the British. The lakes are part a complex web of interconnected North American waterways, which includes the Mississippi River and all its various tributaries on the eastern side of the continental divide. Significantly, from the mouth of the St. Lawrence River, it is possible to travel, with the exception of one ten-mile stretch, entirely by water to the Gulf of Mexico. And only a relatively short land bridge separates the southern shore of Superior from the Mississippi's headwaters.

Just as the lakes played a key role in European colonization, they were crucial to American economic development. It's no accident that many of the centers of American industrial production—Chicago, Detroit, Cleveland, and Buffalo—were located on Great Lakes shorelines. The lakes provided a convenient (if at times dangerous) route for hauling raw materials from the west to midwestern manufacturing centers. It's unlikely that the United States would have become the industrial powerhouse it became without the Great Lakes. American cultural imagery of the movement westward often conjures Conestoga wagons trundling across the Great Plains. And while the movement over land was essential to westward expansion, what became the western territories were first traversed and explored in the north starting within the Great Lakes watershed and then moving to points west, north, and south.

The period of expansive industrialization in the lakes is now over, and there is little, if any, expectation that it will ever return. But its legacies are still omnipresent in the region. For one thing, industrialization here and everywhere has been the handmaiden of environmental distress. And the Great Lakes region has a legacy of pollution and toxic contamination. The infamous Love Canal is located on the Niagara River between Lakes Erie and Ontario. Sarnia, Ontario, is one of the most polluted cities in Canada. Dozens of Superfund sites dot the borders of the lakes. The lakes themselves, while in some respects cleaner than they were at mid-twentieth century, still face numerous threats from contamination and invasive species.

The economic health of the region has also suffered in the past forty years. Deindustrialization has hit the region particularly hard, harder than in many parts of the country. The economic decline that began decades ago has not been reversed, and it is highly unlikely that industrial production on the scale that it once occurred will ever return again. But that doesn't mean that the region is in an irreversible downward spiral. Great Lakes cities like Duluth and Grand Marais are transforming themselves, often drawing on tourism, culture, and the arts as a way to spur new forms of economic development. Larger cities, like Buffalo, are also undergoing transformations with major investments in medical care and biotechnology. In economic terms, the Great Lakes region is a flash point between the old and the new. Nevertheless, the collisions of the environmental and industrial legacies are an aspect of the region's history that I find both fascinating and compelling, and it helped pull me into this journey.

Cycling the Great Lakes turned out to be a remarkable experience. I used the opportunity to read intensively about the human and natural histories of the areas that I cycled through so as to mitigate the impulse to experience and judge them in superficial terms. In my view, the knowledge gleaned from direct experiences and those mediated by the thoughts and writings of others are complementary. The individual body is by necessity limited in its sphere of immediate understanding. In other words, to chart your course, you need some guides, and I have had many of them along the way.

A Great Lakes Bicycle Tour Reading List

Ever since people have been riding bicycles, some cyclists have had the urge to ride them for long distances and to write about it. Thomas Stevens's *Around the World on a Bicycle*, now considered a classic of travel-adventure writing, recounts his journey circling the world in the early 1880s.[1] Stevens, riding a high-wheeled bicycle, was the first person we know to have made the trip. He started out in California with the intent of crossing the United States, but when he arrived at the East Coast, he decided to continue onward. His journey took him to western and southern Europe, on through Turkey and Persia, Afghanistan, India, and China. That he was able to complete such a trip on a single-geared bicycle (a black Columbia Standard cycle) on unpaved roads and trails, with virtually no possibility of finding a mechanic or replacement parts along the way, is to me as impressive as scaling Everest. Fortunately for him, Stevens didn't have to worry about his chain breaking (since there wasn't one) nor one of his hard rubber tires going flat, in the pre–pneumatic inner-tube era.

Stevens's mode of transport did not, of course, insulate him from patronizing and sometimes outright racist attitudes, which were probably common to the experience of many American travelers of the period, but he also at times expresses a surprising level of patience, openness, and cultural sensitivity, even when confronted by hostility from local people, who sometimes threatened violence against him. Frank Lenz, a well-known bicycle racer of the era, tried to repeat the feat several years later but disappeared in eastern Turkey, having been purportedly murdered by marauders in the twilight days of the Ottoman Empire.[2]

Since the early twentieth century, many additions to the cycling-around-the-world genre have been written, including former headmistress and historian Anne Mustoe's *A Bike Ride: 12,000 Miles around the World,* Frosty Wooldridge's *Bicycling around the World: Tire Tracks for Your Imagination,* and Barbara Savage's *Miles from Nowhere: A Round-the-World Bicycle Adventure.*[3] Josie Dew has traveled over eighty thousand miles by bicycle and has written a number of books about her trips to India, Japan, the United Kingdom, and the United States.[4] Dew is a gifted writer, and unlike many of her male counterparts, she does not see cycling as an existential test of masculinity but rather as a vehicle for social encounter.

I love Erika Warmbrunn's *Where the Pavement Ends: One*

Woman's Bicycle Trip through Mongolia, China, and Vietnam.[5] While the places that she traveled, the people that she met, and the landscapes that she experienced are certainly compelling, I was especially taken by the bike that she rode. Access any bicycle-touring website or blog, and an average cyclist may feel inundated by details about hardware: road versus touring or mountain bike, steel versus aluminum or titanium frames, wheel sizes, gear ratios, and passionate arguments about shifter types and disc versus rim brakes. As a nonspecialist but also someone who works on his own bikes, I find this sometimes helpful, but often as not a little over-whelming. Warmbrunn simply found an old used bike, painted it blue, by hand, and took off across the Mongolian countryside. And it turns out she did just fine.

Mark Jenkins's *Off the Map: Bicycling across Siberia* is a classic adventure story by a master of the trade.[6] Jenkins is one of the great modern travel writers, whose treks have included walking across Afghanistan, kayaking down the Niger, and climbing through ice caves in Greenland. His bicycle trip across eastern Russia was the first attempted by a non-Russian after the end of the Cold War, in 1989. As such he caught up close to the start of one of the most significant political and economic transitions of the late twentieth century. Plus, he had a great ride across some of the least populated large stretches of land left in the world. Andrew X. Pham's *Catfish and Mandala: A Two-Wheeled Voyage through the Landscape and Memory of Vietnam* follows his journey across the Vietnamese highlands.[7] I once rode the coast of Vietnam, but Pham gets far off into the countryside, visiting places that are ignored in the usual tourist itinerary. And given his Vietnamese heritage, the book is also one of personal self-discovery.

Of all of the bicycle-touring books that I have read, my favorite might be Dervla Murphy's *Full Tilt: Ireland to India with a Bicycle*. Murphy gives new meaning to the term *intrepid*. She left Ireland, by herself, the second week of January 1963. Why she left in winter is a mystery never explained, but as would probably be expected, she encountered some pretty harrowing weather: intense blizzards in the Balkans and then massive floods on their eastern edge as the snow began to melt. She fended off wolves in Bulgaria, faced down an attacker in Azerbaijan by firing her gun over his head, nearly died of thirst in the Hindu Kush mountains, and was treated with a mixture of wonderment, awe, disbelief, and respect all along the way. She became something of a local celebrity as word of her exploits preceded her. "Dervla going to India," people would acknowledge as she passed them walking along the road. As one reviewer put it, "This vivid journal . . . would have delighted Cervantes with its almost incredible surprises."[8] Nowadays, on tour, when things get a little rough, I think of Dervla Murphy and her courage and resilience. I ask myself, What would Dervla do? To put it simply, she is my hero.

There are numerous books about bicycling across the United States, so many, in fact, that to distinguish yourself you need an original approach. John Seigel Boettner followed twelve- and thirteen-year-olds who bicycled across America to test what they had been taught by their schoolteachers, in *Hey Mom, Can I Ride My Bike across America?*[9] T. E. Trimbath rode his bike diagonally from Washington State to Florida and recounts his travels in *Just Keep Pedaling: A Corner-to-Corner Bike Ride across America.*[10]

This list only scratches the surface. One website lists the sixty-two *best* books on bicycle touring, alluding to the fact that there are many others.[11] Adding books on ancillary topics, such as bicycle racing and the history of the bicycle as a mechanical object, would add significantly to the length of the list.[12]

For anyone that cycles, drives, or skateboards around the Great Lakes, there are some books that should be read in preparation for the journey. Jerry Dennis's *The Living Great Lakes: Searching for the Heart of the Inland Seas* should probably be at the top of the list.[13] Dennis, who grew up in Michigan and spent much of his life traveling around and thinking about the lakes, joined a small crew to take a tall ship, but via motor rather than sail, from Chicago, through Lakes Michigan, Huron, and Erie, the Erie Canal, and eventually up the Atlantic coast to Maine. Dennis recounts historical tales, like the sinking of the *Edmund Fitzgerald*, discusses the lakes' ecology, and provides unforgettable portraits of his crew. The book mixes adventure, history, personal insight, and science. It provides something of an aspirational model for my own effort here.

Mike Link and Kate Crowley walked around Lake Superior and wrote about it in *Going Full Circle: A 1555-Mile Walk around the World's Largest Lake*.[14] Link and Crowley are retired biologists, and their book is bursting with detailed scientific data about the natural history of the lake, the wildlife that populates the land, and the aquatic life in the lake itself. The book constitutes a kind of ecological travelogue, but it also recounts many encounters with a range of eccentric characters along the way.

For cyclists, Harvey Botzman's Cyclotour Series on the Great Lakes is a necessity.[15] Botzman offers guidebooks that give detailed mileage maps and list attractions, side trips, and places to stay. When I phoned Botzman to order one of the books, he was generous enough not only to send it, but to include a slew of maps and other information that he had gathered about Lakes Erie and Huron, the trips for which I was planning at the time. Along with the Botzman guides, any number of helpful postings can be found on the Crazy Guy on a Bike website, where cyclists of all different levels of experience and interest discuss recent trips, post photos, and recommend routes.

I have also consulted various books on the history, geology, geography, and economics of the Great Lakes. These are too numerous to mention, and many are included in the notes for the chapters that follow, but of special note is *The Great Lakes: The Natural History of a Changing Region*, which covers the geological history of the lakes, the forests, wildlife, aquatic life, invasive species, and other ecological threats.[16] The book includes excellent maps and stunning photographs. It offers the best overall introduction to the lakes from a naturalist's perspective of any book available, and I used it as a continual source of reference. More localized texts on Great Lakes geography and geology can also be helpful for understanding the physical and cultural forces that have shaped these regions.

And if you are going to travel in the Great Lakes region, you are going to need an atlas, and the one I would suggest is Helen Hornbeck Tanner and cartographer Miklos Pinther's *Atlas of Great Lakes Indian History,* which I found to be especially useful.[17] This is a very special kind of atlas, however. It's not just a road map. It tells the history of Native American settlements in the region for the four-hundred-year period from before Europeans arrived until the nearly complete displacement of indigenous people by the mid-nineteenth century. The thirty-three colored maps reference everything from the decimation of forests to the impacts of the Iroquois Wars and major disease outbreaks. Over the multiple years that I traveled through the region, I found myself returning to the *Atlas* again and again.

References to the War of 1812 are ubiquitous when traveling through the eastern parts of the Great Lakes region. Before I began my journey, probably like most Americans, I didn't know much about the war, other than uncertain recollections regarding the composition of the lyrics to the "Star Spangled Banner" and a dim memory of the battles of Lake Erie and New Orleans. The war is largely absent from the general American public's understanding and was hardly noticed (in the United States) during its recent bicentennial. Yet it was a significant event in the early years of the American republic.

Many historians consider the war to have been largely unnecessary. Entry into it divided the country along regional and party lines. It expanded American territory to the west at the expense of the Native people that lived there, often in violation of existing treaties. It alienated Canadians and reinforced their ties to the British Empire. It ended with no identifiable victor. In short, it was a fairly disastrous undertaking. Fortunately, there are a number of excellent historical accounts of the war, any one of which provides a comprehensive overview, and all of which are worth reading and helped inform my travels. These include Donald R. Hickey's *The War of 1812: A Forgotten Conflict,* Alan Taylor's *The Civil War of 1812,* Richard Buel's *America on the Brink: How the Political Struggle over the War of 1812 Almost Destroyed the Young Republic,* and Hugh Howard's *Mr. and Mrs. Madison's War.*[18]

Setting the Pace

I love encountering the world on a bicycle because I believe that it fosters an openness that can never be replicated by automobile travel. A bicycle encourages particular ways of touching, seeing, and thinking about the world. But it's also worth noting that there are many ways to encounter the world on a bike. I am not a racer, but I respect and appreciate those who have the discipline, stamina, and speed to do it. The Tour de France is the most famous bicycle race in the world. Winning it turns a competitor into an international celebrity. Cheating in it turns a competitor into an international pariah. While the Tour takes place in the Pyrenees, on the breathtakingly beautiful border of France and Spain, its primary purpose is obviously not geographical, historical, or aesthetic appreciation. In fact, anything that gets in the way of winning would be considered a fatal distraction. A less famous race is the RAAM, the Race Across America, which has taken place every year for three decades. It's not for the faint of heart. Participants must complete the course within twelve days even to be considered as an official finisher. To be awarded this recognition requires that a cyclist cover three thousand miles at a good clip, averaging four hours of sleep a night. Top contenders attempt to get by with as little as ninety minutes.[19]

The Tour and RAAM are at one end of a spectrum of long-distance riding. At the other end are tourers who travel as little as thirty-five to forty miles a day and who luxuriate in the time spent at various locations, talking to people, enjoying the food, seeing local sites, or just hanging out. I have met any number of folks like this on the tours that I have taken.

I find myself somewhere in the middle between these two approaches. One of the reasons I tour is that I enjoy the physical challenge. I simply love riding a bicycle over long distances. As I age, these tests of physical endurance seem to become ever more meaningful, perhaps as a denial mechanism in the face of mortality. I also like the direct experiences of wind and weather, so I'm inclined to ride in the rain and cold when necessary, and the heat as well. Endurance involves more than simply riding. It means riding when the conditions are difficult. At the same time, I enjoy experiencing the places that I visit. Not only do I have a researcher's interesting in knowing more, I also like good food, museums, brewpubs, and architecture. I have an interest in agricultural production and urban design. As a result, I seek to avoid simply breezing through the worlds that cycling opens up. I want to embrace and understand them. These competing desires are a recipe for ambivalence. I both want to push forward and slow down. This ongoing never-entirely-satisfactory balancing act pervades this book.

Touring by bicycle is by its very nature both expansive and limiting. You can certainly see more of the world driving through it by automobile. Cars allow a person to have time to spend in cities and towns and among people and places. A whole genre of traveling writing, from Jack Kerouac's *On the Road* to William Least Heat-Moon's *Blue Highways*, attests to the utility of automobile travel as a means to expand experience and understanding.[20] Robert Pirsig contended in *Zen and the Art of Motorcycle Maintenance* that cars remove one from experience, and he not only proposed a motorcycle as an alternative but also drew upon it as a metaphor to question the philosophical underpinnings that have shaped Western civilization.[21] But a motorcycle hardly seems like a radical departure from modernity.

Motorized transport does, however, entitle a traveler to cover a fair amount of ground quickly. And while the bicycle is clearly a modern technology, it shapes a different kind of experience, both expansive and limiting. That ten-mile side trip to catch a scenic waterfall becomes a two-hour slog on a hot day or in the rain, a large part of it perhaps uphill. This gives a traveler pause. Either because of time or exhaustion, you may miss something that you had intended to see. In fact, you miss a lot, only skating along certain surfaces. On the other hand, that which you experience while moving is taken in at a slower pace and is the result of physical effort, and those experiences are perhaps appreciated more because of that. Moreover, one of the advantages of cycling is that people often want to talk to you. This is especially true in the United States, where bicycle touring is less common than Europe and a tourer is more an object of curiosity. While you might not see as much as you do traveling by car, bicycling creates opportunities, often unexpected ones, that you would likely miss with motorized transport.

Each method of transportation is unique for discovering and understanding the worlds that we inhabit and traverse. Each has its advantages and weaknesses, its positive and negative attributes. Each opens opportunities that can be either embraced or ignored. Each creates gaps that can never be closed, because no region, locale, or landscape can ever be perceived and understood in its entirety. But as is consistently attested to by riders writing in the touring genre and is confirmed by my own experience, bicycling is never boring. Once experienced, it turns out, perhaps, to be exactly the place where most want to be, wherever that is at any given moment.

SAULT
STE. MARIE

MANITOULIN
ISLAND

CHEBOYGAN

LAKE
HURON

PORT
AUSTIN

POINT
FARMS
PROVINCIAL
PARK

SARNIA

Lake Huron

July 25, 2011

I decided upon Sarnia, Ontario, as the place to begin my trip around Lake Huron, primarily because it is the shortest drive from my home in central New York, and it is close to the U.S. border. Also, I discovered that it had a train station with a parking lot where I could leave my car, at no cost, "at my own risk." Ideal. The risks seemed minimal.

It's about a six-hour drive to Sarnia from Ithaca, across the New York State Thruway, over the Lewiston-Queenston Bridge into Canada. It's not exactly a picturesque drive, skirting the edges of Buffalo, St. Catherines, Hamilton, and Toronto, before turning west, until you get to the rural flatlands and rolling hills that separate Lake Erie from Huron and Georgian Bay to the north.

When I needed gas, the station's pumps would not take my credit card. I went to ask about the problem. "The machines won't take American cards," the clerk informed me. "You need to scan it inside." "Don't trust Americans, I see," I joked. She laughed. "I don't entirely blame you." The truth, as I later learned, is that Canadians have the same problem at American pumps. So much for NAFTA.

I arrived in Sarnia in the late afternoon, checked into a motel, and asked for directions to the train station. The clerk directed me to the other side of town. The ride over gave me a chance to check out the place. The city was deserted on a Sunday evening, as I drove by a leafy park running along the St. Clair River, part of the waterway system that connects Huron to Lake Erie. The river flows into shallow Lake St. Clair, which in turn empties into the

Detroit River, which once was one of the most polluted waterways in North America and still faces various ecological threats.

Unfortunately for the residents of Sarnia, a major east–west highway runs through the city's center, acting as an inconvenient and noisy divider between the northern and southern sides of town. Other than that, it's quite an attractive city, with active businesses and stable neighborhoods. With a population of just over seventy thousand, Sarnia is the largest city on Lake Huron. As a general rule, I like Canadian cities. One of the most striking aspects of my travels through the Great Lakes borderlands is that Canadian cities, in general, seem to be in better shape than American ones. You just don't see the boarded-up storefronts and distressed neighborhoods in Canada that are endemic to northern Ohio and eastern Michigan and New York's Ontario shoreline. Canadians seem to take care of their cities.

The French explorer La Salle named Sarnia "The Rapids," due to its location on the river. But oil defines Sarnia as much as water does. Nearby Oil Springs was the location of the first commercial oil drilling operation in the United States and Canada. An oil complex still operating along the river is legacy to this past and was apparently once featured on the back of the Canadian ten dollar bill.

Oil, of course, means chemicals, and Sarnia has a central place in what is known as Canada's "chemical alley." Although the chemical industry has declined here, there are still a number of facilities. As a result, Sarnia, while apparently prosperous, has the heaviest air pollution load of any city in Ontario. Each year, the twenty-three chemical plants nearby release a million kilograms of air pollutants. Sarnia (western tar sands operations excluded) is also one of the leading producers of greenhouse gases in Canada, representing 21 percent of Ontario's total emissions.

Bordering Sarnia is an Aamjiwnaang First Nation reserve, and the health of the residents there has been severely affected by all of the chemical pollution. Live births of males are nearly half of those of live females, the lowest ratio recorded anywhere on earth, and a consequence consistent with heavy exposure to chemical toxins. Miscarriage and stillborn rates are exceptionally high. And the problem isn't confined to First Nations populations. Sarnia residents have higher rates for cardiovascular and respiratory disease than their neighbors in London, Ontario.[1] Of course, you won't find this information on the Sarnia *Wikipedia* page or city website.

What you will find is that Michael Moore interviewed residents of the city for his 2002 film *Bowling for Columbine,* a film that compared gun violence in the United States to the lack of gun violence in Canada. Moore is from Flint, Michigan, so Sarnia was close and accessible enough to be a prime location for tracking down some Canadians. He later returned for more interviews for his 2007 film *Sicko,* which compared the Canadian system of public health insurance with the American private insurance system and was highly critical of the latter.

I found an ATM and decided to take out a fair amount of cash. Conflicts over the debt ceiling increase had been raging in the United States. I was a little worried that there might be a default. The dollar's collapse would make the Canadian part of this trip a lot more expensive.

I then found a Thai restaurant and ate as a violent rainstorm made its way through. It had rained heavily for much of the drive over. I was hoping that it would clear out a little. I don't mind riding in the rain, especially if it's a warm rain, but lightning makes me nervous.

July 26, 2011

The next morning I dropped my car off at the Sarnia train station about eight o'clock. There isn't much to it, just a small building with a waiting area and a ticket counter. The parking lot was virtually empty. I was just hoping the car would be there when I returned. I guessed that my old Volvo station wagon wouldn't be an attractive target for car thieves, and this didn't look like a high crime area. But you never know. I dropped my panniers onto their racks, bungeed my sleeping bag and tent onto the back rack, and headed out.

Fortunately, I spotted a bike shop as I was riding along the river to the bridge to cross to the United States. Somehow I'd forgotten my jersey and figured I'd pick up a new one. One of the guys at the store commented on my S & S couplers. I had them installed after I bought the bike, an old Gary Fisher, used. I discovered them in my quest to find a decent fold-up bike. The fold-ups intrigued me, but I was never entirely convinced one would meet my needs.

I chose the S & S route: a bike shop cuts your frame in half and installs metal couplers that can then be unscrewed to break the bike down, primarily (at least in my case) for airplane travel. I couldn't find a local shop that would do the work, so I shipped it to one in Philadelphia. The procedure cost around $400 and was well worth it. The packed-up bicycle meets airline specifications for normal-sized luggage, saving me at least $100 per flight. Also, in the process of dismantling the bike for travel you, by necessity, learn a great deal about how everything fits together. It can be a little time-consuming, but I've gotten better with practice.

When I told the shop owner that I was headed to the United States to bicycle around Lake Huron, he said that I wouldn't be able to ride across the bridge. He suggested that I consider traveling thirty miles south to the ferry. This didn't seem like an attractive option. It involved a detour that would add a day to the trip, along a route that did not strike me as especially interesting or scenic. But he also said that I might be able to hitch a ride across.

The St. Clair River is only about forty miles long, but the waterway connecting Huron to Erie is one of the world's busiest, with freight being shipped primarily from west to east, including chemicals, coal, and iron ore. Situated in what is still one of the most heavily industrialized areas of the United States, in spite of improvements the river bears more than its share of environmental burdens and threats. These include chemical contamination, sewage, zebra mussel and purple loosestrife infestations, and falling water levels. A decrease in winter ice cover due to climate change poses future problems as well.[2]

The man behind the desk at the bridge office told me he'd take me across once he finished his bagel. But while munching away, he remembered a problem with his truck. He called across the river and learned that someone from the Michigan Department of Transportation needed to make the trip over and would give me a ride on his way back.

As I sat waiting outside, one of the toll workers noticed the couplers and struck up a conversation. He told me that the DOT brought cyclists over all the time. There used to be a sidewalk, but when a major rehab widened the lanes, it was eliminated. The large joints on the roadway were dangerous to cyclists because they could catch a tire, especially when it was hot.

When the DOT worker arrived, I was happy for the lift. Riding a bicycle on the sidewalks of large, high bridges with heavy traffic has never been one of my favorite things to do.

Once over and through customs, I stopped at a gas station to get a Michigan state map. On my way out, a middle-aged man in a pickup asked me where I was headed. He said he envied me. "I've put fifty thousand miles on a bike," he told me. "But I can't ride them any more since I messed up my shoulder." He'd injured it when he slipped on some ice. He was thinking about a recumbent. I've considered one myself, given the toll that touring tends to take on my hands. I encouraged him to give it a try.

Port Huron is the first city, traveling from the southeast, to be considered part of Michigan's thumb. Established by the French, it began life as Fort Gratiot but changed hands after English control of Canada took hold in the eighteenth century. The city was incorporated in 1857 on land that was taken from the Ojibwe after the War of 1812, a war that was as much against Native Americans as it was against the British. In the twentieth century, Port Huron's fate was tied closely to the automobile industry, and as a result, it has been losing population since the 1980s. A local nonprofit has attempted to preserve and celebrate some of the historical homes in the area, and there are some impressive-looking structures, but many look to be in need of sprucing up, if not major reconstruction. The calendar for tours and other events of the Olde Town Historic District seemed to have stopped sometime in 2008.[3]

Nevertheless, I enjoyed a pleasant and very flat ride along the lakefront, drifting past the Fort Gratiot Lighthouse, along with moderate traffic. The weather had cleared out, so no more threat of tornadoes. The front's passage had left the temperature in the mideighties. The headwind was mild. Perfect bicycling conditions, if you like nice weather and prefer not to work too hard.

I bought a sandwich at Port Sanalac, a town that started out as a sawmill town but now seems turned over to tourism, with little shops and restaurants sprinkled along the main street. On my way out of the little lakefront park where I ate, I ran into another rider, a woman who said that she'd been cycling north from Ohio. I was impressed at the distance, but it turned out that she had driven much of it with friends, getting out of the car to ride for stretches. She said the hardest part was southeast Ohio with its steep hills. She was very enthusiastic about the trip, which, from what I could gather, was her first bicycle tour. She had clearly caught the bug.

As you get farther north along the thumb, the geography becomes increasingly rural, and traffic thins considerably. Forestville, one of the few towns along this stretch of the coast, has only about 150 permanent residents.[4] As I rode along, there were times when I would ride ten or fifteen minutes without encountering a car. Abandoned strip motels dot the highway, lending the area a somewhat haunted feel, which marks a sharp contrast to the nearby lake's effervescence.

Lake Huron is the second largest of the Great Lakes, with a total surface area of 23,000 square miles, but it is the second shallowest (after Erie) with an average depth of 195 feet, compared with Lake Superior's 483. If the shorelines of its thirty thousand islands are included, it has the longest shoreline of any of the lakes. Huron, which is named for the Huron people who once populated the area, was the first of the lakes to be reached by white Europeans. French explorers Samuel de Champlain and Étienne Brûlé reached the eastern shores of Georgian Bay in 1615.

My ride around Huron would be unimpeded by large metropolitan areas, and partly because of this, Huron has over time remained less polluted than Michigan, to the west, and Erie and Ontario, to the east. In this regard, the lake's seeming effervescence is not illusory.[5] Still, Huron, like the other lakes, is faced with a variety of ecological threats in the form of chemical contamination and invasive species.

Zebra mussels, about which much has been written, are one of the primary invasive threats, but there are others, including the round goby, a predatory fish from the Baltic region, which was first detected in the St. Clair River in 1990. The bottom-feeding goby has a voracious appetite and eats large volumes of zebra and quagga mussels. While the fish thus serve the positive purpose of eating invasive mussels, the mussels are living filters that absorb contamination that has settled to the lake bottom. As a result, gobies become like little toxic bombs. Since they have also now become a major source of food for lake trout (which have not been able to survive on their own in the Great Lakes since the 1930s), this has allowed contamination to move up the food chain and eventually into the bodies of the humans who consume the larger game fish. At one point, sport fishers recognized the attractiveness of gobies to their prey and began using them as bait. This, in turn, encouraged their spread around the lakes even further. That practice has now been abandoned, but a goby-like fishing lure lives on as testament to their attractiveness to other fish.

As I continued my ride, a house that was caving in from the front and had a couple of trees growing up through the windows caught my attention. It was hard to miss. Noting the unusual nature of the sight, I stopped and dug out my camera. As I pointed to shoot, a loud, deep voice reverberated from an outbuilding next to the house: "No pictures please." It startled me. The place had looked completely abandoned.

Of course, I honored the request, partly out of respect and partly out of unease. But I wondered about the no-picture policy as I rode on. Did people stop often enough that the homeowner was prepared for this? Was he keeping an eye out for surreptitious roadside photographers? Or was this just a spontaneous reaction? I also wondered how you ended up with a tree growing up through your house. Wouldn't you realize at some point that there was a sapling coming up out of the floorboards and cut it down? Was this a matter of intense procrastination? Had the home just been abandoned twenty or so years earlier and now an occupant was back? Was this some strange act of cultivation? I'll never know of course. But sometimes I wish I'd snapped that picture.

Just north of Harbor Beach I found North Park, a nice little municipal park, and decided to camp for the night. The place, across the road from the waterfront, seemed clean and quiet. No one was in the office, and there wasn't a sign stating the fees, so I dropped twenty dollars in an envelope slot, pitched my tent, and took a shower. Plenty of hot water. Afterward, I rode the half mile back into town to investigate and have some dinner. The dinner options included a family restaurant and take-out ice cream/sandwich shop. I chose the latter. There were no customers in the place while I was there, but the waiter said that it had been packed in the afternoon.

After dinner I wandered over to the Harbor Creek Beach House, which houses the local theater and features a meticulous re-creation of a large mural, originally painted in the 1930s. It depicts the area's history, with references to the timber industry, railroads, the growth of agriculture, major shipwrecks, and other incidents that mark both the individual character of Harbor Creek and tie it into the broader economic history and ecology of Michigan's thumb. The mural includes a picture of Supreme Court Justice Frank Murphy, appointed by Roosevelt in 1940 and generally considered one of the most liberal of the New Deal appointees. In his nine years on the bench, Murphy wrote 131 majority opinions and 68 dissents. His most famous dissent was in *Korematsu v. United States*,[6] the now discredited decision that upheld the internment of Japanese Americans during World War II.

The mural offers a romanticized view of hard-working lumbermen, and indeed the labor of the "shanty boys" was difficult and dangerous in the era before chain saws, feller bunchers, mechanical harvesters, skidders, and other accouterments of the modern timber industry. With double-bit axes and handsaws, these men (and they were nearly all men) essentially cleared the forests of Michigan. Much attention is given to the fabled white pine, but Michigan had vast stores of hardwoods as well. Estimates are that over 200 billion board feet of pine, cedar, hemlock, maple, oak, and other species were extracted from the lower and upper peninsulas. While much of the wood was transported across the United States, used to build houses and ships and to make furniture and paper, it was also converted to charcoal to provide fuel for the nascent iron industry.[7]

The fires that followed through the open stump fields of these denuded forests are legendary for their ferocity, swallowing whole towns and killing hundreds of people. The most infamous is the Peshtigo fire, which wiped away the town by that name in northern Wisconsin in 1871. Less well remembered is a fire that in 1881 ravaged through huge swaths of Michigan's thumb, including most of the areas I'd just cycled through. Killing nearly three hundred people, the fire stopped only when it reached Lake Huron's shoreline. On the positive side, if there could be a positive side to such a tragedy, it gave new purpose to Clara Barton's Red Cross, which aided in the relief effort, extending its mission in the post–Civil War era.[8] The Harbor Beach mural provides no images alluding to the fire or the devastation that it caused, focusing instead on the heroic efforts of the timber workers, who unintentionally created the conditions that made it possible.

July 27, 2011

I spent the next day cycling around the thumb's northern and western borders. I'd never been to this part of Michigan, and I was really taken with it. It's one of Michigan's best-kept secrets, often ignored by out-of-staters in favor of the north country or the sand dunes in the west. The thumb tends to be quite flat along its edges. The area is known by geologists as the Saginaw-Maumee lowlands, named for the glacial lakes that once covered it, which left layers of silt and gravel, to which its flatness can be attributed. Moraines, the gravel deposits that were left behind as the glaciers retreated, can be found in the middle of the thumb, disrupting the flatness. Hadley Hills, which are mostly encompassed by the Ortonville Recreation area, is moraine country and consists of 5,000 acres of forests in an area otherwise dominated by farmland. The hills are part of a moraine system that curls inland, following the outlines of Saginaw Bay, along the edges of the ancient lakes that once covered this entire area.[9]

The thumb's tip is largely agricultural, with expanses of wheat and corn fields stretching down into the interior. I got off of Highway 25 for a bit and found myself on gravel roads—not always in the best condition—which took me through little towns that were no more than a stop sign and a general store. The small city of Port Austin, which sits at the northern tip of the peninsula, is lovely. Historic homes, large trees, and an active port area draw business and tourists alike. In general, the upper part of the thumb mixes agriculture and tourism in ways that remind me of New York State along the St. Lawrence River. And like the eastern edge of the Adirondacks, it is no doubt a much less welcoming place in frigid January.

On the way out of Port Austin, camps and small vacation homes dot the highway. The area has long been a vacation retreat for folks in the cities to the south. As you start to head south, the beach opens up on the right, with many public parks, including Port Crescent State Park, which has wooded areas and stretches out along the lake for several miles. People were out enjoying the warm and sunny weather. At times, houses are located across the highway, leaving the beach open for public use. At other points, however, houses are situated on the lake side of the highways, blocking it from view and essentially privatizing the beach front. I wondered how these decisions were made and who made them. Whatever the case, it's a lovely area and made for extremely enjoyable bicycle riding.

On the southwestern edge of the thumb, the highway moves away from the lake into farm country. The wind started to pick up as I was riding and became especially stiff as the highway wended its way westward. By Sebewaing, the summer homes and tourist towns have given way to the world of industrial agriculture.

Sebewaing is a sugar mill town and lies in the heart of sugar beet production in the United States. The Pioneer Sugar slicing plant is on the northern edge of town. The contrast between this area and the northern part of the thumb couldn't be more pronounced. This is a working town. But the city has a deindustrial feel. The Dollar General and other discount stores seemed to be the main outlets, but they were paired with empty storefronts.

Many houses looked to be in need of both minor and major repairs. The place, in other words, looked a little bleak. Even though it was getting into late afternoon, I decided to push on another thirty miles to Bay City.

The wind picked up noticeably as I turned westward. So did the traffic as I moved into the Bay City–Saginaw metropolitan area, and I was blown to and fro by heavy-duty trucks. I was also starting to get a fairly intense pain in my left hand. In previous tours, I've had problems with pain and numbness, so I installed a curled handlebar that allows me to move my hands into different positions. I was still having problems though. The last twenty miles of what turned out to be a one-hundred-mile day were actually pretty tough.

Finally into Bay City, I rode along the main street into a town that hugged the shoreline and was lined with beautiful mansions that are among the most historic in the state of Michigan. These were built by the town's first industrialists from the wealth generated by sawmills, shipbuilding, and mining. It was a pleasant ride along the tree-lined avenue, made more enjoyable with the knowledge that I'd soon be off the bike eating dinner with a cold beer.

I made my way down to the Saginaw River, where there was some kind of festival happening and asked around about a place to stay. One person suggested the Double Tree Inn, which was nearby, but someone else interjected it was booked solid. While a little expensive for my tastes, I figured I'd at least check to see if anything was available.

The receptionist told me that the hotel was full but graciously phoned around to see if he could find me a room in another hotel, with no luck. He also commented on the dried blood on my arm. I honestly hadn't noticed it but realized that it was the result of a fall I'd taken in Caseville. I went to clean it off. While I was in the bathroom, the clerk had reached a state park north of the city, which had plenty of campsites. Unfortunately, it was about a twenty-mile ride, but it seemed like the only choice.

Riding northward, I passed through a typical suburban strip, with fast-food joints, automobile parts stores, and big-box retailers. Fortunately, I also spotted a sign for a small strip motel with a vacancy. In the parking lot I encountered some other cyclists, one of whom was from Spain and had been riding across the United States. He said it had taken him twenty-one days to get this far, which by my rough calculations turned out to have been at least a hundred miles a day. That's a pretty good pace. The record for riding across the United States is seven days, twenty-three hours, set by Michael Secrest in 1990.[10] Secrest was participating in the Race Across America, or RAAM. RAAM has both a solo and team component. The team event is open to anyone, but the solo event has qualifying restrictions. A single rider needs to complete the course in twelve days even to be listed as a participant. Participants pride themselves in their refusal to sleep, which can lead to intense hallucinations. Compared to this, the Tour de France seems like a picnic.

I checked into the fairly shabby motel, took a shower, and figured I'd walk until I found a place to eat. Suburban strips are intentionally designed to be pedestrian unfriendly. With no sidewalk, this one was no exception. I walked on grass about a half mile, until I found a Chinese buffet. A Chinese buffet after a full day of cycling is like a gift from heaven. While the food may not be gourmet quality, there's plenty of it, and it offers all varieties of protein and carbohydrates. And this one even had a liquor license, so I could supplement my Kung Pao chicken and fried rice with a Tsingtao beer or two.

July 28, 2011

The next day's ride from Bay City north had a very different feel than the thumb. The thumb is bicycle friendly, with low traffic density and quaint small towns. The traffic in this part of the state is heavier. But there's more to it than that. I definitely encountered hostility to my bicycle, and me along with it. I noticed this first when a man driving the opposite direction across the highway felt the need to honk and shoot me the finger.

In Tawas City, I pulled out of a convenience store parking lot. Realizing the traffic was heavy and the road narrow, I decided to move onto an adjacent sidewalk/bike path. As I was doing so, someone in a souped-up black muscle car with a large stenciled Detroit Tigers insignia on the back screamed at me. I hadn't seen him, but I have no doubt that he'd have buzzed within a hair's breadth if I'd stayed on the road. By pulling off of it, I deprived him of his opportunity to be a complete jerk, which no doubt angered him even more.

Of course this constitutes only a small minority of drivers. And it has to be balanced against people that go out of their way to be friendly. Earlier in the day, as I was standing outside a convenience store checking my map, a man came up, asked me where I was going, and wished me a great trip.

Still, the acts of hostility and anger stick with you. And I wonder what it's about. Here I am in Michigan, the land of automobiles, and so perhaps bicycles are seen as a kind of economic threat (an idea too ridiculous to consider seriously). Or is this a class divide? Are bicycles in the category of white wine, windsurfing, and brie cheese? That doesn't make any sense. Bicycles have hardly, historically, been the accouterments of the wealthy. They are cheap and available basically to anyone who wants one. George W. Bush was an avid mountain biker. In our divided country, cycling draws in partisans from all sides.

Hostility from people in cars is not, of course, confined to Michigan. I've encountered plenty in my many rides in New York State. It does, however, seem to be confined to the United States. I've bicycled in many places, and I can honestly say that I've never been harassed in any other country, including Canada. Maybe that's part of the problem. Bicycles can be seen as somehow un-American, or European, like President Obama, and as a result some kind of cultural threat.

As I was ruminating about these matters, I passed a Confederate flag flying proudly from a house next to the highway. Why would someone in Michigan be flying a Confederate flag? In a sense, though, Michigan, at least parts of it, is among the most southern of the northern states. Famously, pollster Stan Greenberg found Macomb County, Michigan, to epitomize white working-class disenchantment with the Democratic Party, largely driven by hostility to civil rights and a range of cultural attitudes. I began pedaling a little harder, glad that at least the highway had a wide shoulder.

As you move farther north, the terrain becomes more wooded, and tourism again seems to become a dominant economic activity, at least along the lake. Oscoda is very much a tourist town. I rode through its long strip to Au Sable on its northern border. There I walked into a tree-shaded motel on the northern edge of town and was greeted by a chatty receptionist. When I commented that the motel seemed pretty nice, she responded, "Thanks, but I don't own it. I do clean it though." "Well," I responded, "You're obviously good at it." The place was, in fact, well kempt and spotless. She offered free popcorn at five, and after a shower and short rest, I was back just as it finished popping. Other than the popcorn, there weren't many eating options around town. I settled on a pizza place, which turned out to have not especially good pizza. But, good or lousy, the carbs offered by pizza are always welcome after a long day on a bike.

July 29, 2011

The terrain starts to change again around the Oscoda–Au Sable area. It becomes hillier and woodsier and marks a nice break from the flat areas in the south with their ubiquitous summer cottages. Unfortunately, I started having problems with my back brake, which kept pulling against the rim, even when I released the handle. I stopped at a gas station to try to fix it. I was hoping that I could deal with it without pulling my gear off the back, and messed around with it for a while, until I realized that I'd have to take it apart. As I was working on it, a woman walked up to ask me about my trip.

Her enthusiasm was contagious. She said that she really just wanted to jump on a bicycle and leave her life behind. She was somewhat overweight, which I noticed partly because she kept bringing it up. "I just need to lose the weight," she said. "It's hard to ride a bike, because it's a lot of weight to push around. I need to lose the weight." She also had back problems and was thinking about a recumbent. But she wasn't sure how well it would do on the hills.

I assured her that I'd seen a fair number of recumbents out touring around and figured they would do fine. Here was someone who saw bicycles not as a threat but as a promise, an opportunity, and an escape. Here, in other words, was a kindred soul. I now sometimes wonder if she ever took the plunge and went off on the bicycle trip of her dreams. I sure hope so.

I had intended to keep riding northward, but Alpena caught my attention. I'd only ridden about fifty miles, but I'd been clocking eighty to a hundred in the two previous days, so it seemed like I was due for a bit of a break. I stopped on the main downtown street and sat on a wall to check my map. As I was sitting there, I noticed a swarm of ants. A woman walking by said, "Hey, those ants are going to eat you alive!" She grabbed me by the arm and said, "You should go over there," pointing across the street. "At least there's a bench and some shade." I thought she had overreacted a bit, but I did take her advice.

As I sat on a bench in the small park, I wondered if there might be a place to camp nearby, and asked a man walking by. He advised me that I needed to be careful about biking when it was this hot, but he didn't know of a campsite. He told me to go into the building nearby (which turned out to be the courthouse) and ask someone there. As we were talking, another person rode up on a bicycle and suggested that I go to the fairgrounds, where I could camp by the river. His name was Mike.

He started telling me about his bikes. He had three of them. He named them. He was on a Trek 950 mountain bike, which he called Angela, but also had an Electra three-speed with the gear in the hub, and a Specialized that he used for his winter rat. He didn't tell me the names of his other bikes, and I didn't feel the need to ask. He rode with me to the campgrounds and showed me where the office was inside a small house.

The attendant seemed to have just woken up from a nap. I paid twenty bucks for a campsite, he wrote me up a ticket, and then gave me the bad news. All the campsites down by the river were taken. I'd have a site close to the highway and a couple of hundred yards from the factory across the street. Not exactly idyllic. Still, the price was right, and I was now committed.

I set up my tent and took a shower as I heard loud heavy-metal music start to blast out of the park office, and then headed into town. Mike had suggested a trip to the NOAA Great Lakes Maritime Heritage Center, which turned out to be a small gem, specializing in Great Lakes shipwrecks and the restoration of artifacts that have been found on them. The exhibits were fantastic, extolling the history of the lakes, emphasizing their importance as a major waterway, reaching back to the seventeenth century. Offshore (but you need diving gear to experience it) is the Thunder Bay National Marine Sanctuary and Underwater Preserve.

The waterways here were especially treacherous, earning the name "Shipwreck Alley," and dozens of sunken ships still lie off-shore. Inside the museum, there's a full-sized reconstructed ship's deck, upon which visitors are invited to stand and imagine themselves as members of a crew. A hallway features intricate models of historic ships that succumbed to Huron's waters. One was of the famous *Edmund Fitzgerald,* which was lost to Lake Superior on November 10, 1975, with none of its twenty-nine crew members ever accounted for. In 1976, Gordon Lightfoot turned the tragedy into an unlikely hit song, "The Wreck of the Edmund Fitzgerald." The Great Lakes are in general incredibly dangerous waterways, and it's eye-opening to get a sense of the size and number of ships that sank. Estimates put the number in Lake Huron alone to be over a thousand.

The worst storm to hit Lake Huron, and much of the western lakes, was undoubtedly the fabled "white hurricane" of November 1913. The storm lasted three days, from November 7 to November 10. It occurred during a period when larger cargo and passenger boats were becoming common on the lakes but when weather prediction was still in its infancy. The storm began as swirling mass of low pressure, dropping from the Arctic through northwest Canada and across Lake Superior, a phenomenon now commonly referred to as a "clipper." As the front descended, another low-pressure system moved upward from the southwest. The two systems combined into one massive storm, generating eighty-mile-an-hour winds flowing directly from the north. As it gained momentum, temperatures dropped thirty or forty degrees in a matter of hours.

Ships that had ventured out into the lakes, either before gale warnings were issued or in spite them, were caught in the midst of one of the worst weather events in recorded Great Lakes history. Among the early casualties were the massive 525-foot freighter the *Henry B. Smith,* hauling iron ore, which was lost off the shore of Marquette, Michigan; the *Waldo,* hit by a massive rogue wave near Gull Rock, Michigan; and the *Turret Chief,* whose captain believed his ship to be out on open water, only to have it sink in shallows near Copper Bay, Michigan.

In the end, eleven ships were completely lost, and another twenty-seven were stranded. Dozens of sailors either drowned or froze to death. Lake Huron suffered eight total losses, the most of any lake. Thirty-five-foot waves, seventy-mile-an-hour winds, and blinding snow smashed in hulls and tossed ships around until they either broke apart and sank or were pushed up against the shore on the southern and western edges of the lake. Captain Walter Iler, whose ship, the *Crawford,* survived the storm, watched from a distance as the 436-foot *Argus,* carrying a load of coal, was broken apart by waves and "crumpled like an eggshell." As it sank, it pulled all twenty-eight members of its crew into the icy waters, not far from Port Austin, at the tip of Michigan's thumb.

Ships in the eastern lakes, Erie and Ontario, fared better. As word spread about the ferocity of the storm, they moved into harbor. No ships sank on Ontario, and only one, the unfortunate *Lightship 82,* was lost on Erie. Lightships, as the name suggests, were floating lighthouses. Since they could provide assistance during inclement weather, they generally remained in open water and were constructed to withstand heavy waves and high winds. What went afoul on *Lightship 82* was never determined, but the ship, with the word "Buffalo" painted in large letters on one side, sank in the waters close to its namesake, taking all six members of its crew with it.

It might seem intuitive that the Great Lakes, because of their smaller size, would be easier to negotiate as storms sweep across them than, say, the North Atlantic. But that would be a mistake. The shallowness of some of the lakes and the more confined areas within which the water is held tend to exacerbate the intensity of wave action. On the open ocean, waves will reach higher peaks, but they tend to spread apart, allowing ships some relief and room to maneuver between them. The lakes produce waves with shorter peaks but bunched together, generating more intense bursts of energy, providing little margin for error for crews trying to keep their ships steady. As a result, the shallower lakes—Huron, Erie, and Ontario—are the most dangerous during the stormiest months, which tend to be in late fall.[11]

After the museum, I rode around town a little, got a bite to eat, and then headed back to my campsite. Mike was there. He said that he'd ridden by a couple of times to make sure that I was doing OK. Then I got Mike's story.

He said he'd been clean and sober for about fifteen years and had worked in rehab after that. But feeling the need for a change, he quit his job and went to the local community college, where he took art and computer classes. He loved going to college but was having trouble finding a job now that he was out. He'd been working at the Holiday Inn, where he said they treated him and all of the other employees like crap. People working there for thirty years were still making only eleven dollars an hour.

He had been a finalist for a good job with the Department of Human Services but wasn't chosen. He did, however, have an interview lined up at the NOAA museum gift shop. His father had recently died from cancer, which he probably developed as the result of being an engineer on one of the Great Lakes ships that hauled taconite, a substance that has similar impacts as asbestos on human lungs.

Mike spent his time off work riding his three bicycles and tending his cats. He had a soft spot for stray cats and had taken in nine of them. He told me that the past winter he had read them the entire works of William Faulkner (including the short stories) and then had started on Dostoyevsky. The lucky cats were not only saved from hypothermia and starvation but given a literary education to boot. We chatted for a while, and I wished him well before he took off. I read for a bit and eventually fell asleep listening to the sounds of the Besser Block Company across the way fashioning its cement block-making machines. It's a fairly noisy process.

July 30, 2011

It became windier and windier riding north from Alpena, but also much more heavily forested. It's a beautiful area, with Long Lake to the west and then Grand Lake on the east. The road runs somewhat inland here until Rogers City, an attractive town of several thousand, which is home to the port of Calcite, one of the largest shipping ports on the Great Lakes.

As I left the city, it became even windier, as the road gradually turned west. The terrain starts to become somewhat hillier as well. The combination of wind and hills made for some fairly tough going, but the beauty of the area more than compensated for the difficulty of the ride. At one point a cyclist heading southward turned around and rode along with me to chat. She said that she and her husband had ridden around Huron fifteen years previously. She informed me that there was no shoulder on the road on the Canadian side and that it could be harrowing. "But that was awhile ago," she noted, "and maybe things have changed. A lot of people do it!" I wasn't exactly alarmed by this, but it did make me a little apprehensive. The big wide shoulders of Michigan roads are quite a luxury, and having ridden in a number of places that don't have them, I am very well aware of the difference that a three- or four-foot shoulder can make.

At any rate, this was the most beautiful part of the journey so far, along past Hoeft State Park, Forty Mile Point, and Huron Beach. Here you get a feel for the wildness and vastness of Huron and the Great Lakes in general, with dunes, water, and wind. I had intended to make it to Mackinac City, but the wind was beating me back. Given the choice between hills and wind, I'll take the hills anytime. Wind is relentless and demoralizing, and you never get the equivalent of a downhill or the view from the peak for that matter. I once biked from Hanoi to Ho Chi Minh City into a headwind the entire way, so I have some experience and know how hard it is to get used to.

I spotted a reasonably nice-looking strip motel on the edge of town. When I inquired at the office about a room, a young man, probably in his early twenties, without a shirt and with a raft of tattoos covering his torso, informed me that he couldn't help me but his girlfriend would be around in a minute. She didn't seem to know much either, and the whole situation was fairly chaotic. I wondered if I'd made the right decision. Finally an older woman came in and said that she had a room, but she couldn't seem to find the key. She and the young woman left to try to find it, leaving me with the young man.

He told me that he'd once walked from West Virginia to Michigan. "It took me a week," he said. When I asked why, he said that he'd had no money and needed to be back home. Sometimes, he told me, the police would pick him up and bring him to the state line. This didn't make a lot of sense to me, given that there's only one state, Ohio, between West Virginia and Michigan. Maybe he meant the county line.

I asked him what kind of shoes he wore. "Nikes," he said. "How'd that go?" I asked. " I wore them out." "Sure," I told him, "they weren't made for that." He said his feet were swollen by the end, which didn't surprise me. "Why didn't you hitchhike?" I asked. He said he wouldn't get into a car with a stranger. Personally, given the choice between walking five hundred miles and getting into a car with a stranger, I'd take a chance with a stranger or two. But I had some doubts about the story overall. I don't think it's possible to walk from West Virginia to Michigan in a week.

July 31, 2011

The next morning, a motorcyclist was shining up his bike near my room as I was loading things up. Motorcycle touring seems to be a major activity in upper Michigan. Welcome signs for motorcycles are ubiquitous in motel and restaurant windows. We chatted for a bit, and the biker told me that his niece and her boyfriend set out on a bicycle trip from upstate New York to Alaska, although they only made it as far as Banff in Canada. Still, that's a pretty good trek. I mentioned that they headed straight into the prevailing headwind. He said he'd never thought of that. This is one of the crucial differences, among others, between riding a motorcycle and a bicycle, the necessity of attentiveness to wind direction.

Early mornings tend to be fairly windless, and the ride from Cheboygan to Mackinaw City on a beautiful cloudless day was exceptionally enjoyable. Mackinaw City is a tourist town and a welcome bit of prosperity. I had breakfast at a family bakery at the town center. Typical small-town grumblers were sitting at a table in the middle of the place, complaining about taxes and roadwork. As I was walking out, a man on the street asked me if they served breakfast in the place. I told him that it was mostly just a bakery but had great breads and sweet rolls. That didn't seem to interest him, and he complained about not being able to find a Burger King or McDonald's in town.

To get to the Upper Peninsula, you need to cross the Mackinac Bridge. Bicycles are not allowed, and they shouldn't be, because it's a long bridge with no shoulder and endless streams of traffic. The bicycle rider that I encountered near Rogers City told me to look for a small building that had a phone inside. If you call the number posted there, someone will pick you up and take you across the bridge. It took me a while to find the building, and I probably would never have noticed it had I not been told about it.

I called the number, and then, sure enough, about ten minutes later a friendly uniformed woman in her thirties showed up in a pickup truck and took me across. I mentioned to her that the building with the phone wasn't well marked, and cyclists, or whoever, might have a hard time locating it. "It's on the website," she responded. I suppose I should have thought of that, but I honestly hadn't considered checking it, and I wonder how many other people would. The Mackinac Bridge is an impressive structure. Opened in 1957, it is, with approaches, one of the longest suspension bridges in the world. More than a quarter million vehicles cross it every month.[12]

Once across, I rode through St. Ignace, another tourist town, not as upscale as Mackinaw City, the businesses of which are scattered along the highway. A ferry runs from St. Ignace to Mackinac Island, which has been preserved as a kind of pedestrian oasis, allowing no motorized vehicle traffic. Its claim to historical importance can be traced to the War of 1812, a war that is generally remembered, if at all, only in shreds: the burning of the White House, the composition of the "Star-Spangled Banner," Andrew Jackson at the Battle of New Orleans, Commodore Perry's triumph against the British Navy on Lake Erie.

The war is now viewed skeptically by most historians in terms of the motivations that ignited it, the strategies used to fight it, and its ambiguous conclusion. "Madison's War" exacerbated preexisting regional divisions. Southerners and Westerners, supported it, while Northeasterners opposed it. It has even been referred to as the "Civil War of 1812."

The rationale for the war focused on British incursions into American sovereignty, especially the impressments of Americans into the British Navy. But impressments, while often heavy-handed and widely resented, had a legitimate basis in British concerns about desertions of British sailors to American ships. The conditions for sailors in the British Navy were notoriously dismal. And their American counterparts were better paid. Americans also resented the unprovoked British attack on the American vessel *Chesapeake* in 1807, after it refused to allow boarding for inspection by British naval officers, an attack that resulted in the deaths of three American sailors. Still, the British also seemed eager to avoid a full-scale war. Madison, on other hand, scuttled a last-ditch attempt on the part of the British to resolve things.

The declaration of war vote was fractious and split along political party lines. One of the main political factions supporting war consisted of frontier settlers. Many saw an opportunity to drive Native Americans, generally allied with the British, out of the Northwest Territories. That is how Michigan played a central role in this vision of an expanding America.

Americans believed that Canadians along the southern border were eager to be liberated from British colonization by American forces. The war would be a "second war of independence," in that it would put an end to British hopes of retaking former American colonies, and would incorporate Canada into the United States as well. The supposition of Canadian support for American interests turned out to have been highly questionable. Moreover, American irregulars had an unfortunate tendency to antagonize the Canadian civilians they were supposed to be liberating by burning down their homes and driving them from their settlements.

Mackinac Island played an important role early in the conflict as the site of an American outpost and fort. On July 17, General William Hull successfully defeated British forces at Sandwich, on the Canadian side. Soon thereafter, British troops took the fort at Mackinac by surprise, forcing a much larger American force to surrender and eventually retreat to Detroit. Meanwhile, Hull infamously dithered, choosing not to attack Fort Malden, partly, it is believed, because of his fear of Native Americans. The British regrouped, and Hull retreated to Fort Detroit, which he soon surrendered, leading to an early and demoralizing defeat. The treaty that ended the war, which confirmed a virtual draw, put Mackinac back into American hands.[13]

As I rode north, I left the main state highway and traveled on county road F62. I was annoyed by the elevated ground reflectors strung out along the shoulder, hoping they wouldn't continue for a long stretch. They were hard to avoid, pushing me out into traffic. A few miles north of St. Ignace, however, after passing a large Kewadin Casino, they stopped. Apparently, they were placed to keep late-night gamblers from veering off the road as they headed south.

After the casino, I experienced five-star cycling conditions. The wind was now behind me, as I breezed up along the southeast edge of the Hiawatha National Forest. There were no cars on the road, and I was surrounded by the forests of northern Michigan. The forests here are part of what is known as the Great Lakes–St. Lawrence Forest. It includes all of Michigan, both lower and upper peninsulas, parts of northern Wisconsin, large swaths of southern Ontario, and even areas in northern Ohio and New York. This massive area includes several ecoregions, each of which has its own distinctive mix of deciduous and cover species. In southern zones, maple, oak, aspen, and birch dominate. In the transitional zone, through which I was traveling, between the deciduous-dominated areas to the south and the arboreal forests northward, small- to medium-sized cedar trees are ubiquitous, mixed with juniper and some birch.[14] Riding through the forest, as desiccated as it may be compared to what it once was, was soothing. The trees, although not towering in stature, provided some welcome shade as the day heated up into the nineties. It's rides like these that keep me coming back to touring. There is nothing else quite like it.

Eventually the forest retreats against the agricultural areas of the eastern Upper Peninsula. The road was narrow and at times a little rough, but hilltops revealed beautiful vistas stretching out northward. I imagined seeing Lake Superior far off in the distance, but it was of course much too far away for that. The weather continued to be hot, with temps in the nineties, but the few towns along the road allowed for water stops and a little respite from the sun.

There are two Sault Ste. Maries, one in Michigan and one across the straits in Canada. I elected to stay on the Michigan side, partly because this is where you get the best view of the famous locks. The ride into town does not provide much promise. The southern part of the city appears typically distressed for an older Great Lakes industrial city. Near the water, however, there are signs of economic life, as a string of motels and restaurants provide services to the visitors who come to see the locks. The city seems to have bet its economic future on tourism, which is sensible, given its location near the locks.

The Sault Ste. Marie locks are bounded on the southern side by a park that has a two-story observation deck, offering views of the ships as they move through the narrow channel. Dozens of people were there when I showed up in the late afternoon. In the past, observers could walk up to the channel, but now they are kept about a hundred feet away. (Perhaps a few fell in.) In spite of the distance, it's a sight worth seeing. The massive ships barely squeeze through the narrow channel, as they wait at each juncture to be lowered or raised to the proper level. An adjacent museum offers the history of the locks via displays, photographs, maps, and a short film. Yet, the museum, while well organized and informative, leaves some things out. It has virtually no references, for example, to the indigenous people who once inhabited the area.

What's now often referred to as "the Soo" was at one time one of the most productive fishing grounds in North America. Whitefish filled the rapids of Bawating, providing protein for the Anishinaabeg who populated the region. The United States took control under the 1855 Detroit Treaty, engineered by then governor Lewis Cass, an act that abrogated an earlier treaty. A second version, even more expansive in its claims, was completely fraudulent.[15] But the history of treaties between American officials and Native Americans is sorry indeed. And in this case, as in so many others, economic development trumped legality and fairness. The rapids were simply too much of a bottleneck between resource-rich western territories and expanding factories in the east. Portaging ever-larger ships, loaded with minerals, became impractical.

The building of the locks, and eventually hydro plants, decimated the rapids. A small portion remains but only as a sad reminder of their past grandeur.[16] Before the locks, a volume of water equivalent to that which passes over Niagara Falls filled the rapids. Now the water is channeled, diverted, and domesticated. The completion of the locks facilitated resource extraction from the west and thus played an important, if generally unheralded, role in the closing of the American frontier.

Tourists were out taking advantage of the warm summer evening as I walked along the narrow strip. But it's a bit of a Potemkin village. A short walk away into the surrounding neighborhoods reveals stunning nineteenth-century homes with peeling paint and sagging roofs. The city was apparently trying to upgrade the area by replacing sidewalks and widening streets, which might help with future plans for revitalization.

On the edge of the downtown sits a small fenced-off Native burial ground. To the casual passerby, it might not look like much. But according to the marker, each year a group of Anishinaabeg gather to pay their respects to the ancestors who are buried there. As I stood there, clouds gathering, the burial site provided a meditative counterpoint to the bustling tourist activity a couple of blocks away. I was trying to imagine what it might have been like before European habitation and subsequent industrial development displaced the original inhabitants and tamed the waterway. It wasn't easy.

August 1, 2011

The next morning, I woke up early. I wanted to beat the morning traffic rush over the Sault Ste. Marie Bridge into Canada. There wasn't much, so it seemed that I had succeeded. The bridge has a double-arch span, which for a bicyclist means two short, steep hills to climb. The first arch crosses the American locks, and the second the Canadian. The crossing is only about three miles long in total and provides a dramatic view of the locks and the Canadian side.

On the left as you enter Canada is a large operating steel plant owned by Essar Steel Agoma. The Essar plant, which employs 3,300 people, has apparently had its share of hard times, twice declaring bankruptcy, but it has been kept afloat via interest-free loans from the Ontario government. Now owned by an Indian conglomerate, it's profitable again. A paper mill also operates in the city. You don't see this kind of industrial activity on the American side.[17]

Once over, I was happily surprised to find the welcome center open, and the young woman there was very helpful in giving me advice about camping and route options. She encouraged me to turn south onto Manitoulin Island. It's very busy on the highway after Sudbury, she explained, and the island offers a more picturesque ride. I decided to take her advice.

The city was quiet as I rode through on a Sunday morning. A substantial downtown held a few large hotels, many storefronts, and some restaurants. I saw little evidence of the dilapidation that pervades the American side. I was a little apprehensive as I rode out of town, given what I had been told by the bicyclist in Michigan: The Queen Elizabeth Way (QEW) has no shoulder and a lot of lumber trucks. For a bicycle, the conditions were, in her words, "terrible." Fortunately, coming out of the city, there's an alternative route, with a wide shoulder and moderate traffic, that runs through First Nations territory, parallel to the main highway and close to the shoreline.

A couple of miles outside of town, another bicyclist rode up next to me and asked if I needed some maps of the area. I said, "Sure." Denis (with one *n*, as he informed me) talked nonstop from the moment I met him, and he knew secondary road routes that would allow me to stay off the main highway. The maps that he gave me looked as though they'd been printed on a color printer that was just about to run out of ink and then set out in a rainstorm. He explained, at about a mile a minute, all the different roads and turns and streets, with names, between where we were to Espanola, about 150 miles away. I couldn't keep it all in my head. I wasn't sure how he could.

He offered to ride with me part of the way. His wife was still at church, so he had some time. We turned up a side road, and we were off, as he continued to describe each turnoff and the size of each hill that we were going to encounter. He had quite a bike, and he explained every piece of it, with specifications down to the millimeter. He had three headlights on the bike, one generator driven that he said would light up the entire shoulder and part of the road when fully operational. "I don't believe in a stripped down bike," he told me—stating the obvious.

He gabbed away as I learned that he had worked at the Essar Steel plant, which he explained had recently been bought out by an Indian firm ("*East* Indian," he emphasized). He was near to his seventieth birthday and was the mapmaker for the local bicycle club. He was originally from a town in England that had the first railroad spur. His dad was a railroad man, who immigrated to Canada but returned to England. Denis, who had a fairly heavy English accent, returned to Canada as an adult. He was very interested in the smoothness (or lack thereof) of the railroad tracks that we crossed. The smoothest one he'd ever encountered was some place in England. He wasn't sure how they did it. I never asked what he did in the steel mill, but I assume that he was an engineer.

When he turned around to ride home, I had no idea where I was, and so took a look at the maps he had given me and at first found them impossible to decipher. But I soon realized that the roads that he had marked ran parallel to the main highway, so it wasn't too difficult to figure things out, as blurry as the images were. In the end, they turned out to be a great guide, and I followed them for about fifty miles. Along the county roads, with no traffic, through fields, skirting farms and cottages, it was an idyllic ride—bicycling as it should be. I had definitely scored a great route from "one-*n*" Denis.

When the county road finally emptied out onto the QEW, it was quite a shock, from quiet riding onto a major highway. Fortunately, the previous warnings that I'd been given about the absence of a shoulder did not hold true. The QEW does have a shoulder, albeit a narrow one that at some points becomes *very* narrow. Still, even with the fairly large number of trucks, it was manageable. Canadian drivers tend to be courteous, and the twenty miles to Iron Bridge, a small town of about a thousand, was uneventful. I checked into a strip motel on the highway, and it immediately became clear that even though the Canadian dollar is about equal to the U.S. dollar, prices in Canada were going to be higher.

Along the way, I'd been following the debate over the debt ceiling in the United States. The crazy Republican Tea Partiers were holding a metaphorical gun to Obama's head and threatening the stability of global markets to make a point about the deficit. Things were really heating up, as a number of Republicans, including Eric Cantor, the House majority leader, were contending that a refusal to raise the ceiling would actually *improve* the economic outlook by demonstrating seriousness about the debt problem. Few mainstream economists, including right-leaning ones, agreed with him. But given the kerfuffle, I decided to find a cash machine and take out what I thought would be enough Canadian cash to cover the trip. While unlikely, there was the possibility that the dollar would crash on global markets if the Treasury Department was unable to cover its bond obligations. After watching some of the wrangling on CNN, I walked across the road to a Chinese Canadian diner/restaurant and had dinner. I can't say that I had become a huge fan of the cuisine at this point.

August 2, 2011

The next morning, I cycled to Espanola. I couldn't avoid the QEW for much of it. While drivers are respectful and will generally move into the left lane to offer a little extra room, the problem arises when two trucks coming from opposite directions coincide with the bicycle. That's when you feel the wind in the truck's wheelhouse, and it can be a little disconcerting. Sometimes I take the better part of valor and head onto the gravel to avoid them. The highway through there, which is somewhat hilly, takes you through the small towns of Spanish and Walford.

The Canadian Shield dominates the landscape through this area, with small rounded hills of exposed igneous rock rising up from the fields. The shield, which stretches east to the Adirondacks and north to the Arctic Circle, constitutes more than half of the Canadian land mass. It is the oldest exposed rock in North America, and parts of it date back to the Precambrian era. Small trees grow opportunistically through various cracks. The flatter spaces in between are taken over by picturesque farms, which attempt to coax wheat, corn, and barley from the thin soils. While the views are not as dramatic as, say, in the Rockies, there is something about the ancient character of the land that gives it a quality that is both haunting and reassuring. Espanola, where I decided to spend the night, is a paper mill town. I found a motel, was again shocked by the steep Canadian prices, and turned on the TV to watch more of the debt ceiling battle. John Boehner had worked out some kind of multi-trillion-dollar deal for long-term debt reduction with the president, but the right wing of his caucus was undermining his efforts. Things were getting increasingly insane.

I watched for a while and then headed out for some food. There weren't many options. The Chinese Canadian buffet I took a chance on turned out to be better than the diner in Iron Bridge, and a couple of cold Molson's made the meal more than tolerable.

August 3, 2011

I left Espanola with the paper mill's sulfurous smell trailing behind me. Some kind of front had passed through, and the weather was cooler. I was back into a headwind, though, and hoped to make some distance before it intensified in the afternoon. Southward, through First Nations land, the terrain becomes hillier. The road is surrounded by water, with the Northern Channel on the right and Georgian Bay to the left. The road has a nice wide shoulder, as predicted by Denis, who had said that a very bicycle-friendly MP from the area had lobbied hard for it.

The scenery is spectacular. Ponds that line the roadside are filled with water lilies, a native species with a storied connection to the Anishinaabeg people, who still populate the area. According to one narrative, a great conflict ensued between two suitors for the same young woman. Zeegwun was at first gentle and kind, whereas Bebon was aggressive and cruel. Beaten and intimidated, Zeegwun sought exile but eventually returned and challenged Bebon. Their battles raged for so long that the young woman grew old and died. Upon her death, she was transformed into a water lily, "a constant reminder of the folly of seeking love from war."[18]

I rode about thirty miles before crossing the bridge onto Manitoulin Island, the largest freshwater island in the world. It sits between the North Channel, Georgian Bay, and Lake Huron proper, and it is thought to be one the earliest places for human habitation in North America.[19] The Odawa people (members of the Algonquin or Anishinaabeg language group), its original inhabitants, were driven off the island by the Haudenosaunee, during the so-called Beaver Wars over the fur trade in the seventeenth century. Other Anishinaabeg, including the Huron, Nipissing, and Ojibwe, were driven from their homes along the shores of Georgian Bay as well. The Haudenosaunee did not, however, have the wherewithal to maintain control, and Anishinaabeg gradually began to return, establishing permanent settlements by the middle of the nineteenth century.

Sir Francis Bond Head, Upper Canada's lieutenant governor, apparently with the belief that Canadian First Nations people were unlikely to survive integration into the larger Canadian culture, unilaterally signed a treaty with the Odawa and Ojibwe in 1836 that would make Manitoulin Island their permanent home. The treaty was unique in Canadian history in its categorical rendering of the land to Native inhabitants. And, of course, it was destined to be breeched.

By the 1850s, it was believed that the island contained oil and gas deposits, and energy speculators put pressure on the Canadian government to open it up for development. The categorical Bond Head Treaty was thus superseded by the Manitoulin Island Treaty, which provided minimal economic compensation in exchange for Canadian control of the land. The rationale for abrogating the earlier treaty was that insufficient numbers of First Nations people had moved into the area, and thus the Anishinaabeg, it was claimed, hadn't lived up to their part of the bargain. The Wikwemikong refused to sign and as a result live within unceded territory, still under the terms of the Bond Head Treaty, a situation unique in all of Canada. Their territory constitutes a peninsula on the southeastern side of the island.[20]

Little Current is the largest town on the island, and I stopped there for lunch. I found a fresh loaf of multigrain bread in one of the grocery stores, on which I spread some local jam. This provided strength for the ride along Highway 6, which skirts the eastern edge of the island, climbing up an extension of the Niagara Escarpment, which runs south from there into New York State. About halfway down the island, there's an overlook that provides a bird's-eye view of Lake Manitou to the east.

Fourteen thousand years ago, the Laurentide Ice Sheet, which had covered the area for more than seventy-five thousand years, had retreated to allow the formation of lakes at its southern boundary. To the west, Lake Chicago, a nascent Lake Michigan, formed. On the eastern side was Lake Maumee, an ancestor to Lake Erie. As the ice melted, it still descended southward enough to block outlets for rising water from the ever-expanding and evolving lakes. Water levels were much deeper than today. Lakes Michigan, Superior, and Huron were one massive body of water, now known to geologists as Lake Algonquin.

Manitoulin Island was thus covered first by ice and then by water. Only its highest parts—Little Current, Shequiandah, and High Hill—were exposed.[21] Because of Algonquin Lake's relative geological stability, beaches formed, and their traces can still be found at higher elevations. Eventually drainage paths shifted, not only because ice no longer blocked water flows but because without the ice's weight the land that it covered slowly rebounded to previous elevations. Lake Algonquin's drainage shifted from the Ottawa River system to the St. Lawrence, and the modern Great Lakes were formed. Manitoulin Island has been of special interest to geologists because it provides a rich resource for charting these various transformations.

The wind picked up as the afternoon progressed; clouds moved in, and the hills got steeper. Ten miles north of South Baymouth the road deteriorated noticeably, with a broken shoulder and large potholes. It was cold and rainy by the time I made it into town around five o'clock. The small public campsite was pretty run-down and didn't have showers, so I booked into a little motel near the ferry and hunkered down for the night. There weren't many eating options, so I settled for some fish and chips and then ice cream at a little stand next to the motel.

August 4, 2011

One advantage of bicycle travel is that you can go right to the front of the ferry line. While waiting there, I chatted with another cyclist who'd sailed from the south with a friend and was now headed back on his bike. He said his friend had asked him, "Why would you want to do that?" "Some people just don't understand," he said. True enough, I thought.

The ferry ride across to Tobermory is over what geologists call the "drowned" part of the Niagara Escarpment. In other words, if you could see through the water, you would inevitably notice a large drop from north to south. Soundings have determined that the Yeo-James gorge near Fitzwilliam Island is two hundred feet deep, and the Flowerpot–Bear's Rump valley, near the northernmost point of the Bruce Peninsula, is up to five hundred feet deep. The distance from the top of the escarpment, then, on the northern side of the lake to the bottom of the gorge is nearly eight hundred feet in total.[22]

The foundation minerals that underlie the Niagara Escarpment can be traced back to the Silurian geological period, 400 million years ago. Over a 13-million-year period, when this part of North America was under a shallow sea, the carcasses of small marine animals accumulated, which over time formed into very hard sedimentary rock known as dolomite. This material persists as the cliffs of the escarpment. Where the dolomite was eroded away, from processes that are not entirely understood, the exposed shale was much softer and more easily eroded, creating differences in elevation. The hard dolomite surfaces persisted as bedrock through the various ice ages experienced in the region.[23] The erosive action of the ice steepened the escarpment's cliffs, and slopes formed at the bottom when rocks rolled from the top and landed in the snow at the bottom, which remained after the ice left due to the severe cold in the lake's waters. Glacial meltwater cut channels that became modern waterfalls, which are still visible. And the high waters of the lakes during different phases of glacial retreat eroded caves and arches, which are now visible as well.

During the period of European colonization and settlement, most of the forests that surround the escarpment were cut down. But the flora on the cliffs themselves was mostly undisturbed. It wasn't until relatively recently, however, that it was discovered quite by accident that white cedars growing from cracks in the cliff faces were among the oldest trees in North America. White cedars were highly prized by the region's indigenous people, who used their wood and bark to make canoes and longhouses. Their needles were prized for their medicinal qualities. Tree ring analysis has determined that some of the cliff-clinging cedars on the Bruce Peninsula are more than fifteen hundred years old, rivaling the age of sequoias in the western United States. But these gnarled old trees are relatively small, which protected them from the lumberman's axe.

Due to their inaccessibility and lack of dramatic grandeur, the escarpment cliffs remain one of those parts of North America that have not been subjected to developmental processes. Much of the area is now protected, at least in Southern Ontario. Hiking trails, however, do run along the cliff face, making it accessible to those interested in experiencing this unique environment first-hand.[24] The Bruce Trail starts in Tobermory and runs 885 kilometers to Niagara Falls.[25]

I found the bicyclist whom I had chatted with previously standing in front of a wall map on the ferry. He said that I could turn off the main highway at Mar to continue southward along the shore. The highway had a decent bike lane about halfway to the turn-off, but then it tapered off. He also said that the reports were for a northeastern wind, which would put it at our backs. Unfortunately, he turned out to be wrong about that, which I learned to my great disappointment.

The ride south from the ferry landing was somewhat harrowing. The blue skies that I'd experienced most of the trip had turned to fog and mist. I didn't mind the cooler weather, or even the light rain, but the wind was blowing up as a gale, and I was heading straight into it. The Bruce Peninsula divides the southern end of Georgian Bay from the rest of Lake Huron. It has the largest area of contiguous forest in Southern Ontario and includes a national park and several provincial parks. But given its geographic location, running north to south between two large bodies of water, my guess is that it's windy a fair amount of the time. And as you move southward and the terrain flattens, there's nothing to break up the wind currents.

I was blown around, back and forth, all the way to Mar, and at one point even considered cashing it in for the day. At Mar I turned west for a few miles, which put the wind directly at my back, and it now assisted me over several short but very steep hills on the way to the Huron lakeshore. It was a great relief to get out of the traffic and away from the wind.

A quiet county road brought me to Sauble Falls Provincial Park. I procured a campsite, set up my tent, and ate the last of my multigrain bread, some cheese, peaches that I'd bought on the roadside, and trail mix for dinner. After the fatty fish and chips that I'd eaten along the way, it was a welcome, reasonably healthy alternative.

August 5, 2011

If the day before had been darkness, today was dawn. The sun was shining brightly as I emerged from my tent. My bicycle clothes were still damp from when I had washed them out in the sink the afternoon before. Putting them on was a better eye-opener than three cups of coffee. Others were just getting up as I rode my way out of the park. There's nothing like an early start on a beautiful morning. Cruising along through the early morning dew, my Zen state was broken, however, when I inhaled a large insect. When this happens, which is rarely but still too frequently, you don't see what the creature is. With any luck, it's something completely harmless, but I worry that someday I'll inhale something nasty. Whether or not that happens, even the more benign version of the experience is extremely unpleasant.

I stopped for coffee and a homemade Danish at the little shoreline town of Sauble Beach, which, true to its name, has a large sandy beach. The lake appeared big and blue and beautiful off along the horizon. On the way out of town, I noticed my first flat. It took only a few minutes to repair, but as I was doing so, another bicyclist stopped and offered assistance. I don't remember any time that another bicyclist has passed me by as I was fiddling with my bike on the roadside. The unspoken ethic seems to be always to stop. I thanked him, told him I was fine, finished up, and continued on my way.

The route south from Sauble Beach varies between the main highway and parallel county roads. The coastal roads are smooth, narrow, and completely deserted, as they hug the shoreline. The conditions were excellent, with the sun shining and the wind blowing, as God intended it, from northwest to southeast. As far as I could tell, most of the beaches on the Canadian side are public, and the small cottages that line the road are on the left, making for easy access. These are real beaches, comparable to many that you find on an ocean front, with people scattered all along the wide strip of sand that stretches down to the water.

At different points along the way, wind turbines came into view. They still have the capacity to startle when you see them up close. The turbines pivot into the wind in order to gain maximum efficiency. They were positioned in the direction that I was moving away from, just where I would have liked to have seen them for my own maximum efficiency.

As I pulled up away from the shoreline onto a busier county highway, I noticed a number of "Stop the Turbines" signs. They weren't in every yard, but I saw at least a dozen. One said, "Health Study before Turbines." I'd never heard that wind turbines could cause health problems. One sign, by a farmer's house, said, "Turbines Are an Ill Wind."

There had been, it turned out, a big battle over wind power in Southern Ontario, and some residents were suggesting that wind turbines can damage health by causing migraines and sleeplessness and by generating nausea. Not all residents of the area oppose them though. Some farmers have allowed turbines on their land as a means to supplement their farming incomes. But opposition had been intense enough that the Liberal Party, when in power, backed off a proposal to put turbines out in the lakes themselves.[26] Wind power has been controversial in some localities in New York State but not to the point where it would have much impact on a state-wide election. In my future travels around the lakes, I saw many more wind turbines on the Canadian side of the lakes than the American, especially on the north shore of Lake Erie, encouraging me to believe that this area represented something of an anomaly.

(Full disclosure, two years after this trip, I became an investor in the Black Oak Wind Farm, a small community-owned operation near my home in Tompkins County, New York. Things went relatively smoothly as it made its way through the approval process until it had almost reached its conclusion, at which point some residents near the facility began to object. The ensuing conflict continued for nearly a year and as of this writing has not been resolved. In that way, then, opposition in Southern Ontario proved to be a harbinger of my own experience.)

Wind turbines behind me and back out on Route 21, the QEW, the riding was mixed at best. There wasn't a huge amount of traffic, and parts of the road have been widened and rehabbed, but there are definitely crumbly stretches. Large cracks split the white line, which could only be avoided by riding in the highway itself. The terrain through this area is flat, and there are large farms. Their fields were bursting with wheat, corn, and various other crops in the early August sunshine.

I stopped at Point Farms Provincial Park for the night. The site was a Victorian-era resort, the remnants of which can still be seen in the form of old cedar fences and fruit orchards. It sits on a hundred-foot-high bluff above the lake. The office staff were interested in my cycling trip and fixed me up with a campsite right near the bluff, an ideal location for viewing the sunset. One staff member suggested that discounts should be given for people on bicycles, a policy, I have to admit, that makes complete sense to me.

After showering and eating, I walked down the long stairway to the beach. To the south, it was possible to make out the town of Goderich, featuring a large salt-mining facility. Debris and human bodies washed up on this shoreline in November 1913, days after the great white hurricane passed through. Two boats sank in the vicinity: the *James Carruthers,* with a cargo of coal and a crew of twenty-two men, and the *Hydrus,* carrying iron ore and a crew of twenty-five men. In neither case were there any survivors. But wreckage was also identified from ships that sank on the Michigan side of the lake, having drifted for miles across the open water.

As the sun went down on a midsummer evening, the conditions of which were as distant from an inland hurricane as could be imagined, people gathered to view the sunset and snap photos. Of course, it wasn't that long ago I was on the other side, heading northward, riding along the outside of Michigan's thumb toward Harbor Beach.

August 6, 2011

The last day of the trip would take me from the park back to Sarnia. I was on the road by eight o'clock, a little apprehensive, given the inconsistent quality of Route 21. I decided to stay on it for a while and then, if it deteriorated, try to find a parallel county road.

I stopped in Goderich for some breakfast, another quaint Canadian lakefront town, with well-preserved Victorian houses and a lively town square. The sidewalks were busy with people moving toward work or whatnot. People waved and said hello as I rode around the square surveying the scene. No houses with trees growing out of them around here.

Unfortunately, the highway took a turn for the worse as I headed out of town, so I decided to use the map that I had bought the day before to find a back road. From the look of things, at Bayfield I could crisscross a series of county roads that would ultimately take me into Sarnia. The road I found had virtually no traffic and cut across hay and alfalfa fields. It tracked high along the bluff, allowing occasionally glimpses of Lake Huron a few miles off in the distance. The road runs though quaint farming villages, with coffee shops and antique stores. The problem with riding around on county roads, however, is the possibility of getting lost. And that's exactly what happened. At one intersection, the highway split in a way that did not exactly correspond to the map, and there was no road sign. As I stood looking at my map, someone in a car rolled down the window and offered the use of their GPS. I appreciated the gesture, but it didn't really resolve the problem of which way to turn. I turned left, rode for a few miles, and then turned right up a narrow road toward the west in the direction of Lake Huron. After a couple of miles, the road turned to gravel and then ended at a T in the middle of a cornfield. The clouds were thickening, and it was starting to look like rain, literally and figuratively. I turned left and was relieved to see a sign for Route 11, which was the road that I wanted into Sarnia.

Another miscalculation at another intersection led to a dead end at Huron's edge. Under ordinary circumstances, it could have been seen as a pleasant ride through a small First Nations community to a nice beach, but I was getting a little tired and impatient and wanted to get back to my car. With all the different twists and turns, I was probably adding ten or twenty miles to my trip, turning a reasonable seventy-five-mile ride into one that was approaching a hundred. There is a rule somewhere that says that the last day of a bicycle tour has to be the most difficult, and that seemed to be holding true in this case.

Finally, I saw a sign that said "Sarnia" and figured I must be close to the downtown. But the sign marked the town line, not the city limits, and it turned out to be another ten miles to the city proper. The lakeshore ride into town provides a tour of beautiful old mansions that sit on the shore, and it reminded me of Bay City, Michigan. I should have stopped for water, because I was feeling extremely dehydrated, but I kept thinking I was almost there and could stop and rest soon enough. When I finally made my way across town to within about a mile of the train station where I had parked my car, I stopped at a convenience store and bought a liter-and-half bottle of water. I gulped it down in no time flat. I couldn't help but wonder where it was all going.

My trusty old Volvo was still at the train station, but it had a flat, which seemed a little strange. How often does your car get a flat just sitting there? Perhaps partly because of exhaustion, a mild bit of paranoia set in. Had local kids, seeing American license plates, let the air out of the tires? I put on the doughnut tire, threw my stuff into the back, and headed to a gas station to put some air into it. When I found a place with an air pump, I gave it a shot only to find air pouring out of the broken valve stem. It wasn't a slow leak, and was nothing that I could pin on any local miscreants.

The spare seemed fairly stable, so I stopped for some greasy fish and chips and headed down the highway. Things were going fine until I was just outside of Buffalo, near Batavia, New York. Leaving the tollbooths that cut across the thruway there, another tire blew. I couldn't believe my bad luck. How often do you get a flat tire? And now I'd had two in the space of a few hours. Plus, it was now almost midnight, and my cell phone was dead.

I got out of the car and waited for the state police to show up, which I figured they would do. After about twenty minutes, they arrived. I stumbled on my way over to greet them. One asked me if I'd been drinking. "Absolutely not," I responded. They didn't bother with a breath check. What they did was call a tow truck, and I waited another twenty minutes for it to arrive. By now, it was after one o'clock. Upon arrival, the driver pulled the car up onto the platform and asked me if I had Triple A, which I did. "Plus?" he asked, "Yes, Plus." That would give me a free hundred-mile tow. He'd do it himself, but he had other calls. He was going to take me to the next exit and then get another tower to take me back to Ithaca. I would pay twenty cents a mile after a hundred miles. It seemed ridiculous to me to have my car towed back to Ithaca with just a flat tire. I was doing the mileage calculation in my head and figuring this was going to cost me at least one hundred and fifty dollars. I wondered if there wasn't some other way to do this. He told me that this was really the only option.

He dropped me off in a Denny's parking lot and said it would be an hour before the next tow truck showed up. Fortunately, he was wrong, and the next one appeared before I was even able to grab a cup of coffee from the restaurant. This driver was more helpful and said that if I could find a place to sleep, he'd fix my tire in his shop the next day. There was a motel across the street, so I grabbed my bicycle and my stuff and rode over to it, only to discover that it was full.

I hurried back to the parking lot, just in time to catch the driver before he left with my car in tow. He said that the easiest thing might be just to go to his garage and see if he could fix the tires. This sounded like a plan.

We drove several miles to his house to get the key. Then we drove another few miles back to the garage. He opened it up, unloaded the car, and proceeded to install new valves in both tires as I watched. By now it was close to three o'clock. After he finished, I asked about the price. I was ready to pay anything at this point. "How about twenty dollars per tire?" I cheerfully paid him the cash, thanked him profusely, and was on my way.

In Batavia, I stopped at a convenience store to wash my hands. The clerk wanted to know if I needed a bag for the juice and peanuts that I'd bought. He was very insistent. I said no, and was equally insistent. "What is up with this?" I asked. "You're on a bike!" he responded. I was still in my bicycle clothes.

Down the New York State Thruway at the wee hours of the morning, I was so tired that I missed the turnoff to Ithaca, and drove to Auburn, probably adding an extra twenty miles to the trip. Finally home at seven o'clock, journey complete, I took a shower and fell asleep on the sofa after checking email. Four Great Lakes to go.

FORT ERIE

LONG POINT
PROVINCIAL PARK

DETROIT

AMHERSTBURG

LAKE ERIE

ASTABULA

CLEVELAND

SANDUSKY

MAUMEE BAY
STATE PARK

Lake Erie

May 29, 2012

It was sunny, humid, and very warm as I started my trip around Lake Erie. My departure point was Westfield, New York. I grew up south of there in Jamestown and spent time during my youth shambling around with friends through the nearby Chautauqua Gorge, drinking beer or getting high, or hiking and swimming. The area was crucial to colonization of North America. What is now Westfield was first visited by French explorers in the early seventeenth century as they were seeking a water route from the Great Lakes into what they knew was a vast river system to the south that could take them into the central part of the continent and eventually to the Gulf of Mexico. No water link existed, but the distance between the lakes that were eventually named Erie and Chautauqua was relatively short, though traveling between them involved hiking over a fairly long and very steep hill. Given its strategic location between northern and southern waterways, the Portage Trail is no doubt one of the most important ten-mile stretches in North America.

The path had long been used by North America's Native inhabitants. In 1615, Frenchman Étienne Brûlé purportedly became the first European to travel it. An expedition by Baron De Longueuil mapped and measured the trail in 1739. In 1749 Captain Celeron de Bienville, with a group of more than seven hundred men, cleared trees along the trail and continued southward to the Ohio River, burying lead markers claiming the entire route and all of the Ohio valley for the French king Louis XV.[1] The town of Celeron on Chautauqua Lake is named after the captain. Hikers can still follow the original trail, as I have done on foot. It's about five miles up, then five back down into the county seat, Mayville, which features a courthouse, a jail, a raft of restaurants and shops, and an expansive view of Chautauqua Lake for travelers looking southward.

Westfield was the home of Grace Bedell, the young woman who after attending a campaign event in the town, wrote to Abraham Lincoln with advice to grow a beard. She suggested that his face was too thin and that women would appreciate whiskers and thus would encourage their husbands to vote for him. Lincoln responded with a noncommittal letter of his own. After being elected president and on a return trip to Illinois, he stopped again in the town and asked to meet the young woman who had written the letter. In a brief meeting at the train stop, he asked her if she liked his beard and kissed her on the cheek. A statue depicting their meeting (but not the kiss) is in the town park.

As I cycled toward Route 5 into the even smaller town of Barcelona, Lake Erie was in sight. It was getting hotter and windier, and I knew a cold front was heading in from the west. I figured it was only a matter of time before I encountered a serious rainstorm. Other than the wind and the threat of rain, the scene was bucolic. There wasn't much traffic on the road, which cut a swath through miles of grape vineyards. This area is known as the "grape juice capital of the world." Welch's, the largest distributor of grape juice globally, uses most of these Concord grapes to make its products. Wine making has made some inroads, but this is still primarily a juice region.

Welch's was started by Thomas Bramwell Welch, who perfected the process of pasteurizing grape juice. A Methodist with strong views against alcohol and slavery, he was active in both the Underground Railroad and the temperance movement. He practiced dentistry with his son Charles, and together they started the Welch's Grape Juice Company in 1893. The company received a huge public relations boost when fire-and-brimstone orator William Jennings Bryan, as secretary of state, substituted it for wine at state functions. An even bigger boost came with the passage of

Prohibition. I grew up drinking the stuff, and I have to admit that I still like it. It's an old-school fruit juice in the age of pomegranates, kiwis, and mangoes, but that's OK with me.

As I began to approach Erie, Pennsylvania, I stopped briefly to take a few gulps from my water bottle. I was standing there on the side of the road when a somewhat scraggly-looking man with a beard walked up to me. "Know where I can get some acid?" he asked. I was a little surprised by the question. It seemed odd enough that someone walking on the side of the highway in the year 2012 would be asking a stranger about buying LSD, but that he believed that someone fully outfitted and touring on a bicycle would have some, or know where to get some, seemed even stranger. Then again, bicycle touring may be enough on the fringe and outside the boundaries of ordinary rational conduct that it could, in some minds, be associated with other peripheral activities, such as taking psychedelic drugs.

To be honest, I don't believe that such a conclusion is entirely unwarranted. The same desires that encouraged some to experiment with psychedelic drugs also inspired some to take up long-distance running and other endurance sports. The film *Run for Your Life*, which documents the history of the New York Marathon, makes such a claim. The impulses behind endurance activities and drug taking may express both dissatisfaction with and a desire to escape from the constraints of conventional life and mundane forms of consciousness. Nevertheless, I didn't have any LSD, and if I had, I probably would not have sold it to a stranger whom I met on the side of the road. I politely told him "no" and moved on.

Like so many other cities along the Great Lakes, the area around Erie, Pennsylvania, was first settled by the French, who built a fort at Presque Isle, the peninsula that juts out into the lake north of the city and is now a state park. The first settlers were the Erielhonans, who believed the peninsula to be an outstretched arm offered by the Great Spirit as haven for those caught by storms out on the lake. The Eriez were pushed out by the Haudenosaunee during the so-called Beaver Wars of the seventeenth century. The importance of these conflicts and the fur trade in general cannot be overstated in recounting the history of North American settlement and colonization. Indigenous groups vied over access to hunting areas to supply the seemingly inexhaustible European demand for hats, coats, and boots. As the Haudenosaunee depleted their established areas, they sought new ones, and in doing so, came into conflict with indigenous people to the west. The Eriez were a casualty of this push north and westward.

After the Beaver Wars came the French and Indian War, which was essentially a North American extension of the European Seven Years' War, a huge and complex conflict that involved all major European powers, resulted in over one million deaths, and remade the colonial map of North America. Before the Treaty of Paris of 1783, the French controlled much of the territory to the north and west of the thirteen British American colonies, although the exact borders were undefined and the subject of considerable dispute. After the French loss in the war, the British controlled the entire eastern seaboard and land that was deep into what is now the American Midwest. The entire shoreline of Lake Erie fell under British control. Native Americans still, of course, held land claims, but given their exclusion from the peace talks, those claims became increasingly precarious.[2]

After the American Revolution, this area was highly prized since it offered access to the lake. As a result, it was subject to claims by several states: New York, Massachusetts, and Connecticut. Pennsylvania eventually bought the land from the federal government, settling the issue for good.

Presque Isle played a key role in the War of 1812 as the place where Daniel Dobbins and Commander Oliver Hazard Perry built the fleet of ships that Perry used to attack the British during the storied Battle of Lake Erie. After British victories at Fort Detroit and Mackinac Island, the war, which had been highly controversial from the outset, seemed to be going very badly for the Americans. Moreover, the American shores of Lake Erie were essentially without naval defenses.

Dobbins, an early resident of Erie and an experienced ship's captain, who had been captured and released by the British during the taking of Mackinac, traveled to Washington in 1812 and convinced the James Madison administration to build a fleet at the city of Erie and launch it from Presque Isle harbor. The peninsula served as a protected barrier between American and British fleets. Perry, who arrived at Erie in 1813, worked with Dobbins to build the fleet, cutting beams from local oak trees and bringing in other needed materials from Pittsburgh.

The battle lasted only about three hours, as Perry turned what looked to be certain defeat into an unexpected victory when he rowed from his disabled ship, the *Lawrence,* to another ship, the *Niagara,* and used it to disrupt the British formation. When the British ships *Detroit* and *Queen Charlotte* collided, the battle was over, and Perry became a national hero. One of the ironies of the War of 1812 is that the Americans, who were considered at best a second-rate naval power, consistently defeated the British on the water, whereas the British were most successful on land.

It would be a mistake, however, to think that the Battle of Lake Erie won the War of 1812, as has sometimes been suggested. Madison's War was fought to a stalemate and is now considered by Canadians to be their "war of independence" against the United States. The war did, however, mean that the lakes themselves would be international waters, controlled neither by the United States or the British, or eventually their Canadian counterparts.

Dobbins, who had been ordered by Perry to sail for supplies on the eve of the battle, did not participate. However, he did return to Erie and helped to transform it into an important commercial and manufacturing city. A monument to Perry sits at the end of Presque Isle, and a restored version of his ship *Niagara* is in the city's harbor. The original ship was destroyed, given its deteriorated condition, but some of its materials were used in the construction of the newer one, which operates as a sailing school and also offers public excursions.[3] After the 1812 war and into the twentieth century, the Seneca, a branch of the Haudenosaunee, still held nominal claims to this area but relinquished them in 1970 for a grand sum of $800.

The sky was looking increasingly threatening as I reached the edge of the city of Erie. I decided to stop for shelter near a bus stop until the storm passed. But it rained only a little, and I didn't experience the deluge that the sky had promised. I was right on the corner of a major arterial that took cars around the city if they wanted to avoid driving through the downtown. The traffic there was fairly busy. Somebody yelled something at me: "Chicken shit!" What was that about? Some Americans do love to yell profanities or take out other kinds of aggression against bicyclists. I've never figured out exactly why.

The bus stop was not in the most affluent part of the town. In fact, the convenience store next to it was boarded up. Erie, like so many other cities along these lakes, was once a manufacturing hub but has experienced significant economic dislocations and population loss since it won an All-America City Award in 1972. Along the road into the city center stretched a long row of once-stately brick homes, now in various states of disrepair. As in many of the other cities along the lake, the downtown neighborhoods of Erie have suffered the most deterioration, as affluent residents and businesses have moved to suburbs.

The city center was busy, featuring Gridley Park, two blocks wide, with attractive summer gardens. An obelisk in the park serves as a monument to the park's namesake, Charles Vernon Gridley, a Spanish-American War hero. Across the street, on the western side of the park is the Erie Club, an impressive brick building with imposing columns in the front. The building was originally built by shipping magnate Charles Reed, grandson of the city's original settler, Seth Reed. When his prized steamer *Erie* succumbed to fire in 1841, more than two hundred people died, including his brother-in-law. Mrs. Reed, distraught over the loss of her brother, wanted to leave the area and return eastward. Charles convinced her to stay, so the story goes, by building a mansion for their residence, which now serves as the club's headquarters.[*]

As I crossed to the west end of town and rode along some side streets, I saw block after block of deteriorating houses, often with windows boarded up or dressed with sheets of plastic. Distressed automobiles sat on the streets and front lawns. The tree-lined streets still offer hints of once-prosperous and pleasant middle-class neighborhoods, but these neighborhoods now just seem to be rotting away.

Once out of the city, along West Lake Road, past the state game lands, skirting the town of Conneaut on the Ohio border, things changed drastically. Farms and fields again appeared, and I could occasionally catch a glimpse of the lake to the north. The deluge that I had anticipated never arrived, but at one point I could feel the front pass over, as the temperature dropped a good ten or fifteen degrees. The rainless front did little, however, to quench the thirst of some very parched fields and lawns along the highway.

Ashtabula, Ohio, is about eighty miles west of Westfield, where I had begun the day's journey. I had decided that was a pretty good first-day's ride and decided to spend the night there. In town, I passed the Lake Shore Park, which seemed nice but featured a very prominent "No camping" sign. I rode through the old port to East Ashtabula, across the Ashtabula River (a former Superfund site) and became a little lost in my attempt to find the center of Ashtabula proper. When I finally arrived, I was slightly horrified by what I saw.

Ashtabula was once one of the most important ports on Lake Erie. It was tied into the national rail network and the chemical industry and had assorted forms of manufacturing. But nowadays Ashtabula stands out as one of the more blighted rust-belt cities I have encountered. The downtown area featured several blocks of empty lots and vacant storefronts. These could have provided a movie set for the latest zombie series. I didn't see any motels, so I decided to ask someone standing in front of a convenience store. The person seemed confused. He told me there was a motel over by Walmart. I told him I didn't know where that was. He said it was across from Sheets. I told him I didn't know where that was either. He pointed up the street.

Fortunately, the little motel turned out to be clean and cheap. I took a shower and decided to walk until I found a place to eat. But I was now out in strip-mall territory, which of course means no sidewalks. I walked for a bit on the grass along the highway and spotted a Mexican restaurant in a shopping center. The food turned out to be pretty good, but getting there and back involved a precarious walk on footpaths and across medians and dodging the cars at freeway entrance ramps. Suburbia: open, spacious, antiseptic, and completely alienating, at least for me.

May 30, 2012

The next day's ride to Cleveland was very pleasant, which, apart from a stretch on Highway 20, involved zigzagging along secondary roads that skirt the lake at various distances. Old resort towns like Geneva-on-the-Lake, Fairport Harbor, and Mentor-on-the-Lake maintain a charm that has not been entirely eclipsed by time. Things seemed pretty quiet, probably because it was early in the season. In August the streets and shops were no doubt filled with refugees from nearby cities and suburbs. The weather had cleared since yesterday, making it perfect for cycling. The beautiful blue skies, perhaps recovering from yesterday's storms, seemed devoid of major wind currents.

The route into Cleveland took me through quiet suburban streets lined with old mansions. I was able to avoid heavy traffic almost completely, which I gratefully attribute to the path laid out by Harvey Botzman in his cyclotour guide *'Round Lake Erie.*[5] The lawns and gabled houses of the far suburbs soon give way to middle-class bungalows and apartment buildings and eventually the more economically challenged neighborhoods of East Cleveland. I cycled through Parma, an all-white suburb that refused to allow federally subsidized low-income housing into its jurisdiction in the early 1970s. The decision was challenged by the U.S. Justice Department on the grounds that it was a pretext to keep black residents from East Cleveland out, and thus a violation of the Fourteenth Amendment Equal Protection Clause. The case made it all the way to Supreme Court, which found against the city and ordered a detailed plan to diversify its pool of residents. But after more than thirty years, Parma is still predominantly white, East Cleveland is predominantly black, and Cleveland has been designated the tenth most segregated city in America.[6]

Approaching the urban center, there is another small swatch of graceful old mansions that sit right on Erie's shoreline. The small village of Bratenahl, one of Cleveland's first suburbs, is surrounded by the city on three sides. Its one thousand residents constitute the most affluent suburb, on a per capita basis, in greater Cleveland. Unfortunately for them, Interstate 90 rubs right up against the area, and its traffic noise is palpable on some of the streets. It's one of the starker contrasts between a major highway and a leafy cul-de-sac that I've ever encountered. Usually, it's a city's poorer residents who have to contend with nearby arterials, but here it's the most affluent, which struck me as a small victory for urban environmental justice. The residents of Bratenahl are unlikely, I am sure, to see it in those terms.

Back out on the open highway, the Cleveland skyline soon came into view, as the route alternates between bike paths and access roads that run parallel to the small Burke Airport. On the bike path through a park that leads into the downtown, I stopped to help another cyclist, Ryan, who was having trouble. His chain had broken, and he was unsure about how to run it through the derailleur before recoupling it. He asked me to turn over my bike, so he could see how it worked there. I was a little hesitant, given that it would require me to take my panniers off and undo the bungee cords that held on my sleeping bag and tent. Plus, his level of anxiety seemed disproportionate to the relatively minor crisis he faced. In other words, I found him to be fairly annoying. Fortunately, before I had a chance to lose patience, Molly appeared. A take-charge cross-dresser, outfitted entirely in pink, she calmed Ryan right down, carefully fixed the chain, while managing to avoid getting even a spot of grease on her clothes. I was impressed. Crisis averted, we went our separate ways.

I rolled into the city around four o'clock and found the hotel where I'd booked a room. Cleveland's downtown is a mélange of stores and businesses, still with the look of a midwestern city of the 1940s: Chicago writ small. Some of the old buildings have been taken over by casinos, and gambling and sports are obviously important economic drivers. The Quicken Loans basketball arena is in the center of town. The Browns stadium and the Rock and Roll Hall of Fame are down near the lakefront. Entertainment fuels the postindustrial economy, along with health care, of course. The Cleveland Clinic is just a few miles east of the commercial district.

After dinner, I walked past a bar with throngs of people crowding the sidewalk. This seemed a little odd for a Sunday early evening. Curious, I went in. It was NBA draft-pick night. Attendees could win prizes for matching the picks with the teams. Score cards littered the place. No doubt Cavalier fans were hoping for a good pick, given the recent loss of LeBron James to Miami. (James would return to the Cavs after leading the Heat to two championships. His return marked a considerable improvement to his hometown team, to say the least. The Cavs went on to win the NBA championship in 2016. After being down three games to one in the finals, they pulled off perhaps the greatest comeback in NBA history to defeat the Golden State Warriors, four games to three.)

May 31, 2012

Since I haven't spent much time in Cleveland, I decided to make a day of it. First on my list of sights was the famous Rock and Roll Hall of Fame. Given the beautiful sunny morning, I walked over to the lakefront where it sits. The museum has more than its fair share of critics who see it as too stodgy and conservative, too commercial, and an attempt to institutionalize and tame the exuberance of and danger (at least originally) posed by rock music. There may be some truth in the criticism, but museums tend to be conservative by nature, and popular music is commercial by definition. You just have to take it for what it's worth.

The place was chock-full of schoolkids, out on an end-of-year trip. I couldn't imagine my teachers taking me to a place like this.

My school trips involved a local bakery and the Marlin Rockwell factory. Here, over at the large Rolling Stones exhibit, a young man, probably around fifteen, had his mom take his picture standing near one of Keith Richards's guitars. It doesn't get much more endearing than that. Cleveland was, of course, an important center for rock music, and the term itself was, according to lore, coined by Cleveland DJ Alan Freed when he changed the name of his radio show from Record Rendezvous to Moondog's Rock 'n' Roll Party. It was a fit of marketing genius in its successful attempt to appeal to white teenagers cast under the spell of African American rhythm and blues music.

One of the more eye-opening sections of the museum, at least for me, involved clothing and fashion. I tend to think of rock 'n' roll as a casual art form, but what's clear from all of the exhibited outfits is that successful performers (or perhaps their managers) thought an awful lot about what they wore. They either consciously or intuitively grasped the essential connection between the aural and the visual, and they understood that they were participating in a form of musical theater.

After lunch, I took the train to the Museum of Contemporary Art, which would also give me the opportunity to see the Case Western Reserve campus. The closest train stop dropped me off about a half mile south of the Cleveland Clinic complex. The neighborhood, if you can call it that, between the station and the complex consists of a stretch of vacant lots with a smattering of shabby houses scattered among them. The streets were mostly devoid of human beings. The entry to the clinic area makes for a startling contrast. One moment you are surrounded by urban decay, the next by modern glass-encased buildings. The abandoned cars rusting forlornly in abandoned driveways are replaced with sleek expensive models swooshing around with men and women in suits or medical uniforms. Health care takes up a large proportion of the U.S. economy, and the wealth generated is clearly on display here.

The Museum of Contemporary Art was closed, as its collection was being moved to a new space, so I took a bus up Euclid

Avenue to the beautiful Case Western Reserve campus and found the Cleveland Museum. I'm not exactly an art connoisseur, but I have a layperson's interest, and I like the open space and the quiet meditative atmosphere that museums offer. In most art museums, the historical and stylistic organization of the work grants an illusion of order and progress to our aesthetically chaotic world. The Cleveland Museum isn't huge, but it's well curated, with a strong European collection. The portrait miniatures collection is purportedly among the best in the world, although I cannot say that I could fully appreciate its value. But I did appreciate a day of edification, sight-seeing, and good food and one of America's most underappreciated cities. The next day I'd be back on the road.

June 1, 2012

I woke up early to sunshine and took my rear wheel to the nearby bike shop to have the wobble tightened. It took the mechanic only a couple of minutes to do it. He didn't want to charge me, but I insisted on giving him at least something for his time. It's an art to get the tightness just right, and something I've never been able to master myself. It took me a while to load up the bike. I was on the third floor of the hotel and had the bike locked up in front. After several trips, I was out riding through the western side of Cleveland, along St. Clair Avenue, through the warehouse district, and then over the West Superior Avenue Bridge. After the bridge, I turned right onto Detroit and then Lake Avenues, along the lakefront, an urban environment that seemed intentionally designed for great cycling, even though it obviously wasn't.

The rain started as a mist as I departed greater Cleveland, through the western suburbs and then the small communities of Bay Village, Avon Lake, Sheffield Lake, and Lorain, into Vermilion. The cool, misty rain was pleasant at first, but soon it turned into a downpour, which carried on and off between medium and heavy for several hours. I can live with rain, but such heavy, intense rain for a long period of time can get a little tiresome. Fortunately, the road had a decent shoulder, so I didn't have to worry too much about not being seen by cars. But it was raining heavily enough that if I were closer to the traffic, it would be an issue.

Having to pee, I pulled into a dirt road near what appeared to be the entrance to a county park. When I got back to the bike, the back tire was flat. I changed inner tubes but realized after riding a few hundred feet that the replacement must have had a leak. It's hard to fix a leak on a busy highway because you can't locate it by listening. And I didn't have a sink to dunk the tube into to find the bubbles. But as it turned out, the water falling from the sky helped me to find it. The glue in the patch kit, however, was old, partly oxidized, and not destined to create a tight seal. Before I knew it, I had to add air to the softening tire. Every couple of miles, I got off the bike and repeated this procedure until I arrived in Sandusky.

It was only three o'clock, plenty of time, I thought, to make it over the Sandusky Bay Bridge and find a place to stay on the other side. I'd been a little worried about the trip across because, as is noted on several websites, bicycles are not allowed on the bridge. According to Harvey Botzman's guidebook, however, if you can make it halfway across and the police catch you, they will ride you over to the other side (after a brief lecture). The alternative was to ride around Sandusky Bay, which would take at least a half day.

As I approached the bridge, with my slow leaking inner tube, the traffic became heavier, with long strings of large trucks packing the road. Two or three miles from the bridge, my chain broke. So here I was in the rain with a leaky tire and a broken chain. I pulled the bike down into a culvert, dug out my chain tool, and went to work. It took a bit, but when I finally got it working again, I decided to ride back into Sandusky and find a motel for the night. This turned out not to be as easy as I had anticipated, since I couldn't find any motels on the ride back into town nor in the main downtown area. Someone I asked in the parking lot of a convenience store directed me back to the eastern edge of the city, where I found a place, not especially elegant but dry, with ample space to fix my bike.

Once inside the room, I found my extra chain and put that on, but had more problems with the inner tube patch. The rubber cement that came with the kit wasn't holding, so I went to a drugstore and bought some instant glue, a method that has worked well for me in the past. But it was hardening up the patches, so I couldn't get them to adhere properly. I started putting patch over patch, but each time a new leak would spring up. I spent a couple of hours on this and then just gave up. The inner tube would hold long enough to get me to the bike shop that I had noticed on my ride back from the bridge.

June 2, 2012

The rain had cleared when I pushed my bike out of the motel room into a brilliant early morning sun. The bike shop didn't open until ten o'clock, so I had breakfast in the local diner. Other small businesses lined a street that tilted down toward the lakefront. Sandusky seems like a much more prosperous place than its neighbors to the east. After a breakfast of French toast, orange juice, and coffee, I made my way to the bike shop. The owner and his daughter were friendly and helpful. Unfortunately, I'd put skinny tires on my mountain bike to minimize resistance, and the only inner tubes he had were for wider ones. The owner thought that they would work OK, although he didn't seem entirely confident about the matter. He also told me that police were tightening up on the no-cycling policy on the bridge. Now, if you were caught, they'd bring you back to your starting point. The new policy put a significant disincentive to attempting to cross; still, I figured it was worth the risk.

I followed Botzman's instruction as to how to approach the bridge via an entry ramp that avoided most of busy Highway 2. The bridge is wide, not too steep, with an excellent shoulder. I've definitely traveled over much worse, and if it were up to me, I'd allow cycles. But when I had made it about a quarter of the way across—no cops in sight—my back tire suddenly went flat. I couldn't believe it. I had no choice but to walk the bike back up the shoulder, facing into traffic, down the exit ramp, back to the access road.

For some reason, I was convinced that this had to do with the size of the inner tube, which I thought maybe had gotten folded inside the tire. If I could just get the kinks out, it would be OK. How else to explain why a brand-new inner tube would suddenly go flat after riding on it for only around ten miles? I reseated the tube, rode for a hundred yards, and, of course, it went flat again. I tried again with the same result. I seemed to be acting out Albert Einstein's definition of insanity: repeating the same behavior while expecting a different outcome. I tried the other tube, and voilà, it held. I pedaled as fast as I could over the bridge, and in just a few minutes I was on the other side.

The wind was really starting to pick up as I rode across the Marblehead Peninsula, separating the bay from Lake Erie proper. I had forty miles to Toledo, my original goal. Given the late start, the screwing around with my tire, and the wind, I was wondering if I'd make it. The closer I got to Toledo, the more the wind intensified. It's a flat stretch, so few obstructions to block the gusts. Highway 2 also isn't exactly a peaceful ride, with a shoulder that is narrow enough that I was worried about being blown out into fast-moving, heavy traffic.

After a few hours of difficult and slow going, I saw the sign for Maumee Bay State Park and turned onto County Road 202. The wind was suddenly at my side rather than in my face. Not a tailwind exactly, but still I felt like I was flying down the three or four miles to the park entrance. Once there, I realized I'd made the right choice. Maumee is a gem of place, and this early in the season it was half-empty. Flat dunes and grasslands reach up from the lakeshore. The wind, which had just been my enemy, now seemed a perfect fit for the setting. The deep-blue lake contrasted sharply against the sky, the white sand, and billowing grass.

The Maumee, or Maami, the original Native settlers of the area, were driven off the land by General Anthony Wayne in the 1794 Battle of Fallen Timbers, the final decisive battle of the Northwest Indian War.[7] Maumee was also the name given to the ancestral precursor of Lake Erie, which formed as the Laurentide Ice Sheet retreated. Thus, the area's indigenous people are now celebrated literally in name only, as has been common practice in the American experience. Nevertheless, Maumee Park offers a hint of the unspoiled landscapes that existed here before European settlers, or any settlers for that matter, arrived. At a more mundane level, the campsites were large, offering plenty of privacy. I put my tent up in an area that offered some protection from the wind, showered, made dinner from a mixture of items I found scattered around in my panniers, and then slept very deeply. The next day I hoped to make it to Detroit.

June 3, 2012

The morning was sunny but a bit chilly, as I found my way out to the grid of county roads that crisscross the pancake-flat terrain east of Toledo. It soon becomes clear that Maumee, with its apparent wildness and sweep, is just a stone's throw from greater Toledo's industrial infrastructure. A large and rather smelly BP oil refinery sits just a couple of miles from the park on Cedar Road. Soon thereafter appear the neighborhoods, warehouses, and factories of East Toledo, which line the banks of the Maumee River, probably, at least at one time, using it as a convenient dumping site for a witch's brew of toxic effluents. The Maumee's watershed is the largest of any river flowing into the Great Lakes, reaching as far west as Indiana. American settlers called it the Great Black Swamp and spent incredible effort over many years in the nineteenth century draining it to turn it into land suitable for their agricultural purposes.[8]

I made my way to the Veterans' Glass City Skyway bridge, a modern structure, which lights up at night, marking it as a distinctive feature of Toledo's skyline. It also features a wide bike lane, which runs up and away from the bridge traffic, allowing cyclists the opportunity to take in the view without having to worry about finding a front wheel caught in a drainage grate or being hit by a long-haul truck.

Toledo's skyline is the prominent feature looking southwestward from the bridge's peak. From the distance it looked to be the epitome of a vital, middle-sized, midwestern city. If I'd made it in a little earlier yesterday, I'd have found a place to stay there. But in that case I would have missed Maumee, so I had no real regrets. Across the bridge, I turned northward to Detroit, now skirting the very western edge of Lake Erie.

Eventually the factories and warehouses of northern Toledo give way to flat farmlands. To avoid Interstate 75, the most direct path to Detroit, I rode across a network of county roads that run through places like French Township and Monroe. It's easy to get lost, which I of course did, but the wind, now at my back, helped direct me back on course as I meandered along. I kept thinking that the Detroit metro area would start to impose itself on these rural stretches, but to my surprise, even ten or fifteen miles south of Detroit there were few signs of urban incursion.

Just across the Wayne County line, a traveler enters what is known as "Downriver," a series of working-class communities that lead toward Detroit's city limits. The first is Trenton. Chrysler still makes engines here, and a large power plant presumably employs people as well. But the dominant feature of the city's architecture is the hulking remains of the old McLouth Steel plant. The company was founded in 1918, undertook a major expansion in 1948, and continued to grow even into the 1960s. Once known for its innovation, particularly as an early adopter of computer controls and the first steel plant to use the continuous casting process,[9] its challenges began in the 1970s as cheap Asian imports entered the market and the Detroit auto industry's demands for steel began to decline. The Detroit Steel Company bought it in 1996, and it soon fell into bankruptcy. Several attempts to restart production failed. Its electrical power system no longer works, the copper wiring having been plundered. Detroit Steel hasn't paid property taxes since 2006 and is now more than $4 million in arrears. These days the plant serves primarily as a ghostly tourist attraction for adventurous explorers of modern urban ruins.[10]

After Trenton is Wyandotte, an island of activity and prosperity, sandwiched between the distressed industrial landscapes to the south and River Rouge to the north. The city features small shops and a lovely park in the town center. The city was famous for its production of toy guns up through the 1950s. Michigan Alkali Chemical ran a soda-making operation, a highly toxic process, creating residues, including mercury, that were dumped unceremoniously into the Detroit River.

Next is River Rouge, home to the storied River Rouge industrial complex, still owned and operated by the Ford Motor Company. Everything from World War I Eagle Boats to Model T parts and the Ford Mustang were manufactured here. The plant is infamous for a 1937 confrontation between pro-union workers and company security guards, during the so-called Battle of the Overpass. The subsequent publication of newspaper photos featuring guards beating workers turned the incident into a nationwide cause célèbre and helped to spur the successful genesis of the United Automobile Workers Union. While the original Building B has now been shuttered, parts of the complex still operate, cranking out Ford trucks under a green roof designed by sustainability guru William McDonough.

Bicycling into Detroit along the river's edge, avoiding the main highways, there's surprisingly scant traffic. West Jefferson and West Ford Streets are lined with more abandoned buildings and the occasional operating plant at this southern edge of the once-mighty Motor City. The taller buildings of downtown Detroit, including the Renaissance Center, slowly come into view. Upon closer inspection, however, what seemed bright and shiny from a distance starts to look a little threadbare.

The city's center, a maze of intersecting side streets and wide boulevards, was hard for me to decipher, even with a city map. Stymied in my search for my hotel, I asked a couple of very large police officers for directions. One looked at me like I was from Mars. The other was very pleasant and very helpful with directions. I climbed on the bike and backtracked a few blocks to the hotel.

The staff was accommodating, allowing me to put my bike on the elevator and bring it up to the room. After a quick shower, I walked outside and followed the swarms of people that were heading to the riverfront. Following crowds is sometimes to be avoided, but in this case I had a hunch they were headed someplace interesting. Many of those whom I walked along with sported brightly dyed hair and unusually vivid attire. Following them, I found my way to a big public party celebrating Detroit Pride Day. Out front, dozens of political organizers were fund-raising and leafleting. Many wore Barack Obama T-shirts. Inside, on two stages, I caught a couple of trans dance and vocal shows. The audiences were enthusiastic, and everyone seemed to be having a great time. I hung around for a while and then went in search of food.

Even a few blocks from the city center, Detroit's economic distress becomes undeniably apparent. I was hit up by several panhandlers on my way to a brewpub recommended in the *New York Times* "36 Hours in Detroit." I was approached again several times on the way back. One person, searching through a trash can for bottles, was practically apoplectic. "Why won't anybody help me out?" he yelled out to no one in particular. I walked somewhat warily back to the hotel.

June 4, 2012

My plan on Monday was to hit some museums. I had a list: the Motown Museum, the Detroit Historical Museum, the Detroit Institute of Arts, and more. In search of metro passes, I wandered over to the welcome center in the Cadillac Place, formerly the General Motors Building. The fifteen-story structure was designed by the famous architect Albert Kahn. Built in 1919, it once served as GM's headquarters. It is now a public office building for the State of Michigan. The center itself was closed, so I asked a guard if there was a place to buy bus passes. He directed me to a little store on the first floor, where Beatrice and May held court.

They informed me that they only had monthly passes, and I'd be better off just buying tickets on the bus. It was easy, they assured me. So, with their assurance, I wandered up to catch the

Woodward Avenue bus north. I waited for a few minutes, got on, and paid the fare. No problem. But the ride was something else. From the windows, I viewed an increasingly desolate urban land-scape. I'd never seen so many abandoned buildings in one place before. Some were tall, ten or fifteen stories. Many had all of the windows broken out. In between were large swaths of vacant lots. Scenes like this went on for blocks and blocks. Jane Jacobs wrote in 1961 about Detroit in her classic work *The Death and Life of Great American Cities*: "Detroit is largely composed, today, of seemingly endless square miles of low-density failure." I wonder what she would say if she could see it today.

I hopped off the bus at a stop near Wayne State University, an island of commerce and concentrated activity amid the desolation, and walked three blocks to the Historical Museum. It was closed for renovations. Since the weather was nice, and I wasn't planning any other exercise that day, I decided to walk the two miles or so to the Motown Museum, along Cass Avenue under the viaduct and then left on Grand Avenue.

Exiting the campus involved reentering the world of urban decay. Grand Avenue is dotted with liquor stores, with clients hanging around out in front. Every time I walked by one, I was hit up for loose change. This continued for two or three miles until I arrived at the museum. The Motown Museum is a house on Grand Avenue, a fairly modest but well-kempt blue and white structure. Unfortunately, it was closed on Mondays. Someone was in front trimming the shrubbery, so I asked him about the museum. He said he'd been tending to the landscaping for years but had never been inside. I found this to be somewhat inexplicable. Endowed with a bit more curiosity than the landscaper, I peered in through a window in the front door. I couldn't see anything, not the shadow of a single instrument or even a stray spangle. Very disappointing.

I caught a bus back to Wayne State, where a number of muse-ums are clustered. But the Detroit Institute of Arts turned out to be closed, as was the Museum of African American History. I guess I had never completely realized that Mondays were days off for museums. Since I'd run out of potential museums, I walked

back to the Wayne State campus and had a bagel at the Barnes and
Noble. This area, the Cass Avenue Corridor, was once a thriving
arts center. In the late 1960s, it was the home of Iggy Pop and
the MC5, progenitors of the 1970s punk rock. Detroit has held a
central role in the history of American popular music. In addition
to Motown and the pre-punk scene, it was also crucial to the birth
of techno music in the early 1980s. And, of course, Eminem is
from Detroit. Sitting in the Barnes and Noble on a late Monday
morning, I tried to imaginatively absorb some of Detroit's artistic
glory, hopefully taking in some of it leaking out of local history
books that lined some shelves.

I caught the bus down Cass Avenue to my hotel. I'd arrived
at the conclusion that the best way to see Detroit was from the
seat of my bicycle. I wouldn't be held to the bus map and schedule, and I could avoid the panhandlers. I pulled my bike out of
the hotel and rode up to Eight Mile, the road that rings around
the northern part of the city. Techno music is said to have started
in these neighborhoods, initiated by Kevin Saunderson, Derrick
May, and Juan Atkins, the so-called Belleville Three. The children of autoworkers, they attended school in the affluent, mixed-
race suburb of Belleville, but their dance music caught on in
the clubs along the Eight Mile strip. Eight Mile was the racial
dividing line between black Detroit and the white (often hostile)
suburbs that surrounded it. In his bestselling exposé *Detroit: An
American Autopsy,* Charlie LeDuff calls it a "moat."[11] But moats
can be surmounted, and as the economy shifted in the 1970s and
deindustrialization crept in, black and white youths found new
spaces for social and artistic interaction along Eight Mile Road.
Eminem would eventually get his start in rap clubs there. The
fictional film *8 Mile* documents his experience in the scene and
explores the (often fruitful) cultural collision between white and
black working-class cultures in the 1990s.

The five-mile ride out had involved a route through more desiccated urban landscapes, punctuated by bits of concentrated
activity. There isn't much to see along the road. It's just a road
after all. Still, I snapped a picture. I was sure that no one else

would be interested in it. I wouldn't put it on Facebook—if I ever decided to put snapshots on Facebook—but for me it offered a trace of a culturally significant historical epoch, and this would be the closest I would ever get to it. Just east of here is Warren, once a favored stopping point for white flighters, and if you continue, the road will take you to Grosse Pointe, where several of the Ford heirs have resided, a suburb famous for its historic mansions and churches and still one of the toniest residential enclaves in the United States.

On the way back I rode through the Sherwood Forest neighborhood, home to some of the finest old mansions within the city. Surrounded on all sides by Detroit's deterioration, it is two or three square miles of curved, intersecting streets that feature wide lawns, large trees, and virtually no traffic. The residents have a long history of mobilizing to protect themselves from urban incursions, essentially walling themselves off from the rest of the city. There are two Frank Lloyd Wright houses there. And it offers an almost surreal respite from the rest of the city. I noticed riding out the prominent signs signifying that it was protected by a private security agency. My entry and exit, however, apparently didn't trigger any alarms.

Next, I rode south through Palmer Park and then onto Hamilton Avenue. About a half mile down, I decided to turn left onto a side street to make my way to Woodward Avenue and a straight shot back to the city center. Even what I'd seen so far hadn't prepared me for this. Every other house was vacant. Some had trees growing through the windows. In 2008, there were a reported 101,000 vacant homes in Detroit.[12] More disturbing is that the houses might not be empty. LeDuff informs us that "in this city, crumbling houses are often occupied by drug addicts, the homeless, and even families with children struggling to survive." In contrast to the landscape, the people whom I passed were far from hostile, some waving as I rode by. When I got lost, the person I asked for directions seemed eager to help me find my way back to the center.

I stopped at the beautiful old Fox Theatre. It's still intact and operational with amazingly intricate metalwork and beautiful ceiling frescoes. The theater was featured at one point in a Chrysler Superbowl advertisement starring Eminem, which launched the very clever "Imported from Detroit" campaign.

The last stop on my itinerary was the Michigan Central Station, a couple of miles to the west of my hotel. Online guiding sites recommended it as a must-see destination. And, yes, it is worth the trip. The building is huge and was once Detroit's equivalent of New York's Grand Central. But it has been vacant for years and is now surrounded by a chain-link fence, which hasn't, of course, prevented it from being ransacked. Nearly anything of value in it, including important stone architectural pieces, is now gone.

While I was standing there, someone pulled up in a pickup and started taking pictures. "They going to tear it down?" he asked. "I have no idea," I answered. "I'm from out of town." "Too many buildings gone," he said. "Too much empty land." I asked him if he was an architect or a contractor. "No," he said, "I'm a barber." He gave me his card: Motor City 2 Barber Shop, "tapers, fades, razor shaves, eyebrow arching." Proprietor: Ron-Da-Man. He was interested, he explained, in Detroit's old buildings. He loved them. He lived out in the suburbs now. Too much crime in the city, he told me. He'd come down for some brisket at a place called Slows, and he always liked to revisit some of the buildings when he came into the city. He told me to check out the gargoyles on the Guardian Building, which was near my hotel. Later on, on my way to find some dinner, I searched it out. He was, of course, spot-on.

June 5, 2012

They don't allow bicycles into the Detroit-Windsor tunnel. I called a cab to drive me through it on a cool sunny morning. At seven o'clock the streets were deserted. The cabbie was a Nigerian immigrant. He'd come to the United States to attend college, and stayed. He started his own business providing location services for General Motors executives. He made good money, and he loved

the work. But when GM restructured, his services became super-
fluous, and the business went into decline. Now he was driving a
cab. On the upside, he figured driving a cab in Detroit was better
than in New York: less traffic. He lived in the suburbs but would
prefer a place downtown. It just wasn't possible. "Too much killing," he explained. It was a quick ride through the tunnel and into
what seemed like the other side of the world.

Windsor appeared shockingly clean and neat compared to
Detroit. It's a smaller city, of course, with a population just over
two hundred thousand, but it is a very attractive, highly func-
tional urban space: everything Detroit isn't. It's hard to completely
account for the difference, except as further evidence that Canada
puts stock in its cities and supports the public infrastructure that
makes them work. And Windsor has found a tourist niche. Many
Detroiters come to gamble.

I found the visitors center, grabbed a couple of maps, and
headed south along the river. The Detroit River is just wide
enough to foster an illusion. From here Detroit still looks to be
a muscular and dynamic metropolis. You don't see the collaps-
ing buildings, vacant lots, and wandering vagrants. I continued
to Amherstburg, passing by wharfs and docks that once serviced
Windsor's automobile industry. As on most Canadian highways,
there are no shoulders, but drivers tend to be courteous, and the
traffic was moderate.

The village of Amherstburg has an English feel, with its small
shops and brick sidewalks. It sits at the very mouth of the Detroit
River, which from here widens into Lake Erie. Fort Malden is on
the southern edges of the village and features several restored
buildings, including an old barracks. The fort was overrun by
Americans during the War of 1812 but returned to the British
after it ended. It hasn't been in actual use since the middle of the
nineteenth century.

After Amherstburg, turning east, there is a tangle of county
roads running parallel to the lakeshore. I rode to Glen Eden, then
east to Malden, and then south on Highway 50. The smaller roads
running along the shorelines are often likely to turn into dead

ends, with water blocking the path and no bridge over to the next shoreline finger. I headed straight across to Malden, turned south to pick up the lakeshore road again, and took it to Colchester and points east. Traffic was light. The road is flat, and other than a bit of a headwind, I would have been hard-pressed to ask for a nicer ride. I wended my way along the shoreline for an uneventful ride to Kingsville, where I stopped to have some pizza.

The owner, Joe, was a Lebanese immigrant. Talkative and curious, he seemed quite interested in my trip. He liked to travel himself, and last summer had taken his family to Europe. While there, he wanted to rent a car to drive around the countryside, but his wife just wanted to stay in one place, at the beach or the hotel. He couldn't understand that. There was so much to see. "Go for it." That was his philosophy.

He told me that a woman in her seventies had ridden through town on a bicycle a couple of years ago. She came into the restaurant at around eight o'clock in the evening and talked to everyone in the place. Then she hit the road, at around nine o'clock. She wanted to get some more mileage in. "Really?" I asked. "That's impressive." I've never done much night riding myself. I'm much more about the early start and a good night's sleep. Plus, it seems dangerous, given traffic. Perhaps when I reach my seventies, I'll be more open to it.

I took the greenway/bike path that Joe told me about to Leamington. It was nice to get away from the highway for a bit, but on the way I realized that my tire was starting to go flat. I didn't want to take all my gear off and patch it, so I'd stop every half mile or so and put a little air into it. That seemed to work OK, but leaky tires had been a theme on this trip.

At Leamington, I found a little strip motel and settled in for the afternoon. I patched the inner tube and rode through the small city of about twenty-eight thousand, past a large Heinz tomato-processing facility to the marina. The plant must attract some Mexican immigrants, because there are several Mexican restaurants in town. The one I decided on for dinner turned out to be a mistake. Being the only customer in a restaurant is never a good sign, and I probably just should have left. But I stuck it out as an indifferent owner took his time to get to me. The meal took forever, and it was less than mediocre. The rice seemed to have been spooned out of a can.

June 6, 2012

Up early and out. Given the early start and the beautiful weather, I decided to ride to Point Pelee National Park. While it would take a good chunk of the morning, I felt it would be worth it, and I wasn't in any particular hurry to get back to Ithaca at this point. While I was having a couple of bagels in Leamington at the Tim Hortons, a guy asked me where I was headed. When I told him, he expressed his encouragement. "Seems like it's going to be a nice day weather-wise," he said. After awhile, he got up and came over to my table, smartphone in hand, to show me the weather forecast from Leamington to Toronto. It confirmed a positive forecast. "You should have a lot of fun," he said. I thanked him and headed out the door.

Pelee Peninsula is a very thin strip that sticks far out into Lake Erie. At the end is Point Pelee National Park, which runs along a tree-lined road, with open water on one side and marshland on the other. Unlike in much of Canada, the trees here are deciduous, rather than conifer, and part of a band of deciduous forests that runs from here to the Carolinas. The trees thrive due to the peninsula's southern reach and the moderating climatic effects of Lake Erie. These same conditions make the area habitable to numerous flora and fauna found nowhere else in Canada.

The park road continues about four miles and then becomes accessible only by bicycle or park shuttle. I rode out as far as I could, spotting wild turkeys and dozens of other bird species. Point Pelee is a birder's paradise as an important vector in spring and fall songbird migrations. Off the road to the right were large dunes that shielded any view of the lake, but I couldn't resist stopping occasionally to wander over them to the beach. The last half mile or so to the peninsula's tip is accessible only on foot. It's the southernmost point in Canada. The wildness of Lake Erie, not always apparent from the shorelines, is on full display here. And you can catch a glimpse of Pelee Island off in the distance. I rode back along the peaceful deserted road in the early sunshine, stopping at one point to walk onto an overlook that allows for a clear view of the marshlands on the eastern side of the peninsula. It was eleven o'clock before I was back on the road eastward along the lake.

Unfortunately, a plucky headwind had now appeared. A headwind from the east is particularly annoying, since it runs against the prevailing patterns and deprives a cyclist of a well-deserved reward for riding westward several days. Still, the breeze was nothing like I'd experienced in Ohio, and it was generally a nice ride along the very lightly trafficked roads that ran close to the shorelines. There are many fruit farms through here: strawberries, cherries, and apples. The moderate temperatures make this one of the most productive fruit-growing regions in Canada.

I stopped at a farm stand, bought some apples, and inquired about this year's crop. I was curious because New York had had an extremely warm March, with temperatures in the seventies, followed by a cold snap in April that decimated the apple crop. The woman I talked to, Heather, said with some dismay that, as in New York, things were not good this year. Because of all the crazy weather, they had lost more than half of their crop.

Riding along the Talbot Trail, which hugs the Lake Erie shoreline, you see many large, newly constructed McMansions overlooking the lake. These would appear to be second homes or vacation getaways for wealthy Canadians, or perhaps Americans who are looking for a still-accessible waterfront. No easy beach access, though. The houses all sit up on bluffs, which are residual features left from shorelines of glaciated lakes that preceded Lake Erie, which formed as ice sheets receded: Lake Maumee (14,000 years before present [YBP]), Lake Whittlesey (13,000 YBP), Lake Warren (12,700 YBP), Lake Wayne (12,500 YBP). Lake Erie is in geological terms quite young, having been formed roughly 4,000 years ago. The glacial lakes formed within the contours of the 2-million-year-old Erigan River basin.[13] There's so little commerce here that I began to worry if I could find a bottle of water if I became dehydrated. This must be one of the most sparsely populated areas along the Erie shoreline. It's also apparently one of the most productive in terms of wind power. Turbines are everywhere.

In spite of my late start, I had plans to make it to the John E. Pearce Provincial Park before nightfall. I hoped to arrive around six o'clock, given the rate I was going, fighting against an increasingly stiff headwind. Still, I didn't see a problem in making it, although it would be a long day, my longest yet on this tour. I didn't see any signs from the main highway for the park as I got nearer, which made me a little nervous. At the intersection in the small village of Wallacetown, I stopped into a diner and asked. An older gentleman said that he knew about it, and he believed that I should take the road that headed toward the lake. He'd been living in Florida, though, and hadn't been back in a while. He also suggested that I should try the diner's cherry pie. I assured him I'd be back for it once I got my tent set up.

I rode the three miles to the park, seeing only one small sign along the way. I started to wonder whether there would be camping, something I hadn't really doubted before. I finally found the park entrance, which had no attendant and opened to a very rough road, with a weathered sign indicating that no camping was allowed and that the gates would be locked at 9:00 P.M. I didn't see a problem getting around the gate, so I walked my bike down a steep dirt road to a fence that lined the bluff overlooking the white caps of Lake Erie. It was a seventy-foot drop. A bulldozer stood off to one side. That seemed to be the extent of the park. This was a pretty bleak and depressing place, and I wasn't completely sure what qualified it as a park.

There didn't seem to be anyone around, so I considered guerilla camping, but there would be no shower and no access to the water, and the place was just extremely uninviting. I couldn't see spending the next twelve hours there. St. Thomas was at least two hours away, and it was six thirty, plus I was pretty beat. I would have to backtrack to get to the main highway, a somewhat demoralizing prospect. Still, given the alternative, I decided to take Joe the Lebanese pizza maker's advice and go for it. Fortunately, I discovered the Fingal Line road, which ran parallel to the Talbot Line that I'd been riding. It opened up to fields and farms and would have been ideal under more congenial circumstances.

I arrived at the St. Thomas city line at around eight o'clock and climbed a fairly steep hill that led to the commercial strip, along which I figured I'd find some kind of motel. But after two miles of riding, I didn't see anything. It was hard for me to imagine that a city of this size wouldn't have at least one motel, but you never know.

After reaching the far edge of town, I decided to ask. A man in the Walmart parking lot told me to head back a half mile the way that I'd just come, take a left, another half mile, under a railroad bridge, and I'd see a motel on the left. I followed his directions but found no underpass and no motel. I asked someone else walking along the street. He said the last person that I'd talked to didn't know what he was talking about. The only motel was back out on the edge of town (the way I had come) but a little farther out past the Walmart shopping plaza. There was a Comfort Inn next to a Tim Hortons. I rode back, with my lights now on, and found a fairly seedy strip motel. Still, I was happy to find a place to land, and the price was right. I unloaded my gear, took a quick shower in the dark and musty room, and then walked next door to Tim Hortons. After dinner I returned to the room and had an uneasy sleep. As tired as I was, this was not a restful night.

June 7, 2012

Next morning I was up early and had a bagel at the Tim Hortons, after which I made my way to the nearby supermarket to buy a raft of fruit, snacks, and other food supplies. I was heading southeast at this point, back toward the lake. My little detour to St. Thomas had taken me north of a direct path hugging the lakefront. A half-hour ride brought me to the little village of Port Stanley, a picturesque place right on the water, with a restored inn on the main street. It would have been a great place to spend the previous night.

I got off the bike to make a quick adjustment, when an older gentleman walked up to me and said, "Hey, you aren't trying to get out of town, are you?" I said, yes, I was heading eastward along the lake. "East," he said, "That's good, because people have a terrible time getting out of here to go west. They get lost. It's a complete mess." "Well, luckily, I'm going east," I responded. "Yes, lucky you."

My luck only extended so far, however, because there's a short but very steep hill that leads out of Port Stanley toward the east. At this point, much of the highway runs across a bluff. Streams and small rivers cut through it at various points, carving out gorges that run down to the shoreline. It's in these crevices that settlements sometimes took root and became small villages, like Port Burwell. This results in long stretches of flat riding across the plateau, with occasional steep dips down and back up. On the open highway, you can achieve some momentum that will carry you up the next side. But in a town, there's usually an intersection with a stop sign. The steep ride back up can be challenging. Fortunately, the weather continued to be beautiful, so I had little to actually complain about. What was most striking to me, however, was how few people I encountered. Southern Lake Erie is one (often distressed) metropolitan area after another, but the northern side is mostly farms, orchards, and sparsely developed shoreline.

By the time I arrived at Port Rowan, midafternoon, I thought it might be nice to camp along the lakeshore. I stopped at a tourist booth, and a young woman convinced me that camping at Long Point Provincial Park was a good option. To get there, I had to ride to the west two or three miles and then turn left onto Long Point Road, which runs along a strip of land that separates the marshy Big Creek National Wildlife area from Lake Erie. The wind really kicked up as I cycled along the flat, narrow road. The sun hung suspended in the late afternoon sky, hovering over the marshlands to the west. It turned out to be an eight- to ten-mile ride, as the road circles back toward the east out onto the Long Point peninsula, which is fenced off to visitors.

Long Point Provincial Park is another one of the ecological gems that populate the northern shore of Lake Erie. The Long Point spit has been designated as a UNESCO biosphere reserve due to its significance as a stopover for bird migrations and its abundance of other wildlife, especially turtles, snakes, and the threatened Fowler's toad. The "new" campground, where my tent site was, straddles the peninsula, which is only about a mile wide at this point. The sites are interspersed between sand dunes, the largest of which sit on the edge of the shoreline.

Heavy clouds had moved in as I was looking for my numbered campsite. The park seemed to be mostly deserted. It was still too early in the season to draw in many campers. Before setting up my tent, I walked the path between the dunes to the shore. Lake Erie, which seemed so domesticated for much of the trip, had taken a wild turn. White caps dotted the water as far as I could see. It was a dramatic display of wind and water that offered at least a small glimpse into a once primeval landscape.

Lake Erie is the shallowest Great Lake, and only Ontario is smaller in terms of surface area. Its average depth is sixty-two feet, but it is very shallow on the western end. As a result, Erie has less total volume of water than any other of the lakes. And whereas the other lakes are surrounded mostly by glacially scrubbed rock surfaces, Erie's shores are composed of softer mineral deposits, providing an ideal environment for the development of a rich variety of flora and fauna. There are purportedly forty-six million fish in Lake Erie, versus less than five million in Lake Superior. But, of course, Erie's shallowness, while being especially hospitable to biodiversity, also makes it especially vulnerable to ecological threats. And there were multiple ones, given the number of large manufacturing centers that line its southern edge.[14]

In the mid-twentieth century, the dumping of chemicals, of water warmed by industrial processes, and of sewage into Lake Erie created algae blooms, which depleted its oxygen, resulting in the loss of insect species, like the mayfly, and declining fish populations, as chub and lake herring were displaced by much hardier alewives and carp. By the 1960s, Lake Erie was declared to be dead or dying. It's not that there was no life in the lake, but the life that was taking over was in the form of algae, which squeezed out a formerly thriving biodiversity.[15]

Of course, Lake Erie is healthier today than it was fifty years ago. Partly, this is the result of regulatory actions, especially the Clean Water Act, and the Great Lakes Water Quality Agreement between the United States and Canada. And deindustrialization is in some respects an environmentally friendly process. As a result, phosphorus levels in the lake, the leading cause of algae blooms, declined significantly. Lake Erie's shallowness and its flushing rate have worked in its favor. Erie's cleanup was hailed as the most important act of ecological restoration in U.S. history. Unfortunately, Erie, like the other Great Lakes, has faced continued problems. Phosphorus levels began inching upward in the 1990s, and algae blooms again appeared in 2003. Erie is threatened by zebra mussels and other infestations, and given its relatively small size and depth, it is the lake most vulnerable to the impacts of climate change.[16]

As I set up my tent, a couple of hundred feet away from the shore, I could hear the waves washing against the sand. I felt a deep sense of gratitude to be in such a beautiful park, close to such a wondrous lake, with virtually no other human beings in proximity. After a shower and a pieced-together dinner of bread, cheese, and dried fruit, I did some reading in my tent, while listening to the waves. While not as loud as the ocean, the lake still provided a soothing backdrop for what turned out to be a very sound night's sleep.

June 8, 2012

Next day, I woke up early, broke down my tent, got organized, and went to the washroom to brush my teeth and wash up. I thought I'd return fresh and ready to go after relaxing and eating the croissants I'd bought along the way the previous day. When I returned, the picnic table was covered with a mélange of birds—sparrows, starlings, red-winged blackbirds, and the like—who were busily tearing apart the plastic bag that held the croissants. I shooed them away and then debated whether I should still eat the croissants. Could they spread disease? Hunger, however, won out over my reservations. I couldn't believe how fast and efficient the birds were at getting to the food. No doubt, they get plenty of practice.

The sun was rising as I rode off the peninsula with the hope of making it to Buffalo. I knew it would be a long day, probably at least a hundred miles. I stopped in Port Rowan at a small grocery store, where I picked up some additional breakfast and sat on a park bench on the sidewalk in front to eat a muffin, have some juice, and a very welcome cup of coffee. "Eating on the run?" a woman asked, walking by. "Yep," I responded. "Nice town," I told her. She agreed. She had moved there from Toronto fifty years ago when she was married, and had never regretted it, finding it to be a small, friendly, and beautiful place, albeit a little cold, snowy, and windy in the winter. I wasn't the first bicyclist that had ridden through, she told me. I would unlikely be the last.

A series of county roads took me right along the lakeshore, with a fair number of dips along the way. Some were very steep and fairly long. Still, I wasn't complaining. I was a little worried about getting lost, though, within the maze of generally unmarked roads. At one intersection, I hollered to a guy stopped at a stop sign, as I pointed right. "Reyersville?" "Yes," he said, noting that it was rare for people to ask for directions these days. "Sometimes it's still a good idea," he noted. I've never owned a GPS for my bike. It has always struck me as an unnecessary expense and just another gizmo to go haywire just as you have started to rely on it. Also, it's always more interesting to interact with actual human beings, even if their directions can sometimes be unreliable. And what would bicycle touring be without the serendipity that emerges from becoming lost?

This part of the ride is along the southern edge of the Niagara Peninsula, the strip of land that lies between the western end of Lake Ontario and the eastern tip of Lake Erie. The area was occupied until the middle of the seventeenth century by an indigenous group called the Attawandaron, known by Europeans as the Neutrals due to their unwillingness to take sides between the Huron and Haudenosaunee during the Beaver Wars. But their neutrality did not protect them, given the Haudenosaunee desire for western hunting grounds and trading routes. Outnumbered and outmatched by superior weaponry, the Neutrals essentially ceased to exist as a distinctive people after 1647.[17]

It was nice to have the wind at my back for a change, and I was breezing right along through the fields on the north shore, through the towns of Port Dover and Nanticoke. Coming out of Nanticoke, I confused Provincial Highway 3 with County Highway 3, which threw me off track for a few miles, bringing me to a dead end at the lakeshore. I also had a problem at Port Maitland. The map was a little confusing, and it appeared that a right-hand turn along Port Maitland Road would bring me along the shoreline again for the ride toward Port Colborne, about ten miles east of Fort Erie. I rode along a river for five or six miles and reached what turned out to be a dead end. At the lakefront, there was no bridge to the eastern side of the river. I rode around the area a bit, hoping that I'd simply missed it but knowing that I probably hadn't. Even more unfortunate, the ride back to the bridge was into a fairly strong headwind. There's no bicycle ride less enjoyable than the one that takes you back to the point that you made your wrong turn into a strong wind. It seemed like it took forever. Being lost can open up unforeseen possibilities, but it can also be a pain in the ass.

Once back and over the bridge, I rode down along the eastern side of the river. Only when I again reached the lakefront did I feel like I'd gotten my groove back. Buffalo, at this point, was out of the picture, and I was even wondering whether I could make it to Fort Erie. But it felt good to be back on track. At various points along the winding shorelines, the sturdy upright buildings of Buffalo came into view. Lake Erie appeared to be on its best behavior, with dozens of sailboats out catching the brisk afternoon wind. A healthy fifteen- to twenty-mile-an-hour wind was pushing me along toward my destination.

It was getting fairly late, around four o'clock, by the time I made it to Port Colborne, a town of a little less than twenty thousand. It is on the southern end of the Welland Canal, which was completed in 1822 and connects Lakes Erie and Ontario (and which, incidentally, allowed fish species from Lake Ontario to move into the upper Great Lakes). The canal's presence helped to define the city's identity as an important port during the nineteenth century. Gas finds in the region facilitated industrial development and fostered the emergence of glass making and metallurgy. Tourism has also long been central to the city's economy, and it was a place where genteel Southerners (including reportedly the wife of Confederate leader Jefferson Davis) escaped summer heat, leaving their slaves, of course, to bake in it. I wondered how Canadians responded to Southern slave owners. Likely, Ms. Davis didn't go into town much.

I considered stopping for the night there, rather than Fort Erie, which was still about fifteen or twenty miles east. On the eastern edge of Port Colborne, the only alternative is to get onto Highway 3, which has two lanes and appeared to have no shoulder and a fair amount of fast-moving traffic. I was feeling the day's ride at this point and not sure that I wanted to continue a dozen miles down the busy highway. I stopped at a convenience store to ask if there was somewhere in the neighborhood to stay. The congenial South Asian clerk directed me back to the western end of town. His cousin owned a place, he informed me. If I mentioned that I'd stopped in the store, the cousin would give me a discount. I started back onto the highway turning westward and immediately thought better of it. Tempting as the discount offer was, I couldn't see riding into the stiff westerly wind I was encountering, even if only for three or four miles. I decided to push on to Fort Erie.

It soon became clear that I'd made the right decision. A couple of miles down Highway 3 the traffic lightened considerably and then a nice shoulder appeared. With the wind behind me, I'd make it to Fort Erie in a little over an hour. Given my navigation errors, I figured I would have ridden about 120 miles when all was said and done.

Fort Erie is a town of about thirty thousand, but it felt larger than that as I rode in. Traffic increased as I made my way through its western suburbs. Soon enough, I saw a Clarion Inn on my right, and I decided that while perhaps it was priced a little on the steep side, I was ready to find a place to settle in for the evening. I checked the price, and when I balked, the clerk was willing to bargain. We settled at eighty dollars for the night, at a hotel that, by my standards anyway, was fairly luxurious. The place was huge and completely empty. As the clerk guided me to a storage room where I could leave my bike overnight, I asked her where everyone was.

Fort Erie was once well known for its horse racetrack and a large casino, which would draw Americans from across the border. But, the clerk explained, the casino had recently closed, and now the racetrack fell into bankruptcy. The Clarion was now a large hotel in a small city. Without gambling, there wasn't much to draw in tourists. Staying in a large, empty hotel can feel both luxurious and slightly unnerving. Such places have been the subject of more than one horror film. Stanley Kubrick's *The Shining*, starring Jack Nicholson, kept coming to mind. The scene in which Nicholson has the famous line "Here's Johnny," after chopping down the bathroom door to get at his terrified wife, has been voted as the most frightening in film history.[18] But after a shower and a dinner of fish and chips in an empty dining room, I retired to my room and fell immediately to sleep. If there were ghosts around, they were incapable of waking me.

June 9, 2012

The morning brought rain. I didn't mind it as long as there was no lightning attached, so I loaded up the bicycle and headed out. On the way into the city center, I spotted a Tim Hortons, so I stopped for my usual: two cinnamon-and-raisin bagels, an orange juice, and coffee. The place was buzzing with activity on a Saturday morning. I found a seat near the window where I could keep an eye on my bike.

Fort Erie was founded soon after the French and Indian War,

which gave England colonial control over Canada. While much of the Niagara Peninsula was still under the control of First Nations people, the fort was established to protect the newly acquired area in 1764. After the American Revolution, the British government offered land there to demobilized troops. Fort Erie was captured by the Americans during the War of 1812, one of the few American land victories in the conflict. But the Americans eventually abandoned it after burning it to the ground.

The city went on to become an important stop for the Underground Railroad. And the Niagara Movement, launched by W. E. B. Du Bois, with his associates Mary Burnett Talbert and William Monroe Trotter, was organized in the Erie Beach Hotel in 1905. The immediate impetus was a response to segregation in Buffalo's hotels. But more generally, the movement was a challenge to the accommodationist philosophy of Booker T. Washington. Du Bois and associates drafted a set of principles, which held, among other things, that "we refuse to allow the impression to remain that the Negro-American assents to inferiority, is submissive under oppression and apologetic before insults." The group called for an end to segregation, and while relatively short-lived and small in membership, it wielded a powerful voice for social justice and equality and provided inspiration to the civil rights movements of the 1950s and 1960s.[19]

I rode down Highway 3 to the entry to the Queen Elizabeth Way (QEW), the major cross-Canada highway, which in turns leads to the Peace Bridge. It always feels a little strange to be out on a major highway with a bicycle, the semitrucks whizzing by a few yards away. But there's usually plenty of room, so in spite of the velocity and intensity of the traffic, it feels safe. The Peace Bridge was completed in 1927, named in celebration of a century of peace between the United States and Canada, a peace that had not been violated or even remotely threatened since the end of the War of 1812. Americans are lucky indeed to have such amicable neighbors to the north.

The Peace Bridge became a source of conflict, though, about a year after my trip. The binational agency that has controlled the bridge since its completion, generally without any major conflicts, was heavily criticized by Governor Andrew Cuomo's head of the American delegation, William B. Hoyt. The Cuomo administration was known for its combative style, and it seemed to carry that forward to its dealing with its Canadian counterparts on the bridge authority. The Americans were unhappy that Canadians were reluctant to commit funds to improve the plaza on the American end of the bridge. Canadians claimed that New York was paying too much for the property needed to expand the plaza, well above the appraised value. Name calling ensued. The New York delegation refused to attend board meetings. Attempts to mediate by New York Senator Charles Schumer were unsuccessful. Suggestions were made that Governor Cuomo, given a possible presidential run, was demonstrating his foreign policy bona fides by being tough with, well, Canada.[20]

It's no problem getting a bicycle across the bridge, given its accessibility to pedestrians. But signs direct cyclists to walk the mile and three-quarters distance. In the process, you get a great view of downtown Buffalo, with the Niagara River rapids below, rushing fast to the famous falls, ten miles to the north. Looking southward, you can see Lake Erie opening up in the distance. The weather could not have been improved upon, the views were stunning, and the walk was completely enjoyable.

Once on the other side, it was no problem getting back into the United States. Somehow being on a bicycle seems to bring out the best in border guards, especially if you're carrying a lot of gear. For one thing, it's probably unusual and thus offers a break from the boredom that no doubt constitutes a significant proportion of the job. But also, it's pretty clear what you've been doing. It's hard to imagine anyone stupid enough a carry a significant quantity of drugs or other contraband across the border on a bicycle. Moreover, it was still relatively early on a Saturday morning, with few other people in cars trying to get across.

I've been to Buffalo many times and know the city reasonably well, but I still needed the map to get me started. I rode down Niagara Street toward the city's center on a quiet morning with few people around. At the center point, there's a large traffic circle into which a number of the main thoroughfares feed, like bicycle spokes: Delaware and Niagara Avenues, Court and Genesee Streets. I wanted to avoid the Skyway but also wanted a path that ran roughly parallel with it, along the lakefront, heading south and eventually west. I wended my way over to Louisiana Street as the area turned from commercial and residential to industrial. As I approached the shoreline, I was surrounded by ancient factories, warehouses, and storage facilities. The deep blue of Lake Erie in the near distance provided an almost surreal counterpoint.

As I was about to take a short drawbridge that crosses the Buffalo River, my chain gave out. I was trying to remember if this was the second or third time this had happened. (I eventually realized that the screw attaching the bottom of the back rack to the bike frame was rubbing into the chain, ever so slightly, but just enough to weaken it after a few hundred miles.) In the shadow of a large, old brick factory building, I tore everything off the back of the bike, dug out my chain tool, fixed it relatively quickly, and was back onto the bridge.

The Buffalo River empties the western end of the Erie Canal, so at one time this area was of considerable commercial and industrial importance. As the canal fell out of use and as Buffalo went into economic decline, these old buildings were abandoned. It could now be fodder for Pink Floyd album art. The river was at one time one of the most polluted in the United States. I have a vivid memory of visiting Buffalo when I was in high school and having a headline of the *Buffalo Evening News* catch my eye: "Life Found," it declared, "in the Buffalo Barge Canal." Curious, I read the article, which noted that some kind of small (and very resilient) worms had been detected on the bottom. The canal is still filled with contaminated sediment, which is slowly being dredged as part of a restoration project.

Once over the bridge, Fuhrmann Boulevard runs parallel to the Skyway and even has a bike path. On the right is Buffalo Harbor. Tiff Nature Preserve, a 264-acre natural area sited on what was a city refuse dump, is on the left. Just past the preserve, Fuhrmann

merges with Route 5, to become the Father Baker Memorial Highway and the entry point to Lackawanna. This was once the heart
of the area's industrial production, with large Bethlehem Steel
mills and Ford production facilities, now either torn down or left
to crumble in overgrown fields extending down to the shoreline.
Amid the ruins are several tall wind towers, as a small piece of the
new economy sprouts up in the remnants of the old.

As the sign for Hamburg appeared, the highway became
busier, with little if any shoulder. Suburbs tend to be the most
difficult places to bike, in cities large and small. On city streets,
traffic lights slow things down, and drivers are used to negotiating with pedestrians and bicycles. While suburbs sometimes now
have bike paths, they often don't, partly because commerce hugs
right up against the streets, which tend to be just wide enough to
accommodate two lanes of traffic. Fortunately, in this case, the
busy highway evolved into Lakeshore Road, which as the name
implies, runs close to the shoreline on the right, and features a
series of beautiful old houses on the left. There are many parks
and beaches on the flat, winding highway through there, and a
nice stretch for riding. Clouds appeared, however, and it began to
rain moderately as I entered the last half of the last day of my trip.

Right around Lake View I experienced another flat tire. This
time, I had my extra tube patched and ready to go, so I didn't
foresee any problems. I found a little grassy patch off the road
at an intersection of Highway 20. At this location, people had to
slow for a stop sign before turning onto the main highway. On
three separate occasions, someone in one of the passing cars rolled
down the window to ask if I needed help. Sometimes you face
harassment while riding a bicycle, by irate drivers or just genu-
inely nasty people. But today, it seemed, the good side of humanity
was revealing itself. In the meantime, however, I realized that the
tire was shot, and I was starting to wonder whether it would hold
together for the rest of the ride. The thin tires recommended to
me in a local bike shop didn't have that many miles on them, but
they were clearly not up to the task of touring. Lesson learned.

I passed a large Tops Supermarket, from which I grabbed a

tasty lunch of fruit and granola bars. Civic organizations were selling hotdogs in the parking lot, and the store was filled with Saturday shoppers. The Tops Company was original founded in Buffalo, and along with the Rochester-based Wegmans, tends to be one of the most ubiquitous supermarket chains in upstate New York. In 1991, the Dutch firm Ahold bought it. Ahold, in turn, was eventually caught in one of the largest European fraud cases in history (sometimes referred to as "Europe's Enron"). The company used a series of accounting gimmicks, many of them illegal, to inflate the plus side of its balance sheets. When the fraud became public, the stock price collapsed, and the company nearly went out of business. Ahold eventually sold its Tops holdings to Morgan Stanley as it consolidated its various holdings.

I continued along past Evangola State Park through the village of Silver Creek, which I remember traveling through as a kid, as the family drove many times back and forth to Buffalo when my younger brother spent time in the Buffalo Children's Hospital. I hadn't been through it in many years. It didn't make a strong impression on me when I was a kid, and it wasn't making much of one now. The highway splits here, with Route 5 turning into Lake Shore Drive and following along the shoreline with Route 20 running on a parallel track a few miles south.

Five miles or so east of Dunkirk my chain started to skip, and then the back tire went flat. The double whammy. I pulled my bike off the road down a small embankment. The traffic was heavy, including many large trucks, which I found a little disconcerting and very noisy. Once I got the back tire off, I had a terrible time finding the leak. I put patches in two places where there was no leaking, and I spent half an hour finding the actual one. Then I took a couple of links out of the chain.

I had also been in denial about another problem, which I could no longer ignore. The back hub was making a grinding noise, as though the bearings were being slowly pulverized. I wasn't completely sure about the problem, because sometimes it would stop. But the wheel had become somewhat wobbly as well. I was starting to wonder whether I'd make it back to my mom's place on

Chautauqua Lake, even though I had only about twenty miles to go. Mechanical problems seemed to be accumulating at an alarming rate.

I finally made it into Dunkirk, where I made the mistake of turning south on Route 60 to connect with Route 20 for the final trek to Westfield. I should have stayed on Route 5, which would have led me to the same place but saved a few miles, which were becoming increasingly precious, given my mechanical problems and the sheer exhaustion that now seemed to be enveloping me. Route 60 in this section runs through a suburban commercial strip, with stoplights and traffic.

While I was waiting at a light, two guys in a pickup truck, who looked like they might have dropped out of the film *Deliverance*, struck up a conversation. "Run away from home?" one of them asked. They were good-natured, and I had to laugh. I told them that I sure had and was glad to finally get out of there. They had fishing gear in the truck, so I asked them about their luck. "Terrible," one responded. "The crazy winter has screwed everything up. The fish don't know what to do." I was tempted to say something about climate change but decided against it. Why interject a serious topic into friendly banter between a few strangers? It was a nice moment, and I didn't want to screw it up just to make a point.

In Fredonia, I stopped at a convenience store to grab something cold to drink. A stereo was turned up quite loud and was blasting "Jessie's Girl," the inimitable Rick Springfield hit from 1981. My hands were pretty dirty and greasy from all of the fooling around with the bike. The very nice woman operating the register allowed me to wash them in the store's sink.

The ride to Westfield was uneventful. A few small hills slowed me down a bit, but it was definitely starting to look as though I would make it at least to my starting point. But once there, I had another eight miles to Dewittville on Lake Chautauqua. At this point, another eight miles seemed daunting enough, but I also knew that there was a rather long, steep hill between me and the village of Mayville. I'd traveled over the Portage Trail via car on the way over but would not be so lucky on the way back.

The trail wasn't an easy walk for early trappers and adventurers, and it's not an easy bicycle ride. Since the road tends to wind around a bit, I kept thinking I was close to the top, only to be disappointed when I rounded the next turn. It was a tough end to a tough day. Finally, when I reached the top, I could see the village of Mayville and the lake stretching off into the distance, surrounded by Chautauqua County's fields and forests. It was a beautiful sight not only because of the view, but because I now could experience the downhill side of the climb. Once down, I had couple of more miles to Dewittville, and I was done. I knocked on the door and entered the sunny, warm house.

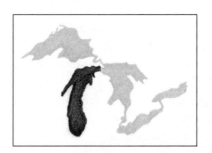

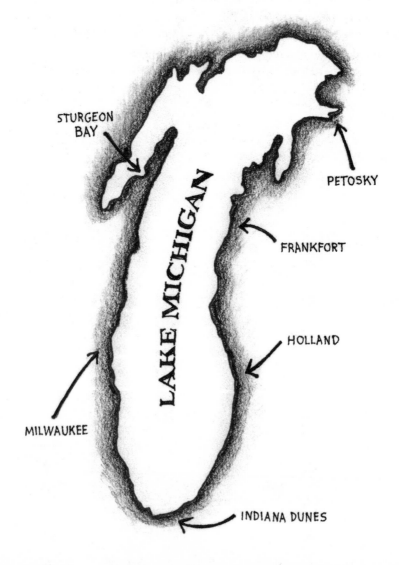

STURGEON
BAY

PETOSKY

FRANKFORT

LAKE MICHIGAN

HOLLAND

MILWAUKEE

INDIANA DUNES

Lake Michigan

Lake Michigan's name is derived from "Mishigami," the Ojibwe word for "great water." I had decided for somewhat arbitrary reasons that it would constitute the third leg of my tour. I had already completed Huron and Erie, I wanted to save Ontario for last, and Superior would take too much time, as the summer was starting to run away from me. This would be a longer trip than the circling of Lake Erie that I had completed earlier in the summer, and it promised interesting contrasts, from the relatively unpopulated northern shore, which constitutes the southern shoreline of Michigan's Upper Peninsula, to metropolitan Chicago in the south. Fortunately, I wouldn't need my passport to travel around Michigan, because it's entirely within U.S. borders. By surface (but not by volume), it is the largest lake contained within the borders of a single country.

From a bicycle-riding perspective, Michigan poses a couple of unique challenges. It has a number of peninsulas and bays, which require decisions about how closely to follow the shoreline. I hadn't felt the need to follow every nook and cranny of the lakeshore, but Huron's and Erie's shorelines are smooth, posing fewer choices. I wasn't leaving with a definitive plan about how I would handle things but hoped to balance time considerations against a determination to see as much as possible. A second challenge is that Michigan lies along a north–south axis. When I circled Lake Erie, I found myself riding west into very strong late-spring winds, which then provided welcome support riding back the other direction. With Michigan, I was guessing I'd experience less direct head- and tailwinds.

Not wanting to deal with the complexities of flying into and bicycling out of the huge Chicago metropolitan area, I chose to fly to Milwaukee from Syracuse. About a mile from the airport there is a scrum of inexpensive motels, and I booked the cheapest. I was happy my room was on the first floor, where just outside, through a sliding glass door, was the motel parking lot, which was ideally suited for my purposes.

I had to break my bike down to get it on the plane, which required putting everything back together in the motel room. The S & S couplers that I had installed allow me to break the bike apart to get it into a suitcase, but that requires deconstructing it almost completely. It's of course easier to get it apart than back together again. It took me less than an hour to get parts back into their appropriate places, but I would need to do some adjusting before leaving the next day. The motel parking lot would be an ideal place for that. Also, the motel was right on the bus line into the city. When I returned to Milwaukee, I planned to spend another night in the same place and spend a day touring the city.

July 22, 2012

At seven o'clock, when I pushed my bike through the glass doors to the motel parking lot, it was already getting hot. Ozone permeated the atmosphere, no doubt partly the result of traffic flowing across nearby Interstate 94. I rode around the lot, adjusting gears and breaks, double-checked the room for stray items, dropped the room key off with the clerk, and headed east on Thirteenth Street into Milwaukee. Small businesses of various kinds lined the street but turned into modest frame houses as I approached the center. At Oklahoma Avenue, Thirteenth Street ends, which I found a little confusing, but eventually I made my way to Sixth Street, which continues eastward. Spanish-language store signage and a collection of Mexican restaurants give testament to the ethnic character of the neighborhood. Next, I crossed under Interstate 94, which runs like a gash along the western edge of the business district. Like so many interstates, it fractured the urban core, and in Milwaukee it provides an ugly and inconvenient obstacle to streets lined with stately, solid nineteenth-century Germanic-styled buildings. I stopped at a Dunkin' Donuts for a couple of bagels, some juice, and coffee. The break gave me a chance to get my bearings.

After breakfast, I traveled the short distance to the lakefront, where a breeze took a little of the edge off the midmorning heat, which was, it seemed, only just starting to build. At Lake Park, a little green gem next to the shore, I picked up a bike path that took me northward running parallel with city streets and stately old row houses. I followed this path through the tidy northern suburbs of Whitefish Bay and Fox Point. The marked bicycle path along the shoulder made for safe riding along the flat highway. There seemed to be some slack in the back brake cable, but otherwise the bike was operating smoothly on new tires that I had bought after the multiple fiascos I'd experienced on the Lake Erie trip. I'd also purchased some waterproof front panniers, replacing the old cloth ones that I'd had for nearly twenty-five years. It was a propitious start to the thousand mile–plus journey that I had in store.

Sheboygan was approximately seventy-five miles from my starting point, which seemed like a good distance for the first day, especially given the heat. Lake Shore Drive is interrupted by Kapco Park, a baseball stadium serving Concordia University, at which point you are pushed out into the busy Northern Port Washington Road. But you can make your way back to Lake Shore Drive once north of the stadium, following it all the way into Port Washington. The small city of around eleven thousand, founded before the Civil War, was once a bustling port and thriving manufacturing center. With the closing of Simplicity Manufacturing in 2008, most industry is now gone. The local economy is focused on tourism, especially charter fishing excursions on Lake Michigan.[1] I breezed through, stopping only for a cold drink, on my way to Sheboygan.

Once north of Port Washington, the bicycle route moves away from the lake into the surrounding farmland. This is true midwestern farm country, with large fields of wheat and corn, a scattering of farmhouses and barns, and the occasional village. The route runs parallel to Interstate 43 with intersecting county roads that run down to the nearby lake.

I took the Sauk Trail Road turnoff into Sheboygan. The road is named after the Ozaagii people, originally from the St. Lawrence River valley, who became the "Sauk" under a regime of French mispronunciation. In the seventeenth century, they were driven westward as pressure on land and hunting grounds increased due to European encroachments. They settled near Sheboygan. By the end of the nineteenth century, the group, now under pressure from American settlers moving into the Northwest territories, sought refuge farther west, in Iowa and Oklahoma, where the remnants of the tribe still remain, residing on reservations.

I was really feeling the heat as I made my way through the village of Oostburg into Sheboygan. A small park borders the southern edge of town. People were spread out along the beach, trying to find some relief from the triple-digit temperatures. I stopped at the local bathhouse to fill my water bottle. A man close by was speaking to his young son, switching effortlessly between Chinese and English. I was envious of his facility. I was also nearing the end of my capacities, and the ride up a modest hill toward the center of town seemed daunting. Once on top, I spotted a small motel on the Sheboygan River, which splits the city almost exactly in half between north and south. The river flows from the western part of the state, down and away from the Niagara Escarpment which ends (or begins, depending on your point of view) about forty miles west of here. The friendly motel manager notified me that he had only one room left. Assuming that it had air-conditioning, I grabbed it, even though it was a little pricey.

I pulled my gear off the bike and locked it out front. In the hallway, I noticed a man and woman, probably in their seventies, chatting near a recumbent bike leaning against the wall. It looked new and pretty flashy, with an orange-and-black painted frame. I asked about it. Preston let me take a look at what turned out to be his Cruzbike Quest, a fold-up model. I'd seen recumbents before but only the three-wheeled versions that ride close to the ground—

the kind that you need to attach a flag to, to keep from getting run over by inattentive motorists. I'd never seen one like this, where the smaller crank is on the front wheel, with the pedals attached to a triangular frame above it, and the chain running between them.

Emily invited me into their room to take a look at her Bike Friday, a fold-up touring bike that has a good reputation for quality and service. I'd never seen one up close and was impressed with the cleverness and the engineering and the quality of the workmanship. But she was getting to the point that she was having trouble getting her leg up over the crossbar, so she wanted a newer model, because they had removed it. She offered to sell me hers. It had just been factory refurbed, so it was in excellent condition. I turned her down but eventually had some regrets about doing so. Bike Fridays are not cheap, and I might have gotten a good deal. Whatever the case, Emily, in spite of her infirmities, was still biking regularly and had just completed a 1,300-mile tour. She was now traveling with a crew of five other septuagenarians, riding around in a van, stopping to take day trips at various points along the way. Seemed like a good retirement plan.

After a shower, I went in search of dinner and found an old-school family restaurant a few blocks from the motel. The place was packed: Greek American food at a reasonable price. It also had air-conditioning, a definite plus. Sheboygan, a city of just less than fifty thousand residents, was first settled by Europeans, mostly Germans, in the mid-nineteenth century. As is colorfully stated in Carl Ziller's history of the area, "It was not until 1846 that the sturdy and industrious Germans set their eyes upon this land of peace and plenty and began to settle here." Many came as refugees from the Revolution of 1848. They became known as the "48ers." The German middles classes tended to support the revolt against the aristocracy, but they came into conflict with the more radical working-class elements, resulting in a split that allowed the aristocrats to regain control. As reaction took hold, supporters of the revolution with means often fled to the United States. Or, as Ziller states, "A great share of the German immigrants came to Wisconsin and no better selection of that share could have been made than the ones who threw in their lot with those that rocked the cradle of the infant Sheboygan."²

Many Germans stayed to fight, at least for a time. Friedrich Engels famously joined the revolutionary forces and fought in the Palatinate with the thirty thousand–strong Willich corps, which was in the end easily defeated by the well-armed and highly disciplined Prussian Army. The result of this final defeat was an influx to the United States of more-radical German émigrés, often from the working classes, who had skills that contributed to the growth of the American industrial revolution. German immigration also helped to generate a backlash of nativist sentiment, as previously settled immigrant groups felt threatened by economic competition and cultural transformation.³

Hmong refugees started to emigrate in the 1970s, and there are now five thousand in the area, making it one of the largest Hmong communities in the United States. Originally from China, the Hmong settled in mountain villages in Laos in the mid-nineteenth century. Many Hmong joined forces with the CIA in the 1960s during the Vietnam conflict to help fight the U.S. "secret war" in Laos. After U.S. forces left Southeast Asia, the Hmong were left to fend for themselves against the Marxist Laotian government, which they had been fighting. While most stayed in Laos, where they established an uneasy truce with the central government, many fled to Thailand and then eventually settled in the United States, with Sheboygan being a primary stopping point.

The Hmong are not a highly visible presence in Sheboygan, at least to someone spending an afternoon there. They haven't had an easy time of it, which is entirely understandable. I've bicycled through the mountains of northern Laos, which are dotted with Hmong villages. I cannot imagine the level of culture shock that someone would face moving from a Laotian mountain village to Sheboygan, Wisconsin. The first émigrés found work in local factories, seldom having the economic means or knowledge of English required to open family businesses. Moreover, smaller midwestern cities, where Hmong often located, had been highly homogeneous and had little, if any, experience with non-European immigrant populations. As a result, racism and discrimination likely intensified the Hmong's sense of isolation. Many younger Hmong found refuge and belonging in gangs.

After a horrific gang rape that occurred in 1999, Sheboygan belatedly, but to its credit, took action, hiring a young Hmong man into the local police department in an attempt to diversify the force. Officer Bruce Lang developed an innovative Hmong-language citizens' academy to reach out to non-English-speaking members of the Hmong community, pointing to the benefits of diversifying small city police departments.[4] Things have improved for the Hmong in Sheboygan and other Wisconsin communities due to local efforts and state support. In 2004, in response to the last ripple of Hmong immigrants, who had been held in a refugee camp in Thailand, Governor Jim Doyle established the Hmong Resettlement Task Force and accepted its recommendations. As a result, the availability of classes teaching English as a second language increased, and bilingual assistance was expanded, with special attention to older members of the community. The state offered help to immigrants to obtain drivers licenses and find employment. Rather than place the burden of assimilation entirely upon the Hmong, often in the face of local intransigence, the state and local communities worked in tandem with refugee mutual assistance programs. In 2006, Sheboygan erected the Hmong Veterans Memorial to commemorate the role that Hmong partisans played in the Laotian war, fighting beside American soldiers.[5]

I walked along the main street, which has attractive old buildings with large windowed storefronts, then down to the river, along a row of storefronts and restaurants, providing services to the owners of the boats docked there. Although the sun was setting, and it was practically dark by the time I returned to my room, the heat was still pretty intense. I wasn't optimistic that the next day would be much cooler.

July 23, 2012

Next morning I started out through Deland Park on a bike path running north along the shoreline. I passed Preston and Emily and their friends, the folks that I'd talked to in the motel the previous afternoon, as they pulled bikes out of their van for an early morning ride. The road northward runs through rural landscapes, often close to the lakeshore. I was starting to think I could make it close to the Door Peninsula, hopefully Sturgeon Bay, by the evening. While it was nearly a hundred-mile ride, things were running smoothly, and I was feeling good, so why not? Interstate 45, which goes to Green Bay, is to the west, which leaves a cyclist on more or less deserted county roads.

This leg of the trip intersects the lakeshore towns of Manitowoc and Two Rivers. The former first achieved notoriety in 1963, when an errant piece of the Soviet Sputnik IV landed on one of the town's main streets. Something had gone awry on reentry, causing the seven-ton satellite to drift into an uncontrolled orbit and break up in its inexorable descent toward earth. Police reportedly noticed a piece of metal in the middle of the street on the corner of North Eighth and Park. First dismissing it as something that fell from a foundry truck, they eventually made the connection with Sputnik's demise. The Smithsonian, after examining it, returned the six-inch hunk of metal to the Russians. A replica is now on display in Sheboygan's Rahr-West Art Museum. A brass ring marks the spot in the street where it landed. Every September since 2011, Sheboygan has sponsored Sputnikfest, replete with costume contests and the crowning of Miss Space Debris.[6]

More recently (and since my ride through the city) Manitowoc has become known as the locale in which the documentary series *Making a Murderer* is set. The series, filmed over a ten-year period, tracks the legal difficulties of Steven Avery. Avery's family owned an automobile junkyard outside of town and were treated with a fair amount of suspicion, and even hostility, by many townsfolk and, apparently, members of the Manitowoc County Sheriff's Office. Partly this was due to Steven's history of juvenile misconduct. He was convicted of committing a brutal rape when he was twenty-three years old, a conviction that was overturned based upon DNA evidence after he had served eighteen years in prison. Avery successfully sued Manitowoc County for his false conviction but was arrested along with codefendant Brendan Dassey for the murder of television reporter, Teresa Halbach, in 2005. Avery's lawyers argued that their client had been framed by individuals working on the prosecution's side of the case. The documentary leaves the strong impression that that may have been true. Nevertheless, both Dassey and Avery were convicted and are now serving life sentences for the crime. The series does not, to say the least, leave viewers with a positive impression of life in this small midwestern community. Riding through on a bicycle, of course, you would be unlikely to discover the darker secrets of this place or any other. And that may just be part of the appeal.

On a happier note, up the road a ways, Two Rivers is in competition with my own hometown of Ithaca, New York, as the recognized birthplace of the ice cream sundae. Since I wasn't wearing any identifying clothing, I figured it was safe to ride through. In the Two Creeks Natural Area, a few miles outside of town, I snapped a picture of several herons. Two Creeks has significance for geologists because there they have found evidence of advancing and retreating glaciers that definitively substantiates warming trends between glacial periods.

Past Kewaunee and Algoma, I finally made it to Sturgeon Bay a little after five o'clock. The town is split by the bay, which created some confusion on my part. I rode unnecessarily north for a couple of miles and then found my way back. On the main highway, as I was about to turn, someone yelled to me from the window of a car. "Hey, didn't I see you down in Two Rivers?" "That was must have been me," I responded. The couple had bicycles on a rack on the back of their car. "Where are you going?" "Around Lake Michigan." "Good for you! And good luck." Encouragement never goes unappreciated.

I finally found the town's main strip and asked someone in front of a bar where I could find a cheap motel. He seemed a little inebriated but gave me what turned out to be accurate directions to a tidy family-owned place that seemed more than suitable for a night's stay. Unfortunately, it was booked up. But the helpful clerk called around to some other places and found me one. When I asked about camping, she directed me to the Potawatomi State Park. It was less than a mile away, but the only entrance was on the western side, which would mean another five- to six-mile ride. She gave very careful directions that took me over a bridge, through a residential area, up some rather steep hills, back out to the countryside, and eventually to the park entrance.

It turned out to be well worth the effort. After acquiring a campsite, setting up the tent, and taking a shower, I took in the view of Sturgeon Bay, a small sliver of water appended to the much larger Green Bay, which separates the lower from the upper Door Peninsula. I ate fruit, granola bars, and other assorted snacks. By the time I was done, it was dark. I climbed into my tent and fell asleep.

July 24, 2012

I was awoken by rain and lightning. Because of the tree cover, I couldn't quite see the sky when I got up to pee. I couldn't tell where the clouds were or whether the storm was headed toward me. It wasn't raining very hard, but the lightning, while somewhat distant, was intense. The worst of the storm never seemed to arrive though, and the next morning I got up and packed a few things for a day trip to the Door Peninsula. That would require a ride back through town and then up the eastern side of the bay.

I stopped in town at little family restaurant for breakfast. A group of town grumblers was sitting close to my table, commenting and complaining about various topics, local politics mostly. Highway construction, or the lack thereof, seemed to be a central topic of the conversation. The restaurant was full of local patrons and tourists, gabbing away no doubt about plans for the day, the week, and the rest of their lives.

I couldn't tell what was going to happen with the storm from looking at the sky, but the wind was strong from the south. That would make for a nice ride up and a difficult one on the way back. I didn't really have expectations as to what I would find on the peninsula itself. I had somehow imagined that it would be a fairly wild place without much in the way of development, but I was partly wrong about that. I took Highway 42, which is wide and busy, leading northward along the eastern side of Sturgeon Bay. After a few miles, I turned west onto Bay Shore Drive, where the traffic was much lighter, with hilly roads traversing farmlands, fields, and the occasional forest.

Tourist traffic was backed up through Egg Harbor. The area was once a central juncture in the fur trade due to the relative seclusion of the harbor and its convenience as a stopping point on the way to Mackinac and points east. Its name is derived from an actual egg battle that occurred in the nineteenth century. Fur traders, it seems, in a flotilla of six boats, began throwing hardtack at one another as they approached the harbor's shoreline. Soon, realizing hardtack's necessity as a foodstuff, they graduated to eggs, which apparently were more plentiful. They even began to pelt unfortunate bystanders on shore. That evening, so the story goes, to commemorate their battle, they christened the site "egg harbor."[7]

Now the area is stocked with gift shops and has a small park overlooking the harbor. I stopped and ate some fruit and bread for lunch. You can see the other side of the shore of Green Bay from there, which is close to the Wisconsin-Michigan border. Green Bay was excavated by the Green Bay Lobe of the Laurentide Ice Sheet, which divided as it encountered the hard dolomite surface of the Niagara Escarpment, the bedrock material underlying the Door. But as the ice sheet grew, it ultimately covered even the Door, leaving small bays, or fjords, as glacial troughs on the Green Bay side as it advanced, and the Lake Michigan side as it retreated. This accounts for the Door's jagged coastline, which provided ideal locations for settlement, first by Paleo-Indians and eventually by Europeans.[8]

The threat, or promise, of rain never materialized beyond a few scattered drops as I headed north past Peninsula State Park and Ephraim, another tourist town. I was having some problems with my brakes that I couldn't seem to fix. They were slack, but when I tightened the cable, they would rub. Partly this was because the rim was a little askew, so I went into a bike shop along the way and asked the mechanic if he could true the rim. The place was busy, and he said I'd have to leave the bike for a couple of hours. I decided I could live with it and pushed on.

I didn't have time (or perhaps the energy) to make it all the way to Northport to view the place that, according to legend, gave the peninsula its name. Several small islands dot the waters between the Door and Michigan's Upper Peninsula; all are, like the Door itself, pieces of the Niagara Escarpment. Other, unseen fragments lie hidden beneath Michigan's waters. The resulting convergence of rock, water, and wind makes for exceptionally treacherous navigational conditions, a phenomenon known to indigenous people long before Europeans colonizers arrived. It was the French who dubbed the area Porte des Morts, death's door, a name that they apparently appropriated from the indigenous inhabitants.[9] The straits lived up to their name. In 1872, eight large vessels were reported to have been lost there.[10]

The European name for the indigenous people of Wisconsin, which some evidence suggests may have been the inhabitants of the Door Peninsula, was "Puans," which was drawn from the distinctive odor the French attributed to either Green Bay or its inhabitants, depending on whose account you choose to believe. These were the Winnebago people, who can trace their origins to the earliest Paleo-Indians, who lived here nine thousand to ten thousand years ago. It was the Winnebago who Jean Nicolet, French explorer and emissary of Samuel de Champlain, encountered in 1640.

While the Winnebago tended to be isolated from direct European contact—trading with Europeans via Odawa intermediaries—that did not protect them from the ravages of European diseases, and they suffered significant population loss over a relatively short period of time after first contact. As a result of their declining numbers and conflicts to the east—the result of the Beaver Wars— the Winnebago were displaced by the Potawatomi in the second half of the seventeenth century.

The Potawatomi established a village on Rock Island, one of the small islands that stretches northward from the tip of the Door to the Stonington Peninsula of the Upper Peninsula. Here they met La Salle on his trek to find the mouth of the Mississippi River. Due to their isolation, Native Americans on the Door were able to maintain their culture and subsistence practices of hunting, fishing, and agriculture through the eighteenth century, even into the nineteenth. But with the inexorable westward movement of settlers, Native Americans' capacity to thrive in an unforgiving northern environment became increasingly constrained. As fish stocks and hunting grounds became depleted and land was cleared for farming and fruit orchards, traditional practices became untenable. By the mid-nineteenth century, the Door's indigenous inhabitants were entirely gone.[11] They were replaced by immigrants, at first mostly from northern Europe, who found the climate familiar, if not congenial, and who established the settlements that formed the basis of the tourist colonies that I encountered on my way along Green Bay's shorelines.

I headed back at Sister Bay, cutting across the center of the peninsula to make my way to its eastern and, as it turned out, its wilder side. Rather than towns, it's mostly parks and natural areas. This was closer to the ruggedness that I had originally imagined. Green Bay offers protection from the wind and waves of the lake, making it ideal for settlement. But on this side, the lake's waters and the wind are unconstrained, resulting in fewer towns and fewer people. When I walked down a path to the shoreline, the water was frothy with whitecaps, stretching out toward an indefinite horizon. Given that the conditions were likely only a close approximation of those faced by travelers through the straits to the north, the peninsula's name seems well deserved.

The route into town brought me close to the waters of Sturgeon Bay, past an operating shipyard belonging to the Bay Shipbuilding

Company. While it reorganized into its present corporate form in 1967, the company can trace its roots back to the nineteenth century. It is the only remaining shipyard on the Great Lakes but builds large barges, rather than actual ships, nowadays. Boats were in different stages of completion as I rode past, eventually to a shopping plaza, where I spotted the Hong Kong Buffet. I couldn't resist, and I ate my money's worth sitting in sweaty bike clothes, afterward riding to the park as lightning lit up the horizon. Back at my tent, I noticed that a number of campsites had been vacated and wondered if they knew something about the weather that I didn't. But it never rained, and I slept soundly.

July 25, 2012

I was up at six o'clock for the ride out of Potawatomi Park. A fairly steep, albeit relatively short, climb gets you up into the surrounding fields. The morning was cool and cloudy. The ride today would be along the lower western side of the Door, along the eastern shore of Green Bay, to the city of Green Bay, and then back north along the western side. I rode along the edge of the bay and then zigzagged across a network of roads, moving southwesterly. I passed just south of Little Sturgeon Bay, where the first European settler, Increase Claflin, established a farm in 1830. I was surrounded by broad hills in wide-open farm country. The warren of roads can be a little confusing, and I ended up dead-ended at the shoreline after having made a couple of wrong turns. Still, knowing the general direction to travel and being able to see the waters of Green Bay, it was relatively easy to get back on track. The wind was behind me, blowing from the north, making for a nice quick ride.

Eventually the city starts to appear through breaks in the trees, as does the other side of the bay. Its bluish-green waters mark a strong contrast with the industrial skyline of the city, which slowly comes into focus as waterfront suburban homes start to appear on the shoreline. Trash collectors were emptying the ubiquitous plastic canisters as I rode by.

Green Bay is an estuary. While estuaries are usually characterized by water flows between salt and fresh water, they can also
result from flow patterns occurring between highly differenti-
ated forms of freshwater alone. Such is the case with Green Bay,
in which warm water flows in from a southern watershed that
includes the Fox River, and colder water with a different chemical composition flows in through the straits in the north. In fact,
Green Bay is considered the largest freshwater estuary in the
world. Estuaries, including Green Bay, are characterized by very
high levels of biological diversity.

Contamination of the bay's waters, the result of industrial production, municipal wastewater, and agricultural runoff, has been
ongoing since the early twentieth century. As early as 1925, residents complained about odors rising from the Fox River, and in
the 1930s "dead zones" were detected. After the passage of the
1972 amendments to the Clean Water Act, some improvements
occurred, as limits were placed upon the volume of discharges that
could be dumped into the bay. Still, it faces many environmental
challenges, including low oxygen levels, high phosphorus loads,
and algae blooms. The primary culprit nowadays is agricultural
runoff. The invasion of nonnative zebra mussels, quagga mussels,
and carp also poses problems, as do the legacies of industrial pollution, which have left high levels of mercury in Fox River sediments. While all of the Great Lakes will be impacted by climate
change, shallower waters such as Green Bay's will be affected
soonest and most severely. The warmer waters and increased
runoff, resulting from predicted heavy rain events, will exacerbate the problems caused by agricultural runoff. In other words,
industrial agriculture and climate change pose the greatest environmental threats to Green Bay.[12]

There are four bridges over the Fox River, which divides the
city of Green Bay in half. I knew I wanted to avoid Interstate 43,
which is the first one, so I kept riding. After a couple of miles down
Webster Avenue, I realized that I must have missed the turns to
all of the bridges. I turned back, riding along side streets running
parallel to the river, through middle-class neighborhoods with
well-kept houses and large front yards. Having trouble getting

my bearings, I stopped to ask a pedestrian how to get to one of the bridges. He ignored me and just kept walking. I found this a little disconcerting. It hardly ever happens. Fortunately, even without his help, I found my way to Highway 172. It brought me across just north of the fabled Lambeau Field, which I could see off to the right, into the town of Ashwaubenon, which struck me as a pretty bleak place, even by Great Lakes standards. I was hoping to get some lunch, but there were no restaurants in sight, mostly just abandoned storefronts.

As you ride up Broadway, the familiar remnants of deindustrialization are scattered all around: vacant lots, abandoned buildings, the crumbling remnants of warehouses and small factories. I couldn't help but wonder how this city could still host a National Football League team. Green Bay was always one of the smaller markets, but now, with depopulation, there are only about a hundred thousand people in the city proper, and it's pretty far removed from any major media market. Still, given all the problems in the world, not to mention the Great Lakes region itself, I wasn't planning to lose much sleep over how the NFL distributed its franchises (as long as Buffalo keeps the Bills, of course.)

As I pedaled northward, and somewhat tentatively, through the construction along Velp Avenue, weaving between cars and plastic barrels, the sun disappeared, and I could see lightning in the distance. I decided to stop at a Taco Bell for some lunch. I hadn't been to one in twenty years, but it seemed to be the only option, and I was starving. As I sat and ate what passes for a burrito there, Fox News leaked out from the television. Back home this would be considered as a political statement, and perhaps an inappropriate one, in a fast-food franchise. Around here, apparently, it's just considered to be "the news." With the presidential campaign approaching, the commentators were really heating up the anti-Obama rhetoric.

Back on the road, it started to rain a little, and then it started to rain a lot. Lightning ensued but never seemed to arrive directly overhead, so I decided just to ride through it, not that I had much choice. Other than the lightning, it was actually pleasant riding through forests and wetlands. It also felt good to be heading north again, now on the western side of Green Bay, with a clear view to the eastern side I'd just ridden down. As I neared Onconto, it looked like it was really going to storm, so I opted for a relatively early overnight stop.

After a shower and a little bit of a rest, I had dinner in the Chinese Buffet next door. The food was both plentiful and mediocre. The rain poured down outside as I sat and ate. But after the storm, the sun appeared, so I walked down the main drag. Political signs for a Republican district attorney candidate were ubiquitous. No doubt this is Scott Walker country. The governor's successful attempts to disenfranchise public employee unions had been met with tremendous opposition and led to a recall election, which Walker won. The votes that kept him in office came from the rural areas and small towns in the state, of which this was no doubt one.

I stopped for a Leinenkugel in a lively neighborhood bar near the center of town. Patrons had their eyes glued to a Milwaukee Braves baseball game, and no one struck up a conversation.

July 26, 2012

The weather was unsettled as I rode out of Oconto in the early morning. Clouds were swirling around through the sky overhead. The darker clouds seemed to be amassing directly over the path into which I was riding. The county road was deserted and seemed a little lonely, given the threatening sky. There was clearly no way to avoid the rain, so I battened everything down and pedaled forward. My gear is protected by waterproof panniers, so it was only my own self that was exposed to the weather. It's only rain, after all. The darkening clouds didn't give way to a storm, however, until Marinette, a town on the Michigan border. Given the rain's intensity as I approached the city limits, I elected to stop at a Hardee's for a cup of coffee until things cleared a bit.

A half hour later, I was riding through the city, when it became clear that the storm was only starting to pick up momentum. As I approached the First Street Bridge, the wind really started to blow, and the sky opened up. I couldn't even see across the half-mile bridge. I turned back and found a sturdy nineteenth-century stone building to stand against, keeping me somewhat out of the downpour. It was, I have to admit, an exhilarating half hour spent waiting out the storm, which unleashed near biblical quantities of lightning and hail. Once it let up, I rode across the bridge into Michigan's Upper Peninsula, under a still unsettled sky. Once out of Marinette, the UP's distinctive ecological features soon become apparent. You soon feel that you are entering into a more northern ecological zone.

As the sky cleared, I rode northeast into a fierce headwind, continuing up Highway 35, with the open waters of Lake Michigan on my right. I continued through the sun and wind to Escanaba. By the time I reached it, the sky had completely cleared. At the intersection of 35 and Highway 2, there are a slew of motels and restaurants. I chose a little strip motel, which was quite cheap and reasonably clean. After cleaning up and resting a little, I walked toward the center of town and found the Hong Kong Buffet, with decent food. It had been kind of a crazy day with all the weather, so it was nice to sit and eat in a place that had a pleasant family-friendly atmosphere.

The city of about twelve thousand has long been a shipping point for iron ore. The Escanaba River runs into the Little Bay du Noc, which provided a convenient harbor for ore-carrying ships. Hiawatha crosses a river by this name in Longfellow's poem. But the real Hiawatha actually lived in upstate New York, making such a journey extremely unlikely. The poem was based upon the exploits of the legendary Ojibwe trickster Manabozho, whose name Longfellow changed to Hiawatha, partly because he liked how it sounded. The change ricocheted into the naming of the Hiawatha National Forest, which covers large swaths of Michigan's central and eastern Upper Peninsula. I don't see this as an inconsequential error. The actual Hiawatha played a key role in formulating the Great Law of Peace, which established the Haudenosaunee (Iroquois) Confederacy, one of the most significant political events in pre-Columbian North America.

July 27, 2012

The contrasts of weather between this day and the day before couldn't have been more pronounced. After a couple of bananas and trail mix for breakfast, it was northward onto Highway 41, a lightly trafficked four-lane road that hugs the Little Bay du Noc. It was a lovely morning, as the eastern morning sun rose up over the bay. The views were so strikingly beautiful that I even pulled out my camera, an accoutrement that I have a tendency to neglect for a good reason: At best, I'm a mediocre photographer. A light wind drifted down from the north, with just a few fluffy clouds overhead. The road travels along through the small town of Gladstone, along a path cut by Au Train-Whitefish Channel.

Starting about ten thousand years ago, the channel opened to drain water from Lake Minong (a precursor to Lake Superior) to Lake Chippewa (a precursor to Lake Michigan), the levels of which fell quite low when the North Channel opened to drainage, the result of glacial retreat. Now dry, it still persists as one of the most prominent geological features of the UP, splitting it down the middle, neatly dividing eastern and western sides. John Hughes has labeled this "the last glacial event to affect Green Bay."[13] Remnants of the channel's delta, known as the Whitefish Fan, have been located offshore, as have several drowned forests. If there is one geological characteristic that ties the entire Great Lakes region together, it is the dramatic shifting of ice, water, and land occurring in unimaginably complex, and sometimes violent, patterns over millennia.[14]

At Rapid River I took Highway 2 eastward through the misnamed forest, running along the southern edge of the Upper Peninsula and the northern shore of the lake. There's something very alluring about this northern landscape, at least on a lovely, warm summer day. Scrubby white pine trees dominate the surrounding forests. None seem to grow very tall, no doubt because they are cut when they reach a certain age of maturity. I took County Road S6 for a closer view of the shoreline. It runs parallel to the main highway and snakes along the northern tip of the bay, running through a bird sanctuary, with a smattering of small cabins interspersed between the trees. Back out on the main highway, the riding was flat and hot. While I'd run into a fair amount of rain in the south, it didn't seem to have made it this far north. The forest floor was parched and brown.

While I was guzzling some water while sitting on the curb at a highway rest stop, Charles, from Chicago, came over to chat. He was out for an excursion with his wife and in-laws, who were visiting from Germany. He was intensely curious about my bicycle, my trip, and touring in general. I filled him in as best I could. He introduced me to everyone in his adoptive family. They all had German accents. The father-in-law turned out to be a bicyclist, and he noted that many people bicycle around Europe, but he doesn't see it as often in the United States. He wondered why. I wasn't sure how to respond. How do you explain cultural quirks? The best I could come up with was that Americans love their cars. "Germans do too!" he responded. It was hard to argue with that. "Well," I told him, perhaps reaching a little, "there *are* a lot of Americans touring on bicycles, but the country's so big and spread out, you just don't see them as often." He wasn't buying it, and I wasn't going to give him the hard sell, since I thought it was a pretty weak argument myself. The rest stop in general was a busy place, full of tourists. Even if we weren't all on bicycles, we were all briefly pulled together by our appreciation of the austere and rugged beauty of Michigan's north shore.

From there, I enjoyed a pretty easy and uneventful ride to Manistique, arriving at midafternoon. I had started early, and an overnight there would put me within a day's ride of St. Ignace, so it seemed like as good a place to stop as any. I rode across the Manistique River, through the old lumber town, and spotted a strip motel on its eastern edge. I was right across the road from the beach and had a great view of the lake to the south. After a shower, I spent some time lazily sitting outside on the little porch to my room, taking it all in on a perfect summer afternoon. Eventually, I made my way to the large supermarket next door, where I stocked up on pasties, bananas, trail mix, cheese, and bread. While eating, I caught some of the Summer Olympics, which were now in full swing. In a close and very exciting volleyball match, the United States beat South Korea.

July 28, 2012

The riding continued to be pleasant from Manistique to St. Ignace. A wide shoulder protects a rider from the increasingly busy traffic. After more than a week of continuous riding, the ninety-mile ride didn't seem especially demanding, even though it continued to be quite hot. There's a long stretch of beaches at this end of the lake. They were packed with people out on a Sunday afternoon. Cars were parked haphazardly all along the roadside. The hillier terrain allows opportunities for overlooks, where you can see this vast expanse of water that constitutes the convergence of three lakes. Superior, Michigan, and Huron are all close here, and it becomes difficult to distinguish the beginning of one from the end of the other. The categories defined by the names are, after all, human conceits, applied to a very narrow slice of geological time, and, from a natural history perspective, entirely arbitrary.

I found a state park icon on my Michigan map, with camping designated, so I turned south on a road that borders the western edge of St. Ignace. It took me to the bottom of a hill near a parking area where tourists can take in close-up views of the Mackinac Bridge. I'd ride over it in the morning but thought it would be nice to camp on the shoreline here, with lower Michigan and southern Ontario visible in the distance. I continued on the road as it turned westward, only to become dirt, and then disappear into weeds. No state park in sight. Eventually I surmised that the park was on an island out in the straits. With no way to get there, I rode back up the hill to the main highway and decided to crash at a motel at the top. Not the most idyllic spot but a nice enough place, and I was starting to feel the ride. After washing up, I found a little store that sold pasties and fudge. Not exactly health food, but I was starved. After eating a healthy share of each, I fell asleep early and woke up ten hours later, around six thirty.

July 29, 2012

I've been over the Mackinac Bridge before. In fact, I rode over last summer, when I was making my way around Lake Huron. On that occasion, I was coming from the south, up to Sault Ste. Marie. What I learned then, somewhat by accident, was that while you can't ride your bike over the bridge, a Michigan DOT truck will take you across. I found the bridge authority office, paid my five dollars, and waited a few minutes until the truck showed up. I had to unload everything from my bike, but after a five-minute ride, I was back on the Lower Peninsula. I turned right at the first intersection off the bridge and was soon riding west on luxuriously low-trafficked county roads along the northern boundaries of Michigan's mitt.

The turn toward the south brought me into a pesky headwind, and the terrain was much hillier than anything I'd encountered since Wisconsin. I rode straight southward down North State Road through ski country. The challenging rides to the top of the steep hills were rewarded with views of forested hillsides opening to the south. These crosscutting hills and similar topography along the Lower Peninsula's western side are glacial moraines, left in the wake of the Laurentide Ice Sheet's retreat, some ten thousand years ago. It was a rugged ride along deserted roads. Along the way, another cyclist, on a sleek road bike, out for a morning ride, pulled up beside me. He lived in Colorado but was in Michigan visiting in-laws. He enjoyed cycling through the area but was having trouble with the humidity. We chatted for a mile or so, and then he took off.

I intersected the lakeshore again at Harbor Springs and continued on to Petoskey, skirting the edge of Little Traverse Bay. The downtown sits atop a hill overlooking the bay's waters. Petoskey has an old-fashioned downtown, replete with diverse and seemingly prosperous small businesses tucked into nineteenth-century stone buildings. On the southern edge of the city, I spotted the Grain Train co-op, where I had an excellent vegetarian lunch, served cafeteria style. A stool in the front window provided a bird's-eye view of the bay. Friendly patrons asked about my trip. The excellent food and atmosphere reminded me of the Greenstar Co-op back in Ithaca.

Out of Petoskey a nice bike path runs to Charlevoix, hugging the southern shore of Little Traverse Bay. It was sunny and warm, but a stiff headwind made for slow going. A number of other cyclists were out taking advantage of the ideal weather. At an old-fashioned hand water pump, where I stopped to refill my bottles, I spent a little time chatting with a lawyer from Washington, D.C., visiting his in-laws. He loved northern Michigan, and he and his wife visited every summer. Her parents owned a small cottage that they had bought in the 1960s when such luxuries were still affordable to middle-class people.

After Charlevoix, I was back on busy Highway 31, where the shoulder disappeared. I had to face the quadruple whammy: narrow shoulder, heavy traffic, strong headwind, and steep hills. It was the toughest going I'd had so far. I stopped at a sign marking the 45th parallel to grab a photo. As I was standing there, someone pulled up in a car and offered to take my picture. I readily agreed. Jason had recently moved from Chicago and was living at a place that his family owned. He said he just couldn't take the city anymore. He was exploring this part of Michigan and organizing a radio blog about its local history and geography. He wanted to interview me and gave me a number to call when I returned home. To be honest, though, I completely forgot about it until I started reading my field notes, sometime in December.

I continued on to Elk Rapids. The city sits on a strip of land between Grand Traverse Bay and Elk Lake. A river joins the larger lake with the smaller one. Boats were docked at every conceivable open spot. I felt as though I was surrounded by them. I took a chance that Elk Lake might offer some places to stay, but the shoreline seemed devoid of campsites, guesthouses, and small motels. With nothing in sight, I rode into town, asked at a restaurant if there was anyplace nearby and was directed south of town. A narrow and flat tree-lined road that hugged the bay brought me back out onto the highway, where as promised, I found a little motel. I made it to my room just in time to avoid a major thunderstorm. After enjoying its fury from the safety of my room, I caught some of the Olympics on the small television and checked on the next day's weather. After the front passed, the wind was supposed to blow from the north, a prospect that I was much looking forward to.

July 30, 2012

The morning ride would bring me into Traverse City, which sits at the bottom of Grand Traverse Bay, which is like a smaller sibling to larger Green Bay on the western side of the lake. The bay was given its name by the French, who crossed the "grand traverse" from one side to the other. The bay is defined and protected on its western flank by the Old Mission Peninsula, the tip of which is about forty-five miles north of the city. As an early account of the area states, "The early French voyageurs in coasting from Mackinac southward found two considerable indentations of the coast line of Lake Michigan on the east side, which they were accustomed to cross from headland to headland. The smaller of these they designated 'La Petite Traverse' and the greater, 'La Grande Traverse.' These names were transferred to the two bays known as the Little Traverse and Grand Traverse Bays."[15]

I'd heard many good things about Traverse City. While the city proper has only about fifteen thousand residents, the metropolitan area includes more than a hundred thousand and sprawls outward to the north. The north route in doesn't give a particularly positive impression, given the tacky tourist stands that string along the eastern arm of the bay. But once past Traverse City State Park and Northeastern Michigan University, you enter a town center that lives up to its reputation as a cultural gem of the northwestern Lower Peninsula. Shops and restaurants line the main street. The local art house was setting up for the first night of the Traverse City Film Festival.

I stopped and had breakfast at a small café and ate blueberry pancakes sitting out on the sidewalk as people strolled by, enjoying what I'm sure is a fairly brief window of warm summer weather. After breakfast, I headed to the western edge of town to pick up the East Traverse Highway, which runs to the dune coast of eastern Lake Michigan. The hill heading out of town is steep, and it would be the first of many as I reentered a rural landscape that posed the most challenging terrain that I'd encountered. A headwind from the west compounded the difficulties. The sun disappeared as the day wore on, and I rode through light rain. As I approached the shoreline, I kept imagining that each steep hill I ascended would bring a view of the lake from its summit. That never actually happened though. Too many trees and too gradual a downward slope impeded the view.

The final descent down Highway 72 to Platte Bay, was, however, in spite of the lack of a breathtaking view, a welcome relief. And the intersection with Highway 22 at the bottom of the hill was right next to the main office of the Sleeping Bear Dunes National Lakeshore. The place was packed, and I spent some time walking around, looking at various maps, brochures, and exhibits, trying to put together a plan of action. I'd hoped to camp inside the park somewhere but was informed at the registration desk that the campsites were full. Given the time of day, I wasn't sure if I'd be able to ride northward into the main park area, see the dunes, and then make it back before dark. I started out northward but soon thought better of it, and decided that I'd view the dunes while riding through the park's southern stretch. This also struck me as preferable to joining the hordes of tourists sliding down the high dunes on the park's north shore. This is what everyone does, but in truth I didn't find the prospect all that compelling.

The ride through the southern end of the park, along North-land Highway, on the other hand, was exceptional: shady, moderately hilly, with a helpful tailwind. I tooled along quite comfortably and fairly quickly arrived in Frankfort, a tourist town, bordered by small Betsie Lake on the south and Lake Michigan to the west. I found a room at a cozy family-run strip motel, showered up, and walked through the town center to the beach about a half mile away. You can walk out to a long breakwater, at the end of which sits the Frankfort lighthouse, originally placed to guide ships in and out of Lake Betsie. From this vantage point, you could see the dunes and bluffs that run up and down this part of the lake.

The high dunes on Lake Michigan are called "perched dunes." Their genesis can be found 4,500 years ago, during what is known as the Nipissing era, when the lake's level was much higher than it is today. The higher waters eroded the glacial sediments that ring the lake, generating sand that was blown up on the surrounding bluffs by prevailing westerly winds. As waters retreated, sand fell back down the sides of the bluffs. Vegetation took hold and eventually stabilized the dunes. While the "high-perch" dunes at Sleeping Bear receive most of the attention from the public, "low-perch" dunes, which start at Manistee and form a long, mostly unbroken line to the southern end of the lake, are of special interest to geologists. They rest upon the sediments of ancient Lake Chicago. Twenty thousand years ago, as the massive ice sheets that scrubbed out the contours of the lake basins began to retreat, early lakes began to take shape, forming like large puddles in the wake of the melting ice. Six thousand years later, Lake Chicago's shorelines reached up near to what is now Manistee, held back there by the retreating, but still massive, Laurentide Ice Sheet.[16] It is upon this old lake bed that the low-perch dunes now rest.

Back in town, sitting at the bar of a local restaurant, I struck up a conversation with Mike. He seemed to have spent more than his share of time at this particular bar, and he wanted to talk, mostly about politics, about which he had various strong opinions. He was a schoolteacher and didn't like what the Republicans were doing to public employees in Wisconsin and Michigan. In Wisconsin, Governor Scott Walker had recently fought a major battle with the state's unions and pretty much won. Rick Snyder, in Michigan, was also challenging public employees in a heavily unionized state. In spite of his antagonism toward Republicans, Mike wasn't so sure he would vote for Obama. For reasons that were opaque to me, given his other viewpoints, he liked Mitt Romney. Strange bedfellows seemed to inhabit Mike's brain.

The restaurant was friendly, and the wait staff drifted in and out of the conversation, treating Mike with a fair amount of good-natured condescension. He described the tourism economy as a mixed blessing. On the one hand, it brought in money, and the townsfolk had the place to themselves after Labor Day. On the other hand, in summer, the town was full of tourists, who sometimes got on his nerves. I drank one too many beers chatting with Mike and then headed back to the motel, watched the Olympics for a bit, and then fell asleep.

July 31, 2012

On the edge of town, I stopped and grabbed a snapshot of Frankfort's harbor, which is just an extension, really, of Lake Betsie. A mist was rising up over the water, partly shrouding the line of docked boats. It was clearly going to be another hot one. From here, Highway 22 winds its way along through a hilly coastline. The tops of hills yield unimpeded views of a deep-blue Lake Michigan. This trip had definitely had challenging terrain, but today's was the toughest of all. Up on the hilltops, where there was shade, it was cool and breezy, but at the bottom, riding through the valleys, the heat was intense. Along the way, Highway 22 enters Portage Bay, a small appendage of Lake Michigan that routes a traveler in a semicircle along its shores, through the small town of Onekama, and back again to the main shoreline. It seemed like an ideal place for a cottage, close to the water, but protected from the unruliness of the main body of Lake Michigan. The road was, in fact, lined with them. After rounding the bay, I caught the Crescent Beach Road that runs down through a forest to the shoreline, and then quite close to the lake itself. The shady road, with cabins and bungalows tucked in between the trees, was a welcome relief from the direct sun that had been beating down on me.

I had lunch in Manistee, which, like many of the towns along this coast, was founded as a sawmill town and served the timber industry throughout the nineteenth century. The Manistee River facilitated the transport of logs from farther inland. In the late-nineteenth century, salt was discovered, so salt mining and processing became a major economic activity. Nowadays, there is still some industry but nothing like when Manistee was once said to have more millionaires per capita than anywhere else in the United States. The economy now is organized around Michigan's huge fruit industry. I had a sandwich in a local café buzzing with people, mostly, it seemed, local residents.

Out of Manistee, you are forced onto US 31 with heavy truck traffic and, well, just heavy traffic in general. It's never pleasant to cycle out on a major highway, but a wide shoulder made it tolerable, and it was only for a few miles, at which point I turned right toward the lake and took a series of county roads into Luddington: County Line Road, Quarterline Road, West Angling Road, New Jebevy Drive. As the day went on, the heat and headwind both intensified. I continued on, up and down hills, fighting the wind along the way.

I caught the edge of Luddington, which seemed like nothing more than a series of intersecting highways surrounded by strip malls and other suburban sprawl. After some wrong turns, I found the path southward, which took me directly to Pentwater on a county road that runs parallel to 31. Just outside of Pentwater, I encountered another cyclist, out for a short afternoon ride. He told me it was a nice ride into the village, with no hills (which turned out to be less than completely accurate). I asked about Mears State Park. He highly recommended it, so that's where I headed.

The park was right on the beach. Tent sites were in the sand. While it's nice to be near the water, sand is not an ideal surface on which to pitch a tent. For one thing, it gets hot. Also, it's very hard to keep sand out of the tent, your sleeping bag, your socks, and your food. Nevertheless, I was grateful to have found a spot so close to the water to spend the night. The park was packed with families, many of whom seemed to have settled in for a long stretch of the summer. Once I set up my tent, it was a short walk to the beach for a leisurely swim in Lake Michigan's warm waters. Nice way to end the day. Once back to my tent, I had some food I'd stored, showered, and went to sleep early. I was bushed.

August 1, 2012

I was awakened about five o'clock by a storm that ran through the campground. Other than a slight leak in the top seam, the tent held up pretty well. By the time I was out of it at six o'clock, the sky was almost completely clear. A problem remained, however: sticky wet sand that I couldn't get off my feet, or my tent for that matter. I found a community hose and carefully washed my feet off, reflecting on the wisdom of my decision to switch from bicycle shoes to sandals a few years back, a suggestion provoked by someone I met riding north to south on the Baja Peninsula. As for the tent, I just stuffed it into its nylon bag. There wasn't much else to do.

After a short ride into town, I found a coffee shop and had my usual coffee, juice, and bagels. The heat was clearly going to continue, so I wanted to get as far as I could while it was still relatively cool. The ride around Pentwater Lake to Ridge Road runs close to the shoreline, past Silver Lake State Park and some impressive sand dunes. I zigzagged my way across county roads to White Lake, which blocks the path due southward. From there, it was further zigzagging to the bridge at Montague, where I was able to pick up a bike path that skirted the main highway. Not only did it keep me off the main highway, it provided an alternate raised route, through wetlands, to Whitehall. As I made my way through town, I saw some signs for Democratic candidates. I hadn't seen one probably since Milwaukee, and it provided evidence that I was heading into the urbanized belt that starts about here and runs, in fits and starts, to Chicago and back up the other side of the lake.

After riding through the pleasant residential streets of Whitehall, I was back into farmland for the ride due south to Muskegon, along Old Grandhaven Road, which runs parallel with Highway 31. Some bike paths crosscut through the area, but I wasn't entirely sure where they went, so I stuck to the highway.

Geographers have proposed an imaginary line running from Muskegon to Bay City, which divides southern urban and agricultural areas in Michigan from "up north." According to this division, southern Michigan constitutes the field of economy, industry, and productivity, while northern areas offer solace and escape.[17] Whatever the merits of the division in a postindustrial era, and the exact parameters of the boundary, my entry into Muskegon seemed to bring me fully back into the industrial/postindustrial landscape. A bike path skirts south of the town center, where factory buildings are scattered around through the surrounding fields. It leads through some railroad yards and then to a warehouse district and docking area. There the path ends, and you are tossed out into a series of suburban highways, which have neither shoulders nor bike paths but are well populated by shopping plazas, car dealerships, fast-food joints, and fast-moving automobiles.

Muskegon is situated within a web of waterways, including the East and Muskegon Rivers, which empty into a bay that divides North Muskegon from the rest of the city. The bay offered protection for Great Lakes freighters and other ships, making Muskegon an ideal location for manufacturing. The city remains the most populous in the state on Michigan's eastern shore.

It's not surprising that the area marks a boundary where population is concentrated and industry took hold. It has been inhabited for a very long time. Humans moved in eleven to twelve thousand years ago along the shores of the nascent Lake Chicago. Given the harsh climate, the so-called Paleo-Indians of the era relied primarily upon hunting to survive, finding abundant caribou but also now-extinct species, such as mastodons and wholly mammoths. The lake at this point held no fish. The northern part of the state became more hospitable to human habitation nine to eleven thousand years ago, with the first inhabitants crossing over from Wisconsin, so it is believed, rather than coming from the south.[18]

About five thousand years ago, as the climate warmed, the Paleo-Indians were superseded by the so-called Woodland Indian tribes, who practiced agriculture—growing corn, beans, and squash—while still hunting in and gathering from the now abundant countryside.[19] The labels, of course, denote an illusion of discontinuity, and the transition involved a gradual shift. But these more recent indigenous inhabitants organized into a loose confederacy and were known as the "People of the Three Fires," the Ojibwe, the Odawa, and the Potawatomi. The Odawa dominated the northeastern shores of Lake Michigan into the interior, the Potawatomi occupied the southern and western shores of the lake, and the Ojibwe were in southern Ontario. Collectively, in their native Algonquin language, they are the Anishinaabeg, or "original people." The Anishinaabeg lived without significant internal conflicts or external threats for hundreds of years. They, like other Native peoples, were unprepared for the disruptions caused by the arrival of Europeans in the seventeenth century, which began a process of destabilization, leading to eventual colonization. Still, their historical influences and continuous contributions are woven into the cultural fabric of the western Great Lakes.[20]

After Muskegon, a series of county roads goes to Grand Haven, where there's no choice but to get back onto 31 to get over the bridge that takes you across the Grand River, the longest river in Michigan, and the valley of which constitutes an ancient glacial riverbed. For nearly a hundred years, the river was treated as a convenient channel in which could be dumped all manner of industrial, municipal, and agricultural waste. One resident of the area in 1889 described it as "covered with a green odiferous scum, mixed with oil from the gas works." Along with so many rivers and other waterways in this part of the country, the river began to change with passage of the Clean Water Act in 1972. Fish and game fishing have returned to the river in recent years, and it has shown, as is often the case, a remarkable capacity to recover from past abuses. Present threats are most likely to come from unregulated development—especially the paving over of wetlands—and agricultural runoff. Large amounts of the herbicide Atrazine wash into the river and eventually find their way into Lake Michigan, where they cause havoc with its flora and fauna.[21]

Once through Grand Haven, the trail leads to Lake Shore Drive, a tree-lined road that offers a pleasant ride into Holland. Sometimes there's a bike path that runs parallel to the road, which tends to be narrow, and sometimes it disappears. A fair number of other cyclists were out on the road, enjoying a ride through semirural and suburban landscapes. It was a nice way to end the day. I made it to Holland and eventually found the house of my friends Boyd and Sarah.

August 2, 2012

I met Boyd when I was in graduate school at the University of Iowa. He was getting his Ph.D. in religious studies, and I was getting mine in political science. We used to hang out with a group of other graduate students, local characters, and some profs at a little bar called George's Buffet, which had no buffet but did have Hamm's and Olympia Beer on tap, and usually a Cubs game on the television during baseball season. Boyd now has a position at Hope College, where he's been teaching for more than twenty-five years. I hadn't seen him in a couple of decades. I reconnected to him via Facebook, one of the few times I've been on it.

Boyd and Sarah live in a beautiful suburban home on a cul-de-sac, with a large pond and wooded area out behind the house. We seemed to reconnect almost immediately and revisited our graduate school days while drinking a few beers. Boyd, like myself, has a particular taste for India pale ales. We spent the day tooling around Holland, visiting the Hope campus, which is beautiful, and spending the afternoon and early evening in downtown Holland.

Boyd taught world religions and was for that reason somewhat alienated from his department, which over time has become increasingly conservative Christian. He had the impression that once he retired, they would completely abolish the world religions courses. Each year, for more than twenty years, he has taken students on a month-long tour of religious and cultural sites in India. They visited practically every part of the country. And he's made connections to hotels and transport companies, which has helped to make the trip more manageable. It has developed a kind of mythic status at the college. Students found it to be a life-changing experience.

I was struck by how different this part of Michigan is from the eastern side, the side that borders Lakes Erie and Michigan. Those old industrial towns, a number of which I'd ridden through earlier in the summer, are beaten up and struggling. On this side, at least around Holland, things are much more prosperous. The economy is organized around tourism and education, plus agriculture, especially fruit growing. Whatever the reason for its success, downtown Holland surprised me with its vitality and general prosperity. It has followed a nationwide trend with its proliferation of microbreweries. Many of its older buildings had been restored, and there was a lot of activity out on the streets, including street theater and musicians busking. Jane Jacobs, author of *The Death and Life of Great American Cities*, would no doubt approve. She once wrote, "You can't rely on bringing people downtown. You have to put them there." Holland seems to have succeeded in doing just that.

August 3, 2012

Boyd is not an early riser, and I appreciated that he was willing to make an exception in my case. We had a traditional American breakfast of bacon, eggs, and toast, and then Sarah laughed as I went through my morning ritual of taping up my toes to prevent my sandals from digging into them.

I started out on the Blue Star Highway headed south but became disoriented and then eventually quite lost. The northern and southern parts of Holland are divided by Lake Macatawa, the wide mouth of the Macatawa River, with higher-end residential areas to the north and commercial and industrial areas to the south. The North Avenue Bridge across is about three miles east of the lakeshore. Even though I thought I had followed Boyd's directions pretty carefully, I still somehow headed westward toward Lake Michigan. I had to backtrack to get myself back to the bridge. There's nothing worse than backtracking. Once over the bridge, I rode along Pine Avenue toward the lakeshore to pick up Sixty-Sixth Street, which then becomes Highway A-2, also known as the Blue Star Highway. Once there, it was smooth sailing on a flat road along the lakeshore.

Along the way, I rode by some metal sculptures, including Rusty the Metal Dog, with big metal teeth bared but still looking surprisingly friendly. The sculptures were created by Louis Padnos, owner of a nearby Iron and Metal Company, a recycling operation with facilities in Holland, Grand Rapids, and Lansing. The company is a family business, and Padnos, now in his nineties and still working, is a self-taught artist. You can find his metal marching band sculpture on the campus of Grand State University at Allendale. I guess the term for this is "folk art," but whatever the case, I found the whimsical dog and other abstract sculptures to be completely appealing.[22]

It was again going to be hot, with expected temps in the mid to upper nineties. But I'd picked up reports in the morning that there was a front headed through that would cool things off, while also, of course, bringing some potentially intense storms. My plan at this point was to get back to Milwaukee in three days. That would involve around 250 miles of cycling, working out to a little over 80 miles a day: very doable. I also hoped to get a healthy leg in today before the storms hit in the afternoon.

On the way into Saugatuck, I stopped briefly to check the map. Someone in a stopped car asked if I needed directions. Things were pretty straightforward this time, and I easily made my way across the bridge to Douglas. As I crossed the bridge, another cyclist came up beside me. It turned out to be the same person who had asked if I needed directions. Jeffords had thrown his bike in the car to drive from Holland and ride down this part of the highway. He had moved here from eastern Michigan, where he'd been employed in the automobile industry. Now retired, he still worked part-time as an engineer, but he had plenty of time for riding his bike. He told me he loved this part of the state and was happy to get way from the Detroit metropolitan area, where he'd previously lived, with its congestion, economic depression, and general decline. He was able to find plenty of work when he wanted it, but had enough of a pension that he only took jobs that he found interesting. It seemed like a pretty nice life. And I could see the attractions of living in this part of Michigan. He was pedaling along at a fairly quick pace, and I was having trouble keeping up with him, given all the gear that I was hauling. I did my best but was not completely sorry when he turned off to head home.

The Blue Star Highway runs through the small cities of South Haven and Lake Michigan Beach and then becomes the Red Arrow Highway at Benton Harbor and St. Joseph. Numerous small state parks dot these roads. The farther south you move, the more touristic it seems, with parks and cottages amid the low-perch sand dune–lined beaches. The highway also becomes noticeably busier, as you feel the magnetic pull of the Chicago metropolitan area to the south and west. Much of this trip had been through sparsely populated forests and farmlands, but that was coming to an end. From here on in, it would be urban/suburban riding, which, like all forms of bicycle touring, has both its rewards and its challenges.

Benton Harbor fell into the national spotlight in 2003 when it erupted into civil violence. As has so often been the case, it was triggered when the actions of a white police officer resulted in the death of one of the city's black residents. Police pursued Terrance Shum, who was on a motorcycle, through city streets, at speeds of a hundred miles per hour. Shum lost control of his vehicle, drove into an abandoned building, and died immediately. Later in the day, a group of three hundred people gathered at the site of Shum's death to memorialize him. When police attempted to disperse them, individuals within the groups reportedly attempted to set fire to the building and hurled rocks at police cars. The next night, both the size of the crowd and the size of the police presence increased. Several people were reportedly beaten by police, and twenty-one houses, mostly empty, were set on fire.

National media labeled the event a "riot," but some local residents were less inclined to do so. Benton Harbor's police chief, Samuel Harris, who is African American, downplayed it. A local white newspaper challenged him, suggesting that it fit the term's definition. The unrest was confined to a four-block area in a mostly abandoned, formerly industrial part of the city.

If anything good came out of the incident, it was that it concentrated some much needed attention on the extreme economic and racial inequality that characterizes the area. It's a familiar story. Benton Harbor was once a manufacturing center, supplying parts for the auto industry. Whirlpool had a production facility there as well. In the 1970s the bottom started to drop out, as the automobile industry declined in the face of foreign—at that point primarily Japanese—competition. Whirlpool shuttered its plant, leading to the loss of a thousand jobs. As jobs disappeared, the city lost its tax base; city services declined; those that had options left, leaving behind empty and deteriorating neighborhoods, high unemployment, poverty, violence, and crime.

At the same time, however, St. Joseph, just south across the St. Joseph River, has continued to prosper. Benton Harbor in 2003 had a 40 percent poverty rate and a 25 percent unemployment rate. St. Joseph had a 2 percent unemployment rate, a negligible poverty rate, and a median household income of $37,000 a year. Benton Harbor is 90 percent black. St. Joseph is 90 percent white. A starker contrast between two Americas, one poor and black, the other comfortable and white, would have been hard to find. Needless to say, similarly stark contrasts existed, and still exist, all over the United States. Often, when civil unrest arises from such contexts, solutions are sought, policies are proposed and sometimes funded, attention is given, and for a brief period, things might improve. But the deeper structural issues remain unresolved. In the case of Benton Harbor, Jimmy Carter flew into town, a new public housing development was proposed and eventually built, Habitat for Humanity constructed a number of new houses, and Whirlpool opened an office downtown that would employ twenty people.[23] But the Benton Harbor that I rode through looked pretty much as I would imagine it had ten years earlier.

The sky was getting darker as I approached New Buffalo at around five o'clock. I didn't see any places to stay in the town itself, so I asked someone, who told me that there was a motel about a half mile out of town. I was hoping to find someplace soon, since it looked as though we were in for a major storm coming in off the lake. I finally spotted the small, somewhat run-down Buffalo Motel just a bit outside of town. As I rode in, a couple on a motorcycle was entering the motel office. Just as I was walking through the door, they were leaving, looking somewhat dejected because they'd been informed that there were no vacancies. In spite of that, I figured there was no harm in asking. I could at least inquire about other places that might be within riding distance. Maybe the proprietor would even let me ride out the storm on the office porch.

As expected, the owner told me they were filled up, and she thought that most of the motels in the area were as well. I asked if she could call around. She agreed and was looking through the phone book when the phone rang in the other room. She came out to inform me that I must have some kind of lucky charm. Someone had just canceled a room because of the storm. I quickly agreed to the very reasonable price of $50 for the room, brought my bike to it, unloaded my stuff, and turned on the Weather Channel, just as the storm rolled though. All kinds of weather alerts flashed across the screen. The motel owner told me that the lake would cool the storm down, moderating it by the time it reached us. That may have been the case, but it was still a good old-fashioned midwestern cloudburst. It passed fairly quickly, so I rode back into the town center to get something to eat.

There were people standing in lines or sitting in chairs waiting to get into most of the restaurants in town. The only quick option was a food stand, where I had a sandwich, a large portion of french fries, and a double scoop of ice cream. Not the healthiest or best food I'd eaten on the trip, but it was filling and provided some much needed carbos after a long day of riding into a hot wind. It was cool and rainy as I headed to the motel to catch a little of the Olympics and turn in early for a good night's sleep.

August 4, 2012

I left New Buffalo early in the morning with the intent of making it someplace north of Chicago's urban core. Beyond that, I really didn't have a clear plan. I ended up riding all the way to Kenosha, Wisconsin, a trip of around 120 miles. It turned out to be an amazing journey, one of the most memorable I've had riding a bike. What I found so compelling about it was the variation that you see and experience as you make your way from east to west and then north through Chicago and all of the surrounding areas. It's a fascinating strip of the American heartland.

New Buffalo, where I found some breakfast, is a tourist town lined with antique stores and specialty grocers. Next is Michigan City, where along a narrow lakeshore lane into the city, you find many vacation homes and condos. It has quite the upscale feel with immaculate nineteenth-century vacation homes and fancy inns and restaurants abutting the shorelines. But the center of Michigan City is old and industrial, and there's a huge power plant located about three miles from, and in full view of, all the vacationers sitting out on their front porches, sipping gin and tonics and mojitos. It's a clear reminder, in case someone might have forgotten, that the area sits on the cusp of one the most industrialized landscapes in the United States.

The Great Lakes have long attracted vacationers, but they also attracted the industrial processes that provided incomes to pay for the vacations. That's one of the great paradoxes that runs through the region, in fact, perhaps through all parts of the Great Lakes. Industrial production generates wealth that allows its participants to escape its negative environmental and aesthetic impacts. But what constitutes an "escape" is at least partly in the eye of the beholder, and the distance that a person can escape is largely dependent upon the level of wealth that a person has achieved. But then again, perhaps Michigan City's visitors, at least at one time, enjoyed seeing the fruits of their productivity. What might strike some as unsightly could also be appreciated as the golden goose, shiny and beautiful if seen from the proper angle.

Once through Michigan City, Highway 12 runs along the Indiana Dunes National Lakeshore. There was little traffic, and the shade was welcome, since it was already starting to get hot. You feel as though you are in a vast untouched wilderness through there, although that's obviously an illusion. I stopped at one point to walk down to the shoreline. An uncluttered and mostly deserted beach stretched out in both directions. But a little farther in the distance, in both directions, were outlines of smokestacks and other accouterments of industrial civilization. The Indiana Dunes' apparent wildness was sandwiched in, and constrained by, the forces of capitalist economic development.

It is amazing that these dunes still exist as a relatively untouched feature of the landscape. Part of the reason (and this is true of Lake Michigan sand dunes in general) is that they were unsuitable for agriculture and thus left alone by early European settlers. Later, when faced with development pressures, the dunes found defenders in early-twentieth-century preservationists. Famed landscape architect Jens Jensen, a designer who left an imprint on many of Chicago's urban parks, was a key figure in defending the dunes. In the 1960s, Senator Paul Douglas was instrumental in keeping the steel industry from siting production facilities there.[24] In the end, it is possible to mourn and celebrate the Indiana Dunes. On the one hand, as a counterpoint, they provide graphic evidence of the impacts of industrial development, but we can celebrate them as at least a small sliver of the wondrous wild habitats that once dominated the area.

Just beyond the dunes, the trees disappear, the highway opens up, and I was fully back into Pink Floyd album–cover territory. The contrast with what I'd just experienced could not have been greater. I was now on the outskirts of Gary, Indiana. While massive factories and processing facilities line the road into the center, the city itself is a complete wreck. There's really no other way to describe it. U.S. Steel, which was the area's economic centerpiece, shuttered most of its plants in the 1980s, and other subsidiary businesses either left with it or withered in the desolate economic landscape that remained.

Andrew Hurley's excellent book *Environmental Inequalities: Class, Race, and Industrial Pollution in Gary, Indiana, 1945–1980* tracks the process by which a coalition of environmentalists from all parts of the city challenged the great steel-making corporation. While successful in getting the company to reduce air and water pollution, and even conditions inside its facilities, the success was ultimately undermined by globalization, which by the mid-1980s turned the once powerful American steel industry into a shadow of its former self. The city of Gary is one of the remnants. The streets are lined with abandoned buildings, and a large vacant hotel sits on the main corner.

There was no reason to stop here, and I just made my way forward, riding over broken glass into the surrounding residential areas, which seemed like a miniature version of Detroit. Block after block of dilapidated and abandoned houses populated the main thoroughfare out of town. Then there was a stretch of vacant fields overgrown with grass and thickets within which sat old crumbling buildings surrounded by fences. The one good outcome was that the overgrowth gave me good cover when I needed to take a pee.

Once past Gary, the urban feel of the Chicago metropolitan area becomes ever more pervasive. I stopped at a gas station/convenience store for a cold drink to take some of the edge off the heat. I was at the intersection of what's called the Industrial Highway and Route 12, with elevated Route 912 rising up above. It felt like an Americanized version of Fritz Lang's *Metropolis*. I'd arrived at a border, after which I would be surrounded by an urban environment for an indefinite period of time. As I was leaving the store, some guy hit me up for fifty cents. I was a little taken aback. It isn't every day that you get asked for change by someone driving a car, and a reasonably nice car at that. And what, you are on a bicycle, so you have money to spare? I gave him a quarter.

Back on the road, a bike path appeared, unexpectedly and somewhat inexplicably. A nice thought, I suppose, but it was hard to imagine many people actually using it. For one thing, it was strewn with rocks, glass, and the occasional tree branch. There were no houses through there. I passed a huge BP processing plant on the right. On the left were vacant lots and abandoned buildings. After a few miles of this, the landscape changes from industrial infrastructures into the city of East Chicago as the bicycle path disappears. The city, on the very western edge of Indiana, has a working-class feel. In fact, it claims to be Indiana's first truly industrialized city. Founded in 1893, it was a site for steel production and a major freight rail terminus. The city's website boasts that it is home to seventy nationalities, but the many stores, bars, and restaurants with signs in Spanish seemed to indicate a large Latino population.[25] East Chicago is still several miles from Chicago proper, and it feels very much like a self-contained city, and not a far suburb.

On East Chicago's northern edge, signs marking a bike path appeared. It's a lane, rather than a parallel path, but it felt nice to have a buffer from the city traffic. I was hoping that it might turn into something more definitive, such as an actual bike path, but the opposite happened. The signs became more scattered and more difficult to follow. At one point, unsure of which street to turn on, I asked some men, who appeared to be Latino, sitting on a front porch, if this was the way to the bike path, as I pointed rightward away from the main drag. They all nodded enthusiastically. But the street dead-ended into a large vacant field, with no sign of any path. It occurred to me that they were trying to be helpful but probably had no idea what I was talking about. Perhaps they didn't speak English. I turned around and got myself back on Highway 12 into the southern part of the city.

The first true metropolitan neighborhood, coming in from the south, is South Chicago. The bike path is clearly marked through there, and I rode along the tree-lined street, surrounded by well-maintained middle-class homes and rows of brownstones. South Chicago is racially diverse, with a large African American population along with some remaining descendants of Eastern European and Irish immigrants. White flight began occurring there in the 1960s, resulting in the white population declining by approximately 40 percent from its peak in the early twentieth century.[26] After a few miles, the bike path veers off from the street and becomes its own entity. It snakes around toward the lakefront, and then downtown Chicago appears in the distance. It's a breathtaking view, with the vast expanse of the lake off to the east, and the tall concentrated skyscrapers of America's third-largest city directly ahead. The Miracle Mile looked to be a mile or two away, but that, as I learned, is a bit of an optical illusion. In actuality, it was more like ten.

The wide bike path along the lakefront was full of people as I made my way through the Hyde Park, Kenwood, and Oakland neighborhoods; some were walking, others were cycling, some were on skateboards, in-line skates, you name it. Little parks and culs-de-sac were filled with families having picnics and barbeques, playing softball or Frisbee. Some folks were sunning themselves on the beach. Others were out in boats. Chicago presented itself in all its diverse and vibrant glory.

As I approached the Loop, I heard music, and I noticed the sights and sounds of Lollapalooza to the left. The now-famous indie music festival, founded by Jane's Addiction singer Perry Farrell in 1991, spent a number of years traveling to different cities, and then, in 2005, settled in Chicago as its permanent home. I took a break to catch a bit of music spilling out from a stage across Michigan Avenue. Others nearby seemed to doing the same thing. A Chicago police officer asked me if I was OK. This was the third time since arriving in the metropolitan area that someone had checked on me as soon as I dismounted my bike. I guess it was the heat. I appreciated the concern. The concert was in full swing. You could hear a bass-heavy rock band at one end of the festival venue and a hip-hop artist at the other.

I pushed onward past the Loop into the Near North Side. At LaSalle Drive, the Lakefront Trail skirts close to the waterfront. I rode among droves of people strung along the beach trying to escape the city's heat. Dozens of food and drink stands line the path, as it follows the waterfront, past Belmont Harbor, until finally emptying out on North Sheridan Road, which is busy, narrow, and devoid of a bicycle path. The neighborhood is one of the few in the northern part of the city to have an increase in its African American population. Solidly middle-class, the residents have incomes in the upper five- to six-figure range.[27] It was, however, quite a shock to be suddenly pushed out into urban traffic. But before long, the road widens, and the riding becomes safer and more tolerable.

The ride through Chicago, south to north, involves crossing intersecting, multiple lines of class, race, and ethnicity. The neighborhoods I encountered in the southern parts of the city were primarily Latino and African American, and mostly middle- and working-class. The northern parts of the city into its suburbs are predominantly white and generally more affluent. The Loop, the urban core, is where the interesting collisions can sometimes occur. Lincoln Park, once dominated by Puerto Rican immigrants, is now populated by the ascending urban professional class. After Lincoln Park is Evanston, dominated by the leafy Northwestern University campus, which runs for a mile or two along the highway. After this, more tree-lined streets, old mansions, lakeside parks, golf courses, and country clubs: Wilmette, Winnetka, Glencoe, Highland Park. The forested hundred-acre Lake Forest College campus blends effortlessly into this sequestered suburban utopia.

I noticed signs with bicycles covered by the universal "no" symbol. At first, I was having trouble making sense out of this, until I realized that residents were actually prohibiting bicycles from their city streets. I guess they wouldn't want their idyllic enclaves contaminated with noisy and unruly cyclists (and who could blame them?). I found the Green Bay bike trail and rode it for a couple of miles, but it kept disappearing, so I returned to the suburban streets and figured the locals would just have to put up with me. Since the streets were completely deserted, I wasn't too concerned about being stopped or arrested, and I quite enjoyed my foray into self-propelled, two-wheeled criminality.

If there's one problem with this route, it's that all the commerce is off to the east on Highway 41. Since riding here was so pleasant, I didn't want to leave the path to head over to the noise, heat, and traffic that I knew ran on a parallel path just a few miles away. But as a result, I encountered no accommodations—no camping, no cheap motels, just an endless suburban expanse of large lawns and six-bedroom houses. Still, at this point I'd been riding for more than ten hours, and I was starting to feel it. The northern Chicago suburbs eventually blend into more rural countryside, leading into the city of Winthrop Harbor, but I still didn't see any places to stay. I kept riding, and before I knew it, I had crossed the border into Wisconsin.

After another hour's riding, I was in Kenosha, a completely different world than the one I'd just ridden through. A four-lane highway sweeps down through an industrial landscape before taking you into the city center. I was back into the terrain of de-industrialization and hoping to find a place to stay. A couple of guys were standing outside of a McDonald's having a smoke, so I rode up and asked if they knew of any motels nearby. One muttered something unintelligible and walked away. The other said to just keep on going, and I'd find a spot a couple of miles down the road. I couldn't miss it. After a bit, I passed a small square building with the word "Motel" painted on the front: a true economy of wording. Definitely not posh, but I'd pretty much reached the end of my rope, having ridden, I figured, well over a hundred miles in ninety-degree heat.

The manager was exceptionally accommodating and even helped me get my bike into the room. I was grateful for the assistance. The room was only $45, with a $5 key deposit. Not the cleanest place, but I had noticed a family restaurant next door. So after I showered up, I walked up the short hill to eat a huge fish dinner. Back in the motel, I switched on the news to learn that there had been a shooting at a Sikh temple in Milwaukee. This attack seemed especially vicious, carried out, as it was, by a white supremacist in a temple, of all places. And I, of course, was headed to Milwaukee the next day.

August 5, 2012

A beautiful sunny morning greeted me for the last day of the ride. I loaded up my gear and rode to the family restaurant that I'd eaten at the night before. After a healthy filling of French toast, I rode into the cool morning air, past the edges of northern Kenosha, and into a rural landscape that I hadn't experienced since before Chicago. I began to realize how close to Milwaukee I'd ridden the day before. Usually, on the last day of a ride I find myself riding over a hundred miles to make it to a final destination before dark. But today I had the luxury of taking my time. In a way, it seemed a bit of a letdown, after yesterday's long and varied journey.

Racine is the last city of any size before you get into the southern Milwaukee suburbs. I stopped at a park and rested a bit, taking in the view. Back on Highway 32, I rode it to 7 Mile Road in Milwaukee's far southern suburbs. On the right were ranch houses, and on the left, farms. I turned right onto Thirteenth Street, which I knew would take me past my motel. It was fine for a while, but eventually the traffic intensified, and the ruts made it difficult to keep the bicycle on the very edge of the road. I wondered why such a narrow road had so much traffic. Later I learned that the main road into the city, running parallel and to the east, had been the one on which the temple shooting had occurred. The city had shut down sections of the street in the Oak Creek district, thus forcing the traffic onto Thirteenth Street, where I was riding. After a somewhat harrowing half hour, I made it safely to the motel I'd reserved near the airport. It had been a fifty-mile day, the shortest of the trip. The shooting had occurred about a half block from my motel.

After checking into my room, the first order of business was dismantling my bike. I figured I'd get that done, because I wanted to spend the next day touring Milwaukee. It takes about an hour, and as I was completing the task, I had the Olympics on. The American women's soccer team was playing a tight match with Japan. It was an amazing game, with the Americans making a comeback to win the match. I'd only caught snatches of the Olympics here and there, but I was glad that I had the opportunity to see this game. It was a real barn burner.

August 6, 2012

The next morning, I was up early and took the 19 bus into Milwaukee. It's a half-hour ride, which takes exactly the same route that I had cycled two weeks previously. A woman on the bus asked me for some change. I gave her what little I had in my pocket, got off in the central business district, and spent some time walking around to get my bearings. Milwaukee follows the model of most midwestern cities, with a cluster of taller buildings in the middle, from which smaller ones radiate outward. The *New York Times* "36 Hours in Milwaukee" gave rave reviews to the Milwaukee Art Museum. But since it wasn't open when I arrived, I walked under Interstate 794 to the Third Ward, a somewhat upscale neighborhood with art galleries and design shops located in old brownstones. With time to spare, I had a great breakfast at the Public Market, while catching a little more of the Olympics.

After breakfast, I headed to the museum. The modernist building is itself a work of art. The War Memorial Center, which houses most of the artworks, was designed by American architect Eero Saarinen. The newer Quadracci Pavilion was designed by Spanish architect Santiago Calatrava. I spent a good part of the day there and saw most, if not all of the exhibits. One featured poster art from nineteenth-century Paris. While we associate this work primarily with Toulouse-Lautrec, the exhibit focused on his many contemporaries and showed the evolution of the poster form over time. It provided a view of the development of commercial art and advertising, the veritable selling of dreams. While the early posters focused primarily on dance halls, they evolved into depicting various commodities. The posters could be considered as an early form of pop art. My favorite, of course, were the bicycle posters. Bicycles, it seems, were early on marketed as a form of escape and liberation, especially for young women. In fact, most of the bicycle posters featured women, sometimes depicted as goddesses.

The museum also has a great permanent collection of German expressionist art, a somewhat neglected school of painting, which ran parallel to French impressionism. German expressionism was a precursor to cubism and surrealism. The influence of German expressionist film, especially F. W. Murnau's classic pre-horror film *Nosferatu,* is more widely known. The museum also has a great folk art exhibit, apparently one of the best in the country.

After the museum, I was back out on the River Walk in the ninety-five-degree heat. I stopped at the Milwaukee County Historical Society, a beautiful old building with a few exhibits related to local history. Mostly I just needed to find a place to pee. The shops of Grand Avenue, which were originally marketed as a destination for shopping in downtown Milwaukee, were disappointing. Some of the storefronts were empty, and others were low-end discount shops. I got hit up for change several times on the way to the bus stop. The bus ride back to the motel took me through some lovely old ethnic neighborhoods. Milwaukee, like many Midwestern cities, seems to have real gems tucked into its various seams.

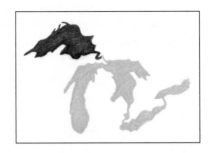

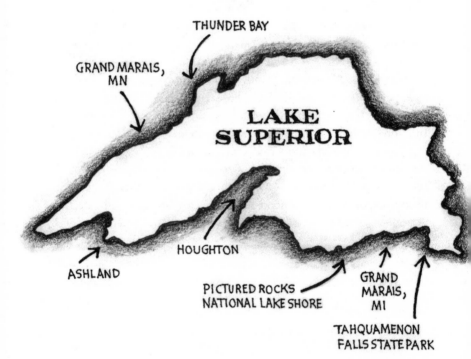

THUNDER BAY

GRAND MARAIS,
MN

LAKE
SUPERIOR

HOUGHTON

ASHLAND

PICTURED ROCKS
NATIONAL LAKE SHORE

GRAND
MARAIS,
MI

TAHQUAMENON
FALLS STATE PARK

Lake Superior

July 22, 2013

I drove on a warm, sunny day from Ithaca, New York, to Sault Ste. Marie, Ontario. I debated for a while about which route to take. One option was to cross the Niagara River in the vicinity of Buffalo, head across southern Ontario, then into Michigan, driving through the center of the state to the top of the mitt. The other involved crossing into Canada, then driving along the eastern coastline of Lake Huron, skirting the edge of Georgian Bay, and then westward. I chose the Canadian route, which was probably a mistake. Things are fine until Sudbury, when the Queen Elizabeth Way empties into the Trans-Canada, which is two lanes, within which are interspersed occasional passing lanes. It's a busy road, slow going. I didn't get to the Soo until ten o'clock in the evening.

I had booked myself into a cheap room on the Canadian side that I found online, which, as far as I could tell, was right in the middle of town. But I couldn't find it. Someone I stopped on the street wasn't especially helpful. Eventually, I figured out that I needed to go around back and into an alley to find the entrance to the place. It was the dormitory for Algoma University's medical school. The rooms were quite nice, although I had to pay cash, which required going back outside to find an ATM. Once I settled in, the only dinner option seemed to be Tim Hortons, but eating at this point was an absolute necessity, so I had no choice.

July 23, 2013

Next morning, six o'clock sharp, I was back at Tim Hortons, this time for my traditional bicycle touring breakfast: two raisin bagels, orange juice, and a small coffee. Then I packed up the Volvo and drove to the Sault Ste. Marie Airport, which, I had discovered online, had long-term parking at reasonable rates. It was ten miles west of town, so I'd have to ride back in to get across the border into Michigan, since I had decided to start my trip by riding westward along the southern side of the lake. My reasons for doing this were only somewhat arbitrary: I had ridden the other three lakes in a clockwise direction, and I wanted to be consistent. It was as simple and slightly ridiculous as that.

I parked my car at the lot of the small airport, loaded up my bike, and rode down the hill from the airport to Second Line Road and then into the city. It was a morning made for a bicycle ride, as I passed through fields and wooded areas into town. At the first shopping center I encountered, I stopped to buy sunscreen lip balm, an essential accoutrement that I had neglected to bring. I immediately noticed the higher Canadian prices.

The Esser Steel Algoma plant is on the right as you head east. The plant was started by an American at the turn of the twentieth century and has been in continuous operation since then. But it hasn't been easy going. The company had declared bankruptcy twice in the past two decades and was bought out by the Indian firm Esser Global in 2007. It's one of seventeen steel mills still operating in Canada.[1]

I followed the signs down to the Sault Ste. Marie International Bridge, which I'd crossed from the other direction two years ago, when I had rounded Lake Huron. At that time, I'd stayed overnight at Sault Ste. Marie, Michigan, a somewhat drearier place than its Canadian counterpart, but it abuts the famous locks, which are a significant tourist attraction and definitely worth a visit.

A steel truss arch bridge crosses the St. Marys River. It's just under three miles long. Crossing by bicycle is allowed, but there is no bike lane, just a narrow shoulder marked by a painted lane only on the north-to-south side. It's wide enough to accommodate both car and even truck traffic and a bicycle. But on the day that I arrived, construction was occurring, which narrowed the lane considerably. Once I got up to where the construction started, which turned out to be the steepest grade of the bridge, I had to pull into the lane, preventing cars from driving around me. I imagined a line of angry drivers fuming behind me as I held them up on their way to work. But the work crews helped me out. They held up traffic as I pedaled my fully loaded bicycle as hard as I could. Cars were piling up behind me, but no one honked. In fact, someone from the other direction yelled, "Go, go!" from a car window. As I approached the peak, a workman called over, "This is the worst part." Then the construction ended, and it was an easy glide down to the customs stop at the base of the bridge.

The border officer was curious and, then, when I told him where I was headed, supportive. "You've got a beautiful day to start," he told me, stating the obvious. Once through, I stopped at the tourist office and picked up a map of Michigan's Upper Peninsula. The helpful woman behind the counter gave me directions to get to Brimly, which would lead me to the state highway. I had been looking forward to this trip. It would be my highest mileage of these lake rides. While Michigan has a longer shoreline than Superior, you would have to follow nearly all its various nooks and crannies to match the smoother path around Superior. In other words, with Michigan, you have the option to skip some parts, which I chose to do. With Superior, it's all pretty straightforward. I did want to stay reasonably close to the southern shoreline, rather than make a beeline across on Highway 41, which is possible but seemed much less interesting.

The ride to Brimly was on a flat, low-trafficked county road. It felt good to be back on my bike, even as I began to feel the heavy afternoon heat. As the day wore on, temps climbed into what seemed like the nineties. There was a stiff breeze blowing from the south, which I surmised was bringing all that heat with it. Brimly is just a small grocery store and a few houses. The road turns north there, at which point I had the hot wind directly at my back.

A couple of miles later I was in Bay Mills, where I stopped for lunch at a place that had a "Don't Frack" sign in the window. Hydraulic fracturing of natural gas—fracking, for short—had been a major political issue back home in central New York, and given that I had serious reservations about its environmental and economic impacts, the sign made me feel welcome. A few customers, locals it seems, chatted at tables around me as I waited for the pasty that I had ordered to warm up. Pasties are a semicircular pastry filled with various combinations of meat, onions. fish, potatoes, turnips, or rutabagas. The dish originated in Cornwall, England, and was often eaten by the tin and copper miners there. When some of them immigrated to Michigan's UP to work the copper mines there, they brought the pasty with them. Other ethnic groups, including Finns, Swedes, Irish, and Poles, adopted the pasty and added their own unique variations.[2] I had been pronouncing the word with a long *a*, but the waitress corrected me to shorten it. The pasty I had was just OK (frozen and microwaved), but the specialty of the house was smoothies, of which the place had a bewildering variety. I settled on peach, which was delicious and took an edge off the heat.

After lunch I continued riding, taking a county road that traveled close to the shoreline of Whitefish Bay. This is Ojibwe territory, with signs marking community centers and other associated agencies and businesses. Ojibwe is the English language name for one branch of Native Americans (and Canadians) who refer to themselves as Anishinaabeg, or "first people." According to Anishinaabeg oral histories, they moved from the mouth of the St. Lawrence River in the mid-seventeenth century into areas around Lakes Huron, Michigan, and Superior, as they split into three groups, designated by colonists as the Ojibwe, the Odawa, and the Potawatomi, or, in Anishinaabeg terms, the Three Fires. Encounters with Europeans led to intertribal conflicts and further regional and cultural fragmentation.[3]

Today the Ojibwe, like other Native Americans, tend to live on reservations, an enduring legacy of colonization, one of which I was riding through. The terrain was flat, and the road eventually entered the Hiawatha National Forest. From there it skirts the shoreline of the bay in an east–west direction: sand and water to the right, forest to the left. People were out on the beaches, trying to get some relief from the hot weather. Fortunately, a canopy of trees kept the direct sunlight off me for much of the fifty-mile ride along the shore.

Lake Superior Shoreline Road eventually empties into State Highway 123, which runs northward along the western side of the bay. My goal was to camp somewhere in Tahquamenon State Park, which at 46,000 acres is the second largest state park in Michigan. It runs for several miles along the bay and then stretches northwesterly along the Tahquamenon River. The Tahquamenon River makes an appearance in Longfellow's poem *The Song of Hiawatha*, even though the actual Hiawatha lived in central New York and, as far as we know, never traveled to what is now Michigan. Longfellow's confusion about Hiawatha (or more likely his deliberate misappropriation of the name as a form of "poetic license") pervades naming practices in this area and is even reinforced by the Michigan Department of Natural Resource's website. In its description of the park, it states, "This is the land of Longfellow's Hiawatha—'by the rushing Tahquamenaw.' Hiawatha built his canoe." Perhaps this is the land of Longfellow's literary Hiawatha, but it has no real connection to the land where the actual Hiawatha lived.

I chose a campground near the mouth of the river, which I understood would be less crowded than areas near the falls. After showering I rode five miles to Paradise to find something to eat. The highway crosses the river along the way. It's a very rugged and beautiful landscape. A strong hot wind blew me quickly into the little town, where I had a fish dinner at a crowded family restaurant. Afterwards, I found a small grocery store to stock up on a few things and then fought the wind back to camp. I then hunkered down in my tent to wait out the storm that I knew was approaching, expecting it to be pretty fierce.

July 24, 2013

The night brought plenty of lightning and thunder but very little rain. I started out in the evening sleeping on top of my sleeping bag but was completely scrunched down in the bottom with the zipper up to the top by morning. It was freezing by the time I got out of the tent at six o'clock. The sun was shining, but a strong and now very chilly wind was blowing from the north, which was, more or less, the general direction in which I would eventually be headed. Starting out, fortunately, it would be due west, over to take a look at Tahquamenon Falls, which I fully expected to be one of the highlights of the trip.

I had breakfast in a diner in Paradise, overhearing several men involved in a very detailed and passionate discussion of ATVs that they were giving serious consideration to buying. As I got back out on the road, I couldn't believe the difference from yesterday. The early morning sunshine had given way to clouds, and it seemed very, very cold. I bicycled in Iceland once with conditions something like this, but I went prepared for it with enough Gore-Tex and fleece to keep a polar explorer warm. But I hadn't anticipated those sorts of conditions on this trip, so I hadn't packed for it.

The road west kept the wind from being directly in front of me, as it brought me to the lower falls. There was virtually no traffic, and the forests that surrounded me were lush and beautiful. From the road, it's about a mile downhill to the lower falls: no charge for a bicycle. The lower falls form on two sides of an island that splits the Tahquamenon River. The rivulets flow over a series of steps in the rocks. From various observation decks it's possible to get a panoramic view. You can walk down to the river, where there's swimming, although no one was braving the water on this chilly day. The water gets its somewhat nasty-looking brown color from the upstream cedar swamps that surround it. I wanted to take some pictures, but my camera's battery was dead. When I went back to my bike to grab my cell phone, that turned out to be dead as well. I'd have to settle for postcards.

After spending some time at the lower falls, I hopped on the bike and headed to the upper falls, about four miles away. It was raining fairly hard by the time I got there. That didn't stop me and a fairly good-sized group of other tourists from tramping down the footpath to see the falls, huge hemlock trees lining the way. The pathway starts below the falls and skirts along the gorge that overlooks them as it moves toward the top. This allows a visitor to get a range of views of an incredible natural spectacle.

In terms of volume of water, this is the second largest waterfall in the eastern United States. But the elevation, at 50 feet, is much lower than Niagara's at 167. But whereas Niagara Falls is surrounded by kitschy tourist stalls, gambling casinos, and Superfund sites, Tahquamenon is nestled in a mostly roadless national forest, miles from any even medium-sized city, with the only commercial development being the park headquarters and a restaurant. Fabled conservationist and nature writer Ben East brought the falls to a larger public's attention when he published winter photographs of them covered in ice in 1929. It was largely due to East's efforts that the area was named as a state park in the 1930s.[4]

I wanted to go north to get back to the shoreline, but there's no road that will take you directly there. Rather, you have to zigzag your way southwest on Highway 123 until you find a road that will take you across and then back up to the lake. Riding south, with the cold wind behind me, was exhilarating, as I cut through the scrubby pine forests that mark much of the terrain through there. Along the way, I spotted a group of cyclists heading north into the wind. I didn't envy them. They waved, shouted out, and wished me luck. When the highway turned west and I caught the crosswind, it made for some pretty difficult riding. My hands were soon completely numb.

I made it to County Road 407, which turned west and would, if I followed it, take me north to Muskallonge State Park. That had been my original plan. I started that way but soon thought better. Riding over twenty miles into the twenty-five- to thirty-mile-an-hour headwind with temps in the low fifties seemed a bit daunting, given how cold I already was. I took the coward's way out and rode south to Newberry, with the hope that tomorrow might be a little warmer with a little less wind.

At Newberry, I found a motel. The owner told me that just a

few days before there had been a horde of people cycling through the town undertaking a ride across Michigan. Some cyclists had stopped in Newberry, rather than the planned overnight stop, because of the heat. And now the temperature was a good forty degrees cooler. I walked the length of the town, which took less than a half hour, had some pizza, and did a little reading before I went to sleep.

July 25, 2013

I tried getting up at six o'clock, but my body just wouldn't respond as directed, so I fell back to sleep and rolled out of bed around six thirty. It was cold outside. I could tell because it was pretty cold inside the motel room as well. The three bananas that I'd stashed away made for a tasty breakfast starter, but I wanted something more and hoped to find it on the way out of town, something with some carbos attached. As I rode southward, in the brilliant morning sun, I noticed that the sign on the local bank said forty-nine degrees. I headed to a convenience store, grabbed a stale apple fritter, a bottle of orange juice, and a cup of passable coffee. I stood in my bike clothes and ate in front of the store. No one seemed to pay me much attention.

I pulled out of Newberry wearing my light fleece pullover and a rain jacket for extra warmth. The wind had completely subsided. I continued southward until I reached Highway 28, and then turned west. Since I'd been thrown somewhat off track by yesterday's weather, I wasn't entirely sure which route I would take, but I knew that I wanted to head north to the lakeshore. I turned north at Seney on Highway 77, which would take me to Grand Marais, Michigan. The ride across on 28 through pine and hemlock forests on a semibusy highway was a welcome change from yesterday's wind and cold. The right turn north to Grand Marais took me along a wide and deserted highway with a wide shoulder. The conditions were ideal, especially as temperatures warmed up into the seventies by early afternoon.

Once in Grand Marais, it became clear that I wouldn't be able to make it all the way to Munising, so I decided to make an early day of it. I thought maybe I'd be able to camp somewhere in the Pictured Rocks National Lakeshore area. The forty-mile stretch of protected shorelines, established in 1966 by an act of Congress, begins here and ends at Munising. When I asked about the options at a local gas station/market, the woman behind the counter gave me a map, informed me that there were plenty of campsites, but she was pretty sure they were all full.

I decided to stay in town and try to make the hundred miles to Marquette the next day. I found the local city campground, sited on a large open field, with an friendly manager. She recommended various sites, and I chose one close to the showers and bathrooms. The park was full of families for whom this was obviously a nice getaway. Even though the grounds were in a residential area with houses right across the street from my tent, the place felt sequestered and comfortable. As I was setting up my tent, I noticed that people in one of the houses across the street were moving back and forth between it and a large tent a couple of sites down from me. They had turned the park into an extension of their front yard. In public policy studies, they refer to this sort of arrangement as a "public/private partnership."

After setting up the tent and organizing my gear, I rode to the Pictured Rocks National Lakeshore, found a visitor center, and asked the ranger if he could recommend a bike ride within ten or so miles. He directed me to the Log Slide Overlook, with the Devil's Slide. A lovely afternoon ride on the deserted park road brought me past Grand Sable Lake to the overlook entrance. Grand Sable was the name given to the area by French explorers. Translation: big sand.

I followed a footpath about a half mile out to sandy cliffs, from which you can see miles up and down the lake. To the west is tree-covered Au Sable Point, and to the east is the Grand Sable Dunes, a massive formation of sand and gravel extending five miles along the shoreline. Quite a view. Then there's the slide: 350 feet down. It was originally fashioned to drop timber, often the mighty white pines from rapidly denuding forests, down to awaiting ships, but it's been decades since it was actually used for that purpose. Now it is primarily a source of entertainment. Several people were climbing up when I got to it. Others arrived, and I watched them take the plunge. I chose not to leap, however. It's a short trip down but a long climb up through the sand. I wasn't sure that I'd be able to make it back up in my bicycle sandals, or maybe I was just too tired after cycling all morning, or maybe that's all just a lame excuse. Whatever the case, the vista was itself worth the trip.

Back in town, after a shower, I went to the local brewpub for a fish dinner. I chatted with some tourists next to me at the bar. They were planning a fishing trip the following day on a chartered boat. They were up from Chicago and hadn't had a lot of experience on the water. The charter service offered fishing lessons, and while they didn't guarantee a catch, they were pretty optimistic. The couple really just wanted to get out on the water. This was also their first time to this part of Michigan, and we traded superlatives about it.

After dinner, I walked through town and down to the marina. People were out fishing on the docks. Boats were lined up all along the harbor. Grand Marais is really a lovely spot, and I was glad that I had decided to spend part of the day there, but I was also looking forward to riding along the national lakeshore the next day.

July 26, 2013

It was fairly chilly when I awoke. A woman out for an early walk said hello as she passed along the street that ran beside my tent. I was just starting to catch a few warming rays of the sun. It didn't take long for me to pack my gear and head to the village. The local diner wasn't open yet, so I went to the central gas station and got some juice and coffee and a packaged roll. Not much of a breakfast, but it would get me started. Then I rode south along the pictured rocks shoreline, retracing part of the path that I had taken yesterday afternoon. The sun was shining, and I was shaded by the pines, hemlocks, and northern hardwoods that lined each side of the narrow Au Sable Point Trail road. It snakes around through the park, out along Au Sable Point, where the old lighthouse still stands, with lightly rolling hills, and, on this day, the mildest of headwinds. I encountered little early morning traffic.

A couple of miles down Miners Road takes you to an overlook where you can catch a view of Miners Castle, one of the more noteworthy sandstone formations among many scattered along a twelve-mile stretch on this end of the park. These formations can trace their origins back to the inland sea that covered what is now the Great Lakes region five hundred million years ago. The skeletal remains of the small Cambrian creatures that inhabited the lake settled to its bottom, piling up to great depths. Compressed over the ages, scrapped clean by glacial advance and retreat, they have been transformed into the worn, majestic, and colorful cliffs, arches, and caves that dominate the shoreline landscape here.[5]

At Munising, given the nice weather and the agreeable terrain, I didn't feel especially tired, so I decided to continue the additional fifty miles to Marquette. I stopped at a pizza joint and got two very large and greasy slices of pizza, which, while not the healthiest lunch, would provide fuel for the rest of the ride. Highway 28 travels north along South Bay, before turning due west to Au Train Bay, where it skirts along Superior's shoreline to Marquette Bay. It's a fairly busy highway with a generous shoulder. The shoreline is lined with beaches, and many people were out enjoying the summer weather, even though it was starting to cloud up. I stopped a few times to take a pee, walking up among the trees away from the road. At one point, as I walked back, I noticed a large black spot on my leg and pulled it off. Blood squirted out. Realizing that it might be a tick, I gave a quick thought to Lyme disease. But since I had acted fast, I wasn't *too* worried. Ticks are certainly nasty little buggers though. People complain about cockroaches, but I'll take a two-inch cockroach over a little dot of a tick any day of the week.

I was definitely getting tired by the time I made it to Marquette. As I approached, I noticed a very large hill between me and the city center but then noticed a convenient bike path that follows the shore, allowing cyclists not only to avoid the hills but also to catch a glimpse of some of the old neighborhoods that hug the shore. The path was obviously part of an effort to transform this once industrial waterfront into something more tourist friendly. As with so many cities in the region, Marquette recognized that the water could be a significant attraction even while still supporting industrial uses.[6]

A huge eighty-year-old ore dock, once used to load ore from train cars onto ships, was jutted out into the lake, visible evidence of Marquette's history as a port town. Massive amounts of iron and copper were shipped out of this port. The city had recently hired a firm to inspect the dock to see if it could be repurposed. Proposals included retail and condominium development.[7] Part of downtown redevelopment involved the siting of a Hilton Hotel on a small hill overlooking the waterfront. I was tempted, but being as cheap as I am, I rode past it. The city's downtown and neighborhoods are on a hill that rises up from the lake. The downtown seems to have been the object of a fair amount of redevelopment money as well. Most of the old sandstone buildings have been restored, and the city's website boasts of a hundred shops and restaurants on the main street. I rode around the streets above the town center for a bit, taking in some of the beautiful historic houses with gabled roofs and large front porches, some of which were no doubt built to house the families of the mining and lumber barons that founded the city.

On the top of the hill on the edge of town, I found a discount motel near a series of shopping plazas. I booked into the place just as the sky opened up with a fairly serious thunderstorm. After the rain subsided, I found a family restaurant, which offered a whitefish dinner, a local delicacy.

Back at the hotel room, I found another tick on my leg, one that I'd missed before. From a little research online, I learned that Lyme disease is endemic to Michigan, including the Upper Peninsula. Now I was starting to get just a little more concerned.

July 27, 2013

The next morning I faced a fair amount of construction on the way out of town. It was somewhat treacherous riding between the traffic cones and then sometimes onto the narrow highway, brushing close up against the cars. I wanted to make it to Houghton, even though that would be another hundred-mile day. I figured I could always stop along the way if things became too difficult. The weather was turning again, with a forecast for the sixties that day and down into the fifties the next. It was raining lightly as I headed out on Highway 41. Lumber trucks breezed by me, carrying their loads sideways because the trees were too small to warrant a lengthwise stacking. Probably those logs would be turned into paper pulp. Timber production is obviously still an important part of the economy in the Upper Peninsula, although gone are the days when two-hundred-foot-tall white pines dominated the landscape.

I cruised along, catching the edges of Negaunee and Ishpeming, over to Humboldt and Champion, touching the eastern tip of Lake Michigamme. At L'Anse, you skirt along the bottom edge of L'Anse Bay, which is a part of the larger Keweenaw Bay, which borders the eastern side of the Keweenaw Peninsula. I had to make a decision whether to stop or continue up the peninsula to Houghton. There's a nice little state park on the bay, but given that it was only two o'clock and there wouldn't be much to occupy my time for the rest of the day, other than sit in the tent and read, I decided to push onward. Besides it was starting to clear up a little.

Five miles down the road the illusion of clearing became apparent, and it really started to rain hard. No turning back now, but it was getting windier and colder as some kind of front was making its way through. I still had about twenty-five miles to go but was now determined to make it and really didn't have much choice. There wasn't any place convenient to pitch a tent. I stopped at a small roadside park near the lake to gobble down a couple of power bars and noticed another tick on my leg as I was getting back on the bike.

I was starting to think that if I didn't get Lyme disease, it would be a miracle. The website I had scoped out had said there would be a rash and then flu-like symptoms. If I started to notice these, I figured I could find a hospital in Duluth where I could load up on antibiotics, which is the main treatment for the disease. One of the earlier bites seemed to be swelling up, as though it could be infected. Apparently it takes two or three days to feel the symptoms. Nothing to do but wait to see what, if anything, would happen.

The last few miles into Houghton were tough. I was freezing and extremely tired at the end of a second hundred-mile day. The highway into town travels along Portage Lake and then the Houghton Canal, which separates the southern part of the peninsula from its northern tip. The canal was dredged in 1873, allowing ships to enter from the west, pick up their cargo, and exit without having to travel around the entire peninsula. Inside the city proper, you pass Michigan Technological University, with its tidy modern campus. The school was founded as the Michigan College of Mines in 1885 to educate engineers for the expanding copper industry. Its emphasis is still on science, technology, and resource management.[8] The entire town has a funky northern vibe. The main downtown area, about a mile from one end to the other, hugs the side of a hill, the bottom of which ends at the canal's edge.

I stopped at a Travel Lodge on the western end of the downtown, but it was full. The helpful clerk called around and found a room for me at the Franklin Square Inn. At the inn I asked where to keep my bike. The clerk suggested locking it up somewhere in the hotel's parking garage. Of course, I didn't have a lock, but I found my way back behind the building to where the garage was located, pulled my gear off the bike, and found the room. I could worry about locking it later.

Inside the room, I immediately filled the bathtub with hot water. It was time to try to warm up a little. And soon enough I was able to feel my hands and feet again. A quick nap and I headed out to survey the downtown. All of the storefronts seemed to be occupied by various businesses, which included everything from clothing to hardware. After chowing down at a Chinese restaurant, I dropped into the local bike shop. I needed a lock, but I also wanted information about riding the northern part of the peninsula. One of the young employees gave me a map and several ideas, the most challenging of which would involve a hundred miles to the tip and back.

It's clear from the storefronts and the general feel of Houghton that this is a jumping-off point for many outdoor activities, from cycling and skiing to backpacking and kayaking. But the history of the place is rooted in copper mining. Like much of America now, it represents the ambivalence we feel about appreciating the beauty of natural spaces while still wanting to plumb them for the utilitarian offerings and celebrating the history of excavating them. As with so many places that I've visited along the Great Lakes, it has a complicated history full of sometimes hidden and sometimes apparent contradictions. After my brief tour of the town, I returned to the hotel and entered a nine-hour dreamless sleep.

July 28, 2013

I got up in the warm hotel with the full intent of riding a good distance up the peninsula. I could see it was raining fairly hard, but I was determined. Ever the optimist, I hoped that it would clear and warm up as the day wore on. The route north crosses a bridge to Hancock and follows the other side of the canal. It seems like the poor cousin to Houghton, with shabbier storefronts and a generally rundown feel. The road north runs up a very long and steep hill, with views of the two cities off to the right as you approach the top. As I made my way upward, the rain fell harder and harder. I felt as though I was being enveloped in a cloud. It's hard to imagine worse weather in July, although having never lived in this part of the country, who knows? Maybe this is the norm.

At the top of the hill are the skeletal remains of an old mining complex. One of the buildings promised tickets for a tour and info about the copper mining facilities that dot the area. I was tempted, but no one seemed to be around. I waited for a few minutes, partly to get out of the rain and cold, and then got back on my bike and headed to Calumet, a relatively short and easy fifteen-mile ride to the northwest. At the city limits, a local bank office featured a time and temp sign. The temperature was forty-five degrees. My hands were already frozen.

The only open copper mines in this area these days serve as tourist sites. The valuable ore from the mines was scoured out decades ago. The Great Lakes and the copper mining industry in the United States are indelibly linked. Copper country at one time stretched from here to Montana and Wyoming. The ore from the western mines was rough, and it had to be refined before it could be loaded onto trains and then ships for the trek eastward to manufacturing centers. But in this area, the copper could be found in nuggets and flakes that could be more easily removed from the rock in which they were embedded. Edwin J. Hulbert, on an expedition through the area in 1864, found "float copper," large pieces of copper that were dug up and carried forward by glaciers, near what is today Calumet. He easily found investors to finance the purchase of land and started digging. He soon discovered a huge deposit of copper and began operations under the name Calumet Mining Company.

Immigrants from all over Europe flocked to the area for work, but the largest group was the Finns. Finns were willing to undertake the most backbreaking and least well paid jobs, seemingly without complaint. And while many of the new arrivals were unable to speak English, the Finns, with their strange-sounding language, which included a written alphabet too complicated to comprehend even by other Europeans, often faced greater discrimination than other ethnic groups.[9]

Calumet, named for the Calumet Mining Company, now boasts a population of less than a thousand people, but that wasn't always the case. Named for the mining company in 1929, before that it was Red Jacket, named after a Native American chief from the Seneca tribe in central New York. The city reached a peak population of over twenty-five thousand in the early twentieth century primarily due to mining activities. It has been in long-term decline since then, as labor strife and declining ore stocks slowly eroded away the area's economic foundations. The city was the site of the tragic Italian Hall disaster.

On Christmas 1913, striking miners, mostly Finns, Croats, and Italians, gathered at a Christmas party on the second floor of the Italian Hall. The primary reason for the party was to hand out candy and presents for the area's children, for many of whom this would be their only chance to receive a gift or treat. Five hundred to six hundred of the seven hundred people gathered were children. In the midst of the festivities, someone with a cap pulled over his eyes came up into the hall briefly and yelled "fire," causing a panic and stampede down the narrow staircase that led out of the building. Bodies piled up on top of one another as people on the bottom were crushed and suffocated by those on top of them. Sixty-two of the dead were children. Of the eleven adults that died, many were clutching children in their arms in a futile attempt to save them from a fire that didn't exist.[10]

No actual culprit was ever charged with the crime, but many of those present said that the man who instigated the panic wore a Citizens Alliance pin. The Citizens Alliance, a quasi-vigilante body, organized actions, sometimes violent ones, against the strikers. While trying to present itself as a group of independent concerned citizens, it was in reality a front for the mine owners. Historian Steve Lehto has concluded that a strikebreaker named Edward Manley shouted the fatal words. He may not have entirely realized the chaos that he was going to unleash. In fact, he was almost caught in the melee himself as he was trying to make his escape. In an attempt to explain why a strikebreaker was in the hall the night of the incident, local papers, controlled by the company, wrote about him as a hero who heard commotion and climbed up through a window to help, a story that was inaccurate to say the least. He left town soon afterward and was never heard from again. But whether he only wanted to bring the party to a premature end or intended real harm, there was enough deliberation to consider this the largest mass murder in Michigan's history.[11]

Woody Guthrie memorialized the incident in his song "1913 Massacre." The tune was later adopted by Bob Dylan in his own song titled "Song to Woody." Guthrie paints a picture of warmth and festivity with a child playing the piano, a welcome break for the hard lives of the copper miners. But the "copper boss thug men" break into the scene and scream "there's a fire." A woman in the crowd responds that "there's no such thing. Keep on with your party, there's no such thing." But some miners grab their children in fear and run down the stairs to a door the "gun thugs" hold closed. As the panic spreads, "The scabs outside still laughed at their spree." And in the end, "the children that died there were seventy-three." Guthrie's version is exaggerated, with his depiction of gleeful scabs celebrating the deaths of children, but he's on target with the basic and horrifying facts.

The technologies of copper mining started to shift in a dramatic way in the 1950s. Much as with coal mining, the development of massive machinery allowed digging operations that made the dirty and dangerous tunnel mining obsolete. In the West, this resulted in the creation of huge craters, as the trucks and diggers slowly burrowed their way farther and farther into the earth. In Butte, Montana, home to another famous copper mining strike, the ensuing bowl filled with water to create a toxic brew that is immediately fatal to any animals, such as landing birds, that are unfortunate enough to come into contact with it. But by the time this transition occurred, the copper mines in Michigan had been exhausted. As a result, Michigan's surfaces have been left mostly undisturbed by mining activity, and the open landscapes offer few reminders of the conflicts that once occurred and their tragic consequences.

I stopped in a café to grab a bite to eat and warm up. It was also a small art gallery. I ate a fresh scone and drank fair-trade coffee as I took in the various artworks on the wall, none of which, unfortunately, grabbed my attention. Still, the place felt warm and comfortable. The old brick structure with its high ceiling seemed to be a fine example of the city's nineteenth-century building stock. I was reluctant to leave but knew that eventually, one way or another, I'd have to reenter the cold and rain. After eating, I rode around town a bit. Parts of it were well maintained, if aging. But some buildings were crumbling and abandoned. Calumet is exactly what you might imagine an old mining town to be, infused with the determination and tragedy that marked the lives of those who created it, and freighted with the conflicts that once defined it. The ghosts of the Italian Hall's disaster seem still to haunt the place, especially on a day as cold and damp as this one had turned out to be.

After touring Calumet, I decided, somewhat reluctantly, that the weather simply wasn't appropriate for a thirty- or forty-mile ride north. Part of what is offered are the views, and given the fog and mist, it didn't seem as though I'd be able to see much farther than the edge of the shoreline. I turned back on the road toward Houghton. Today would be a proverbial rain day. By the time I arrived at the hotel, though, the sky was starting to clear, and there was even a patch of blue. I wasn't dedicated enough to turn back around, but the clearing weather at least boded well for tomorrow.

I spent the rest of the day tooling around town, going into various shops and stores and walking up the hill into residential neighborhoods. At a local hardware store, I bought a lock to go with the steel cable I'd found at the bike shop the day before. Mostly, it was a pretty lazy day. I took a nap and lamented the bad weather that prevented me from getting a longer and closer look at the peninsula.

July 29, 2013

The weather had looked somewhat promising the previous afternoon, but it was cloudy and a little drizzly when I got out the door of the hotel at around seven thirty. I went back in the room and glanced at the local radar on the television. There was definitely rain in the area, but I didn't want to spend another day hanging around Houghton. I was feeling restless and figured it was time to move along. Somehow I was certain that things would improve as I went southward, away from the shoreline. As I headed up the hill out of town, I noticed a temperature sign on a bank: forty-five degrees. Well, it was early after all. No doubt, it would warm up as the day wore on.

Ten miles into the ride, in the Porcupine Mountains, I started to think that I'd made a mistake. It was freezing, probably in the forties or maybe even the upper thirties in the mountains, and the rain was coming down harder and harder, as the wind picked up. I'd never cycled for a long period of time in conditions quite this dire before, and I was getting a little nervous as to what might happen. My hands and feet were becoming increasingly numb.

Part of the problem was that I hadn't really prepared for weather this cold. I had on a cycling jersey, a light fleece pull-over, and a nylon bicycle jacket. I needed heavier fleece and maybe some Gore-Tex. Whatever the case, this was what I was stuck with, and I had to make the best of it. I kept looking west in the sky, up over the trees, hoping to see some breaks in the clouds, but to no avail. At times, the rain was torrential. People honked as they drove by and gave me the thumbs up. I had very mixed feelings about this. On the one hand, it was nice to have support. On the other, I would have much preferred a warmer, sunnier day when I wouldn't have needed it. That people felt compelled to offer me their encouragement was indicative of how miserable the conditions actually were. It wasn't just me imagining things.

On the up side, the area is beautiful. The Porcupine Mountains area holds the largest track of old-growth eastern forests west of the Adirondacks. The short, steep hills reminded me of the curved backs of porcupines, which is perhaps how the area got its name. Under the right circumstances, this would be a fantastic ride through beautiful forests, but under these, the countryside seemed almost sinister. I began to look forward to the climbs up the steep hills, because I knew that this would warm me up a little bit.

About thirty miles south of Houghton, I had a decision to make. I could continue southward into the Ottawa National Forest, or I could turn north to Ontonagon. The southward route looked to offer no towns large enough to have a motel for at least thirty or forty miles, or maybe more. Ontonagon, on the other hand, was fairly good sized. Hopefully, there I could find a place to dry off, warm up, and spend the night. After consulting the map two or three times and noting a road sign that said thirteen miles to Ontonagon, I decided to head in that direction. In the meantime, I also desperately had to pee, but I was a little worried that if I got off the bike, I'd never get back on. My hands were so cold and numb that I wasn't sure if they would actually get me back pedaling on the bike. On the other hand, I really didn't have a choice in the matter. I got off the bike, emptied my bladder, and ate a power bar.

The northwest direction took me through farmland and directly into the wind, with no trees now to block it. As I started out, I was starting to shiver, deep down. I was half wondering whether you could freeze to death or get frostbite with temperatures above freezing. Probably not, but that wasn't providing much solace.

I made it to Ontonagon around two o'clock, after what amounted to a sixty-mile ride, improperly dressed, under deplorable conditions. I found a small, somewhat rundown motel in the center of the village. A sign on the door said no check-ins until four o'clock. I was hoping that there was some wiggle room. Once inside, another sign said to ring the bell, which sat on the desk in the front office. I rang it. Someone bellowed from upstairs: "You want a room?" This didn't bode well. "Yes," I yelled back, as I saw a large, bearded man, looking a little like Grizzly Adams, tumble down the stairs. "What?" he asked, "Why would you want a room on a beautiful day like this?" He was joking, much to my relief. In fact, he turned out to be quite a nice guy, who, more importantly, had a vacant room. He showed me a room in the apartment house next door. I was glad I wouldn't have to be living there, given the cramped quarters and shabby furniture, but it was fine for one night. Forty dollars. Hard to argue with that.

"Never expected to see anyone on a bicycle today," he said. "No one even on a motorcycle." He repeated this several times in a way that made me a little self-conscious. I wasn't sure if he was expressing admiration or merely thought I was some kind of a kook. Back at the front desk, my hands were too cold and numb to fill out the form. He told me to come back when I'd warmed up a little. I told him that I was glad he didn't hold to the rule about four o'clock check-ins. He explained that was the owner's rule. He wasn't around this week, luckily for me. Nobody liked him. And in all likelihood, he'd have made me wait. I said that I saw another motel down the street and could just have easily have gone there. "Good point," he said and chuckled.

Eventually I did warm up, and later on walked down the main street (the only street really) and found a modest family restaurant for dinner. I had a ham and potato casserole, the day's special. I mentioned to the waitress that I'd never eaten it before, but it was ideally suited for the cold, dreary weather. She told me it was a Finnish dish, called kinkkukiusaus. The recipe calls for ham, potatoes, whole cream, and cheddar cheese. A real artery clogger, but it sure tasted good on a wintry day in July. It was no doubt an ideal meal for hungry Finns, having returned from a long day working in the UP forests and mines. When I'm home, I am almost exclusively vegetarian, but when I travel I am pretty flexible. It's not always easy to find good, filling vegetarian food when touring around on a bicycle. I'm also a believer in the precept that eating local food is an entry point into local culture and, in that sense, almost a traveler's obligation. Former chef Anthony Bourdain's show, "Parts Unknown," is one of my great guilty pleasures.

Back in the hotel room, I turned on the Weather Channel with a fair amount of trepidation. The forecast was for seventy-five degrees and sunny. I found it a little hard to believe but certainly hoped that it was accurate. I wanted to get back on track with some longer rides, headed on my way to Duluth at the western edge of Superior.

July 30, 2013

Things started out spectacularly: blue sky and morning dew. Highway 64 starts out along the lake for ten or fifteen miles and then takes a sharp turn southward, at which point it becomes practically devoid of traffic, rolling gently up and down through the Porcupine Mountains. The conditions were exceptional, especially in comparison to the day before. Entrances to small mines are marked along the way, even though this is a protected area. At the little town of Bergland, which sits at the northern tip of Lake Gogebic, I stopped for some lunch. Gogebic is the largest inland lake in the state of Michigan, at over thirteen thousand acres. In the heart of the UP snowbelt, it boasts three hundred inches of snow per year. Having grown up in another snowbelt, south of Buffalo, New York, I can appreciate the number. In Jamestown, a hundred-inch year would be considered snowy. Three hundred is hard to imagine.

Antonio's Restaurant, in the center of town, was full of locals, all of whom seemed to know one another and none of whom paid much heed to an obviously out-of-town cyclist having a sandwich and ice cream in their midst. Soon enough, I was back rolling along Highway 64, which turns west until Wakefield, where it empties into Route 2, the major federal highway that cuts across this part of the UP. I rode gentle hills through the village of Bessemer and then the small city of Ironwood, which sits on the Wisconsin border. From there the highway turns north again and meets the shoreline. The elevation gradually increases, so you can again glimpse Superior off in the distance.

Eventually I arrived at Ashland on Chequamegon Bay, after what turned out to be about a 110-mile trek. A long ride, but it was very gratifying after the past few days of cold and wet weather. The head wind was a bit of a bother, but that's something you have to expect when riding westward across practically any part of the United States.

At Ashland, I found a room on the western edge of town, conveniently located next to a Mexican restaurant. It was Henry Ford's birthday, and on the TV Joe Scarborough was complimenting him for having the foresight to pay his workers enough to buy Ford automobiles. This idea has been debunked, however, the truth being that workers didn't like working on assembly lines, and Ford had to pay them more to maintain a stable workforce. Ford was also, of course, a notorious anti-Semite and crypto-fascist.

After taking a shower and resting a bit, I proceeded over to the Mexican place to chow down on a huge meal of enchiladas and tacos, punctuated by a couple bottles of Dos Equis beer. I figured I'd check out the town the next morning after a good night's sleep.

July 31, 2013

The next morning was again bright and pleasant. I decided to ride up the hill into Ashland for breakfast, given that I only had about a seventy-mile ride to Duluth. I rode around town looking for a place to have breakfast and in the process discovered that many of the buildings were covered with large murals representing different aspects of local history. I'm a fan of public art, so I spent some time riding up and down side streets to take pictures of the various scenes represented.

The murals were painted by two artists, Kelly Meredith and Susan Prentice Martinson. The first, completed in the summer of 1998, depicts the Ashland National Bank building as it looked in 1892. Fifteen murals have been painted since then, with projects still ongoing. Some depict images of people: lumberjacks and railroad workers. Others feature old buildings. They create a surreal feel, especially early on a Saturday morning when there's no one around. I felt as though I was the object of observation in some strange nineteenth-century panopticon.

After the mural tour, I found a bakery/coffee shop that offered homemade muffins and rolls. The young man who was working there asked me about my bicycle clothes, and I told him about my trip. He was interested and said that he had done some touring around parts of the lake himself. Jason was a student at Northland College and determined to become a writer. He told me that a couple of his friends had cycled around the lake in May but encountered significant snow at Duluth. He also knew a couple of people who had left a couple of weeks ago to kayak around the lake. That seemed pretty daunting to me, and I told him so. In fact, it's hard for me to imagine. He suggested a book—Mike Link and Kate Crowley's *Going Full Circle*—which tracks their 1,555-mile walk around Superior. Walking seemed even more improbable to me than kayaking, given what I had seen of the rocky, jagged shoreline. But when I returned home, I bought the book, read it, and was blown away, not only by the physical feat that these two retired naturalists and environmental activists completed but also their intimate knowledge of the lake's natural spaces and human inhabitants. Perhaps it's Superior's vastness and that so much of its shoreline still holds the allure of a wilderness that pose an irresistible challenge to some people to circumnavigate it. I could definitely feel the magnetic attraction.

The day turned out to be sunny and warm with a fair headwind on a not particularly picturesque and well-trafficked highway. There's no way to avoid divided Route 53 entering the Superior and Duluth metropolitan area. It's crazy busy, with massive trucks speeding along, one after another. Fortunately, I only had a few miles on it until my exit, much of it downhill, as the road falls off of the escarpment that rings the southern edge of the lake through here. I pedaled as fast as I could.

The city of Superior sits on the Wisconsin side of this western edge of the lake. It appears to be the industrial sibling to more residential Duluth. The road was terrible. For one thing, it was a multilane highway with a curb, removing any option for riding on the shoulder. Plus, there was heavy traffic of the worst kind, including lots of large trucks. Big cracks in the cement road were at best half-heartedly filled with a little asphalt. I tried to get off on parallel city streets but encountered a repaving project that made the one I found to be nearly impassable. Finally, I found a bike path that took me through the northwestern part of the city and down to the bridges that cross to Duluth.

Superior is separated from Duluth by Saint Louis Bay, the endpoint of the St. Louis River, the largest river to flow into any of the Great Lakes. A short bridge takes you across a finger of the bay, and then there's a longer, steeper one that crosses the border from

Wisconsin to Minnesota. The shorter bridge was a breeze, but I was a little nervous about the longer one that I could see ahead of me. The John A. Blatnik Bridge, named for an area congressman, is two and a half miles long, and with a high, nearly 250-foot peak to accommodate shipping traffic into the bay. I went up the entry ramp and rode along a debris-strewn shoulder. The view was striking, and the ride a little harrowing, with the hills of Minnesota reaching down and then disappearing into the lake. Halfway over, on the other side of the bridge, I noticed a cyclist coming from the other direction on a bike path. Looking around I now noticed another one on my side of the bridge off to the right. I couldn't get over to it at this point. Not sure how I missed it, but now I was at the top of the enormous span, so it was an easy glide from there on down.

West Michigan Street into Duluth runs along the lakefront. It's bordered on the left by a steep hill, which is the very southeastern edge of an ancient lava flow, known as the Duluth Complex, which constitutes the bedrock for northeastern Minnesota. The complex formed during the midcontinent rift more than one billion years ago, when what is now the North American continent started, but ultimately failed, to split apart.

The interstate runs parallel on the right but sometimes crosses the north–south street grid in unexpected ways. I didn't have a city map, so I found myself cutting up and down on various side streets, sometimes blocked by the hill on the left, sometimes by the interstate on the right. Eventually I managed to find the old town center and a Quality Inn built on the hillside. When I checked in, they were in the process of making popcorn, which was offered free to all the guests. I helped myself to a bag, took it up the fairly steep incline to my room, and headed back for a second.

Duluth is named after the French explorer Daniel Greysolon, Sieur Du Luth, who explored the St. Louis River region in the 1670s. Before Europeans arrived, the area was occupied by a diverse array of First Nation's people, but as the European fur trade expanded, the Anishinaabeg, who had become primary trading partners with the French, became dominant, not only here

but all along the north shore of Superior. The area also became
known as the Seventh Stopping place by the Anishinaabeg, one
of the places to which they migrated on their way westward as
European settlements continued their encroachments into the
eighteenth century.[12]

Duluth went through several booms and busts in the nineteenth century, but a large influx of Scandinavian immigrants
arrived, starting in 1869, to work on the Lake Superior and Mississippi Railroad. The city began the process of being fully integrated
into the rapidly expanding American industrial economy of the
later part of the nineteenth century. As these changes occurred,
Duluth, like many other Great Lakes cities, became a hotbed of
labor activity and played an important role in the development of
Minnesota's Farmer-Labor Party.

As new immigrants arrived in the early part of the twentieth
century, from eastern and southern Europe, Duluth also experienced ethnic conflict. And in the 1920s, the Ku Klux Klan elected
several candidates to positions in local government. While fostering white supremacy was an important element of Klan organizing, some Duluth Scandinavians found an appeal in their
anti-Catholicism. Duluth workers were largely integrated into the
national multiethnic union struggles and successes of the mid-
twentieth century. But, as in so many places, the steel mills began
to shutter in the 1970s and 1980s, and there is very little industrial
production left in Duluth now.[13]

After a shower and a brief rest in the clean and sun-brightened
room, I headed out to see what the city had to offer. Duluth's main
streets are scaffolded onto the side of the lava flow, running down
to a flat area that goes out to the water's edge. The city center is
old and a little shopworn but not distressed in the manner of, say,
Ashtabula, Ohio. But there weren't many people out on the streets.
The interstate divides the downtown from the waterfront, but it's
accessible via a series of sidewalks and stairs. The waterfront itself
has undergone a major revitalization. The lakeside path was busy
with tourists, some no doubt staying at one of the numerous mid-
range hotels in the area.

You can follow the path onto the North Pier and out to the lighthouse at the end. From there, it's a great view of the city sprawling up and down the hillside, its stolid early-twentieth-century brick and stone buildings reminiscent of a dozen other medium-sized Great Lakes cities. A long strip of sand separates the mainland from the open waters of Lake Superior, creating a channel, called Superior Bay, which provides natural protection for ships docked there. In 1870, the city of Duluth dredged a canal to allow ships easier access to the bay. A bridge, now known as the Aerial Lift Bridge, was constructed across the canal. Unlike a conventional drawbridge, the lift bridge remains in one piece as it is elevated to a height of 172 feet, allowing even the largest ships to pass underneath.[14] As I walked back toward the shoreline, I watched it slowly rise to let a sailboat through.

I found my way to Lake Superior Maritime Museum, where I learned, among other things, about the massive ore docks designed to load ships with iron and copper ore. I'd seen one of these impressive structures in Marquette and had been curi-ous about it. Trains would unload the ore into "pockets" on the dock. The pockets would each have a chute that could be opened, allowing the material to flow into an awaiting ship for transport to points eastward for processing. The ore dock in Marquette is 1,200 feet long and 60 feet wide, with four railroad tracks running along its top surface. As steelmaking and copper production in the United States have gone into decline, so has the need for the docks. Many are now gone or remain as unused, rotting hulks, the peripheral casualties of deindustrialization.[15]

The old warehouses and other buildings along the Duluth shorelines are now filled with restaurants and shops. I found a camping supplies store and purchased a stuff sack for my sleep-ing bag. The other one had lost its waterproofing capacity. After a dinner of Vietnamese food, I found a deli that sold smoked fish. The clerk assured me that everything offered had been caught in Lake Superior. I bought a pound of smoked lake trout, which I would save for later. Duluth turned out to be a very pleasant experience.

August 1, 2013

A bike path north and eastward takes you out of the city. It empties onto Congdon Boulevard, which runs through northern suburbs into rural areas and small townships. I took the propitious
weather conditions as a positive sign for my return eastward. The
old Highway 61 runs parallel to the newer one, making for great,
traffic-free riding all the way to Two Harbors, which is about thirty
miles away. At that point, you are thrown onto the newer version of 61, which is much less bicycle friendly but still tolerable.
The fact that the wind was now behind me was much welcomed
as I breezed along the strikingly beautiful terrain. People I had
encountered on the southern side of the lake told me that the
north was different, and they were right. The geology is different
here. Huge rock formations spill out from the shorelines, jutting
up from various heights as they disappear into the deepening
water. It's breathtaking scenery, unlike anything I had encountered to this point along any of the shorelines I had ridden.

The geological formations known as the Duluth Complex
are especially visible and are the result of massive changes that
occurred in the very distant past. The ancient continent of Laurentia began to break apart 1.1 billion years ago, a process called
"continental rifting," creating the midcontinent rift. While the rift
failed in its bid to separate the continental core, it created a 1,200
mile gash in the earth's crust, one of the world's deepest. As it
did so, volcanic material, or magma, spilled out from beneath the
earth's surface. The Duluth Complex is the result of this process.
The valley, known as a "rift valley," created by the splitting, filled
with sandstone in a process that took millions of years.

The southwestern tip of the rift is in central Nebraska. From
there it extends northeastward into Minnesota, curves across
through Lake Superior, then cuts a southern swath through the
center of Michigan, and ends on the northern shore of the western
tip of Lake Erie, just below what is now Detroit. The rift has been
called North America's "broken heart" and a "spectacular failure."
Geologists have taken a renewed fascination in it in recent years,

paying particular attention to the question of why it failed to rip Laurentia apart. The rift's importance lies beyond the purely scientific, since the magma that flowed from it made the iron and copper ore that fueled economic development in this region in the nineteenth and twentieth centuries. It is still visible in various geological formations that mark the western half of the Superior lakeshore.[16]

When glaciers descended starting about 900,000 years ago, taking about 100,000 years to do so, their mile-thick sheets scrubbed out the softer sedimentary rock that had filled in the rift valley, leaving the huge bowl that became the Lake Superior basin. As they retreated, generally taking only a few thousand years to do so, they left glacial fill in the form of eskers, kames, and moraines. The fingers of volcanic rock, which were resistant to the powerful ice flows, now stretch out into the water, remaining as the dominant visible feature of the landscape. They are haunting and beautiful. I peddled over a hundred miles, up and down the moderate hills of igneous rock, until I arrived at Cascade River State Park.

The park is huge, and at the point I reached its boundary, I'd had about enough for one day. The final ride to the entrance was grueling, and then once in the park, it was up a steep grade on a gravel road to get to the campsite. Too tired at this point for any serious exploration of the twenty-three miles of hiking trails the park has to offer, I simply unloaded my stuff to set up camp. The mosquitoes were horrendous, the worst I had encountered on the trip. I did my best to shoo them away or smash them as they landed on my legs, but it was a losing battle. I hurriedly set up my tent, gathered some clean clothes, and headed to the showers. Afterwards, I sat at the picnic table by the campsite and ate some of the food I'd gathered in Duluth, including the delicious smoked lake trout. But the mosquitoes constituted a major distraction and soon drove me into my tent at dusk. I needed the rest, so it wasn't the worst thing that could have happened. But my legs were at this point bumpy and bleeding from the dozens of bites that I had received. In spite of that, I slept soundly.

August 2, 2013

The next morning, I rode into Grand Marais, Minnesota, for breakfast. After tooling around a little to check out the various possibilities, I finally settled on a bakery near the highway. The sweet rolls were delicious and the coffee enervating. Grand Marais (French for "Great Marsh") seems like an ideal place to spend some time, with its well-established art colony and easy access to the forests and hills of northeastern Minnesota. Like its namesake in Michigan, it's an appealing little lakefront town. With a population of only thirteen hundred, and a good distance away from Minnesota's urban centers, it doesn't feel overly touristic but has enough activity to make it feel alive. It is unsurprising that it has won multiple awards from various magazines, such as "America's Coolest Small Town."[7]

As I made my way out of town, I noticed someone walking up the shoulder from the other direction. He flagged me down to ask about my trip. He was a cyclist and said that he and his wife had cycled across the United States a few years ago. He seemed to be in his sixties. I told him that I liked the area and had known almost nothing about this part of Minnesota. He was moving, he told me, to Alaska. It was too crowded around here, and he needed a change. I wished him luck and continued on my way to Thunder Bay. Clouds crept into the sky as I made my way northward. At the Canadian border, it appeared that a major storm was on the horizon, but it turned out not to be as bad as it looked. I hung out for a bit in the Ontario tourist center as the rain blew by. On the Canadian side, you start a pretty significant ascent, several miles upward. It was tough sledding, but, fortunately, as I made my way along, the sky continued to clear, so that by the time I arrived at the top, I was able to appreciate both sun and the shoreline's panorama as it stretched along into Ontario. It was the most spectacular view I'd yet been lucky enough to have experienced.

Riding in Canada is often challenging because of the lack of shoulders on the highways. This road turned out to confirm the norm. It wasn't only the traffic that made for a harrowing ride through the hills and farmlands along the lake. The weather had changed to a mix of clouds and sun. As the clouds would gather up, they'd occasionally drop copious amounts of rain, sometimes attached to significant outbreaks of thunder and lightning. There was not much along there in the way of protection, so there was little to do but ride through it. Fortunately, while the rain was a system shocker, when the sun came back out, it would warm things up considerably. Still, it was a tough ride to Thunder Bay. I also had a slow leak in my back tire and decided to stop and occasionally fill it with air, rather than patch it at this point.

When I arrived at the southern edge of town, for some reason I chose Chippewa Road, which veered off from the main highway, because a sign indicated the downtown (or so I thought). This turned out to be a mistake in that I became somewhat lost. But on the other hand, it took me through Fort William First Nation Reserve, a Chippewa community, the boundaries of which encompass an approximately fifty-square-mile area that runs along the southeastern edge of Thunder Bay down to the lakeshore.

The land was set aside for occupancy under the 1850 Robinson-Superior Treaty, which recognized the rights of the Chippewa at Fort William to a large swath of land that runs south of here to the Minnesota border and north to where the Arctic watershed begins, which encompasses all of Lake Nipigon. They were granted cash settlements, annuities, and hunting rights on all public lands within the territory in exchange for agreeing not to interfere with the property rights and activities of white settlers. In 2005, the Canadian Supreme Court ruled that under the terms of the treaty, Fort William Chippewa would have to be consulted with regard to any activity that might adversely affect their treaty rights. The ruling had potentially wide-ranging implications, such that any proposed business activity in traditional Fort William Chippewa territory would require approval from the chief and council.[18] While this might be a cause for conflict in some places, the Chippewa's relationships with public and private entities within their territories have been positive and can be seen as a model of how such relationships can be established and sustained.

I rode somewhat aimlessly, until I spotted a bridge that seemed to lead in the general direction of the city's center. I eventually found myself on a busy suburban street, Arthur Street, that was lined with big-box stores, motels, and other accoutrements of suburban sprawl. I took a room at one of the motels and asked the manager how to get to the downtown. He told me that there really wasn't one. Thunder Bay was an amalgam of two cities, Port Arthur and Port William, and so it didn't have a downtown proper. I later learned that the consolidation occurred in 1970 after a half century of wrangling. The clerk said that there was a kind of downtown area in Port Arthur, and I decided I'd ride through it the next morning. In the meantime, I checked into my room, fixed my leaking tire, found a passable Chinese restaurant, and turned in for an early sleep.

August 3, 2013

The next morning, I decided I'd try to see what the downtown of Thunder Bay, or Port Arthur, actually looks like. I asked the person at the front desk of the motel the best route, and he directed me across the QEW, which runs toward town, to Pole Line Road. Somehow I missed the turn and ended up in a housing development without an exit, before finally finding my way down the hill into the city. When I got there, it was quite the cycling nightmare, with extremely busy streets, lots of large industrial trucks, and no shoulder. This mix of industrial and commercial sites seemed to stretch on forever, though, in reality, I think it was only a couple miles. I missed the left turn that runs along the lake, rather than into it, and wound up in an industrial park before realizing my mistake. Back on track, I rode along the waterfront, which was now on my right, featuring a beach and what seemed to be a pretty nice park. But with no bike path, I was still confined to the busy parallel street. I finally spotted what appeared to be the old city center, but there wasn't much to it, and what little was there seemed a bit run down.

Thunder Bay sounds like such a romantic place. The name evokes images of Lake Superior waves crashing against ancient igneous rock flows, but the reality is less inspiring. Cycling through it offered little hint of anything other than commercial and industrial development. This is a working port town, and probably not a tourist mecca, but there's of course nothing wrong with that.

I found myself on a street that signage indicated was headed toward Highway 11, or the QEW. I had planned to turn before I reached it along Lakeshore Drive, as was indicated on the map. As I was cruising along, someone ran out of their house toward me and hollered at me to stop. I wasn't quite sure what to think. Should I stop? The man was half-dressed, and he seemed slightly hysterical. I decided to stop nevertheless. "Don't go up that hill," he told me. "Don't go up that hill." "Why not?" I asked, completely perplexed by his actions. "Because you can't ride on the main highway," he said. "There's construction on the highway, and they won't allow bicycles. You'll ride up that big hill, and then you'll just have to ride back down." I appreciated his thoughtfulness and his telling me this, even though it didn't appear to be that big of a hill. And I had actually planned to turn onto Lakeshore Drive anyway, so he did confirm my decision. Still, it was hard for me to understand why he had become so excited.

Lakeshore Drive runs parallel to the main highway, and it was clear that at some point it would empty into it. At one crossing point, I decided to head over to see what it was like. I could see traffic through the trees, and it seemed busy but not completely crazy. When I made it over, I found a wide, divided, multilane highway with comparatively little traffic and a gravel shoulder, forcing me to ride in the right-hand lane. It was a weird experience. Apparently, they had completed the lanes for the new road but not the shoulders yet. After riding a mile or so, I decided to head back to Lakeshore Drive and take it as far as possible. This required traversing down a dirt road and carrying my bike through some bushes. And once I made it back, I saw that it ended about a half mile later anyway, with barricades between it and the QEW.

I also saw someone leaning a bicycle up against the guardrail that separated the two roads. It turned out to be Gary. He looked a little goofy, with big red goggles and a helmet that seemed a bit too big for his head. He turned out to be a very nice guy. He was from Berkeley, retired, as he told me, "early and minimally," and he had decided to do a bicycle trip that started in California, went north to Canada, eastward all the way across to the Maritime Provinces, then down the East Coast, across the southern United States, and back to California. A Vietnam vet, he'd been on the road for five months. He was traveling, he said, about forty miles a day. What he most appreciated was going into all the little towns along the way and checking things out. When I retire, I'd enjoy that kind of touring, something more attentive. On the other hand, I like the challenge of hundred-mile days. It's always a balance between touring as a form of physical challenge and stopping to pay attention to the world around you. I wasn't sure at this point whether I'd achieved the proper balance.

While I don't particularly like having a partner when bicycle touring, I always think that it's a courtesy to at least travel with someone that you've met for a spell. I figured I would do so with Gary. We walked up to the intersection of the main highway and hopped on our bikes. Gary had a well-stocked mountain bike, with big fat tires. I took off at what I thought was a reasonable speed, traveled about a hundred feet and looked back. Gary had gotten only about half the distance, at best. I waited for him and told him it was nice to meet him and wished him good luck. It was clear we weren't going to make good traveling companions, which was something of a relief. It didn't seem to bother him in the least. And, fortunately, the highway construction had ended at precisely this point, so I was back onto a normal Canadian highway, with the wind behind me and the sun and a few clouds overhead.

The ride to Nipigon turned out to be a mixed bag in terms of road conditions. Sometimes there was a shoulder, sometimes not. In other words, it was typical of the Trans-Canada Highway. I rode through clouds and sun, over a mix of hills and flats. It was a moderately difficult ride across a beautiful Canadian landscape.

At the visitor center in Nipigon, I asked about camping and was told about Marina Park. It's not that easy to find. A road off the main highways takes you to the town center, and then it's over a bridge, along a street that runs along a canal, and a left turn down to the water. Once there, it turned out to be a very pleasant surprise. I checked into the small building that constituted the park headquarters. A young woman there apprised me that tent camping was five dollars a night, ten with a shower. I took the upscale option. She also informed me that I could camp anywhere in the open field down by the water, which is the Nipigon Lagoon.

The area was large, about the size of a baseball field. While there were camping vehicles across the road, where I set up, there wasn't another soul. I couldn't have asked for a better spot. It was also the weekend of Nipigon's Blueberry Bush Music Festival. People were setting up food tables and a sound system about a hundred feet from my tent. I bought a ticket for five dollars on my way back toward town after something to eat. For dinner, I had found a little diner in the town center. It was a classic place, something right out of the 1950s. Everyone seemed to know one another. I had the fish fry.

Back in my tent, I read and listened to the music. Things started out with a talent show. Most of the contestants were young women, each of whom sang a popular song, changing it in some way to incorporate references to blueberries. The judges didn't just award a prize but offered a critique that involved both positive and negative assessments. It turned out that according to the judges, every performer was really quite good, but one was just a little better than the others. The young woman that I was rooting for from my tent won, with a local guitar whiz coming in a close second. After the talent show, the main act turned out to be a Canadian folk bluegrass band. They were professional, with excellent musicianship, tight harmonies, and witty banter. I fell asleep listening. Sometimes you strike gold.

August 4, 2013

Up and out early, I rode back to the highway and found a Tim Hortons. I'd have my usual, two toasted raisin bagels with butter, orange juice, and coffee. While I was sitting there, Amy, on her way out, came over to chat. A young British woman, she was cycling across Canada. She asked me about my trip. I told her and said I'd been on the road for a couple of weeks. "Still fresh," she quipped. She was on her twenty-ninth day. She was hoping to make it to Toronto, her final destination, in a week. I wondered whether that was possible, although I didn't express my doubts. "You'll probably pass me," she said as she left the place. "I doubt that," I told her.

Nipigon turns out to be something of a dividing line between flat to moderately hilly terrain and more challenging riding. The hills increase in size as you head eastward, and I encountered a fairly steep one a few miles out. But, in exchange, you gain a close-up encounter of the spectacular northern side of the lake, with St. Ignace and Simpson Islands stretching out into the blue water. It is the most striking landscape that I'd seen to this point. On one of the flat stretches, I stopped at a gas station to grab a quick snack. The man behind the counter said that I was wise to get a little extra energy to make it up the next two hills. "Bigger than the last one?" I asked. "Yep," he said. "That one's just a puppy." He turned out to be right of course, as I encountered two very long and steep climbs. The first was slightly more difficult than the second, but they were both challenging. At one point, I thought I saw Amy up ahead, but then she was gone. She might have pulled off into Terrace Bay.

On one of the flat stretches I saw a group of four bicyclists riding in the opposite direction. I stopped to ask where they were headed. "Vancouver!" they responded. They were riding straight into a headwind, with a couple of thousand miles farther to go. I'm not sure that I would want to ride across Canada, given the highway and traffic and all, but if I were to do it, I would definitely start in the west and go east. My guess is that it only gets windier as you get to Manitoba and Alberta. It would be a long, hard slog.

My own day's ride, on the other hand, would be relatively short. I decided to stop at Marathon, partly because it would be another hundred miles to the next town of White River. Besides, it had been a tough day with the hills. A drag race in town had filled up most of the rooms in the two motels, but I managed to grab one of the last available. There wasn't much there, other than a small shopping center. I had dinner in a Chinese restaurant with barely passable food. Marathon was not a particularly memorable stop.

August 5, 2013

The day started out chilly but without a cloud in the sky. It's a beautiful ride along the lake through here, but nothing comparable to yesterday. I wasn't sure how far I would go, perhaps just to White Lake Provincial Park. But once I got there, I decided to push onward. After the park, the road flattened out, and with the wind behind me, I felt revived and decided to continue to White River. It would be a hundred-mile day under what approached ideal conditions.

White River is just a stoplight, a motel, an ice cream joint, and a few random stores. It's also the birthplace of Winnie-the-Pooh. The motel owner told me that they had a big festival every year, and the place filled up with fans. There's a big statute of the famed children's character in the middle of the town strip. After a shower, I walked the length and passed by a young girl having her picture taken in front of it. She was obviously very excited. After dinner in the motel restaurant, I turned on the television news. It had been a year since the Sikh shooting in Milwaukee. Last year, I rode into the city after a tour around Lake Michigan the day after it occurred.

August 6, 2013

The morning started out cold and cloudy. Somewhere in the neighborhood of White River, the highway starts to turn southward, and the terrain starts to shift. The Canadian Shield, so familiar from my previously trips, becomes a prominent feature of the landscape. I love its rounded and worn features. It seemed almost like an old friend. When I started out in the morning, I had imagined that I might make the 180 miles to the Soo in two days. But the turn southward pushed me into a stiff headwind. It became clear as the day wore on that it would be three days of riding.

I was feeling a bit tired from yesterday's long ride to White River, so I only made it as far as Wawa, a little town that has a large statue of a Canadian goose guarding the way in. Wawa residents were disappointed when the completed Trans-Canada Highway bypassed their downtown. A local businessman had the idea of erecting the goose to alert passersby of the town's presence. It is now reportedly one of the most photographed monuments in North America. Unfortunately, it has been deteriorating, and in spite of attempts to repair it, it will eventually have to be replaced entirely.[19]

Wawa came into being as a gold-mining town. According to legend, in 1897 Louise Towab, married to a trapper named William Teddy, noticed some shiny objects in the bottom of a bucket of lake water that she had brought back to their cabin. Returning to the place where she drew it, they found a vein of gold. Teddy took $500 to reveal the location of the site, which didn't make him rich, but which did set off a gold rush to the little Mormon settlement. Before long, a hotel, a hospital, houses, and the other accoutrements of prosperity appeared. But by 1906, the gold was mined out, and the town became virtually deserted. William Teddy was broke after taking a trip to Montreal and spending his small fortune on the various vices that it had to offer. Before he left, Louise convinced him to buy her a new stove and a barrel of molasses, so at least she got something out of it.[20] Wawa now has a population of about twenty-nine hundred, with mining, logging, and tourism as the main sources of economic activity.

I found a small, clean motel, showered, and took a nap. Later I rode to the town center and had a plate of lasagna. It wasn't the best I've ever eaten. It also took nearly forty-five minutes for me to get the food. I should have had the pizza, which everyone else seemed to be eating, and which looked pretty good.

August 7, 2013

I slept for almost ten hours. I guess I needed it, but I felt great as the morning began, so much better than the day before. Sometimes you just need to listen to your body and get some rest. I trundled over to the local Tim Hortons for the usual. It was dark and raining, not hard but steadily. Looked like I had a miserable day ahead, not quite as bad as the ride through the Porcupine Mountains but moving in that general vicinity.

As I left the Tim Hortons parking lot, a woman, two young daughters in tow, said, "Nice day for a bike ride." "Appears to be," I responded, trying to put a good face on it. When I pulled out into the street, another woman was pulling into the parking lot with a couple of kayaks roped onto the top of her car. "Nice day for a bike ride," she said. "Nice day for kayaking," I responded. We both laughed.

In spite of the somewhat nasty weather, I was looking forward to the ride through Lake Superior Provincial Park. It follows the northeastern coastline of the lake. It is also huge: six hundred square miles, fifty miles from the entrance just south of Wawa to the exit, north of Sault Ste. Marie. It's a beautiful ride but extremely hilly. With a consistent ten- to fifteen-mile-per-hour headwind, up through the mountains, it turned out to be the most physically grueling day that I'd experienced.

The road from Wawa south to Sault Ste. Marie was a mere one-lane highway from the advent of automobile traffic until the 1930s, when the Canadian government took the initiative to widen it. It would take an entire day to make the hundred-mile trip. The work, done by men with pickaxes and shovels, was difficult and protracted. At one point, a new Liberal government fired all the day laborers and replaced them with inexperienced party loyalists, further slowing the work's progress. In 1937, heavy machines were brought in to speed up the process, but with the advent of World War II, the project was put on hold. In 1941, conscientious objectors, primarily Mennonites, pickaxes and shovels in hand, continued the work at fifty cents a day, plus room and enough pork and beans to keep them adequately nourished, if not entirely happy about it. Still, the route was not completed until 1960, when the "gap" was finally closed, taking with it a 20 percent portion of the cost of the entire Trans-Canada Highway.[21]

Fortunately, as soon as I got onto this historic and very expensive highway, the rain stopped, although it continued to be overcast and dreary. I figured it was just a matter of time before it started again. But while high up in the hills it was quite misty, with a very light rain, it never rained hard. I was feeling lucky, as I continued up and down against the wind, up 6 percent grades, which yielded breathtaking views at the peaks. At one point, I saw a wolf run across the road ahead of me. Then, right before Montreal River Bay, the highway sweeps down a very steep incline, which at the bottom requires a sharp left turn. Just as I descended down to the shoreline, the sun broke through the clouds, and the temperature jumped up a good ten degrees. Unfortunately, that did nothing to diminish the increasingly fierce headwinds. The highway flattens out from there, as it draws close to the shoreline. I had half a mind to call it an early day, given the winds, but decided to push on.

Just near the park exit, I pulled over to a rest stop to eat some fruit and power bars. A French Canadian couple were there giving their dog a walk. The man, who said he was from Wawa, asked about my trip. I told him that I thought the area was beautiful and had enjoyed my ride through the park. He said that they had experienced very serious floods in the spring and were still recovering. Parts of the road had been washed out. He asked me where I slept, and I told him I had a tent and sleeping bag but also stayed in motels. He said that he'd met someone at a rest stop who was walking around the lake with a shopping cart. "A shopping cart?" I asked. "Yes," he responded. "He kept all of his stuff in a shopping cart and slept under the bridges." I told him that I thought that was a little crazy. He said that Lake Superior can cause people to do crazy things. I couldn't argue with that.

As the day wore on, the clouds returned, and it looked like a serious storm was headed off the lake. I stopped at a little roadside motel on Pancake Bay. The owner said they'd just hosted a big wedding and that the place had been packed. The guests had kind of torn things up after getting drunk during the reception, but he had a clean room for me. What he offered was basic and fine as far as it went, especially given that he wanted only thirty dollars. Then he said, "You carry your own water, don't you? There's a problem with the well here, and you shouldn't drink the water." I definitely needed water and had very little packed away. That would be a deal breaker if I couldn't get water. But he hustled up some bottled water, which was good enough for my purposes. I went to sleep with the knowledge that it would be just another fifty miles or so to Sault Ste. Marie.

August 8, 2013

As you traverse south from Pancake Bay, the road for a while still follows the shoreline, but after fifteen or twenty miles, you move straight south as the shore curves westward. The highway is pretty flat, and it's not a particular interesting ride. The weather was sunny and warm, as summer seemed to have returned in full force. I was looking forward to getting to Sault Ste. Marie and my car, still, I hoped, parked at the airport parking lot.

As I was riding along, appreciating the flat highway, after all of the hills that I'd climbed over the past few days, I noticed what appeared to be a large hill intersecting the highway off in the distance. I was hoping that I wouldn't be climbing over it but would pass around it somehow. But as it turned out, there is indeed a very steep hill crossing the highway on the northern edge of the Soo. It might not have been the longest I'd encountered, but it was probably the steepest. The highway just went straight up for two or three miles, a final parting challenge from Lake Superior's varied terrain. Traffic was also increasing as I made my way closer to the city. At least I had a downhill glide as I reached the metropolitan area, with all of its shopping malls and truck traffic.

Of course, Sault Ste. Marie was not the final destination. Once there, I still had to ride the ten miles to the airport, which required a right-hand turn out of the downtown, straight into a pretty strong headwind. It seemed liked years ago that I had started out on this road, full of expectations, riding the opposite direction toward the bridge to Michigan. I definitely now had a fuller and much better perspective on an area that had previously been fairly mysterious to me.

I rode the entryway to the airport and was happy to see my Volvo station wagon sitting where I had parked it. I took the gear off my bike, threw it in the back, gathered up my wallet and passport, and headed to the highway, more than ready for the seven-hundred-mile drive to Ithaca, a little bit wiser about the world around me and about myself than I had been before I left. And in the end, I suppose, that's really what it's all about.

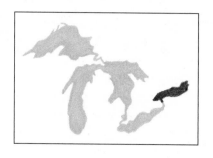

KINGSTON

PORT HOPE

BURLINGTON

LAKE ONTARIO

OSWEGO

LEWISTON

NIAGARA on the LAKE

LAKESIDE
STATE PARK

Lake Ontario

June 22, 2014

In the summer of 2014, I embarked on a trek around Lake Ontario, the last of the five lakes for me to circle. It's the closest to home, and it's the lake with which I am most familiar.

My first relatively long-distance bicycle tour was the Iowa RAG-BRAI (the *Des Moines Register*'s Annual Great Bicycle Ride Across Iowa) in 1989. The race introduced me to the concept of longer touring over multiple days, camping along the way. The next summer, I packed up my old Fuji road bike with a sleeping bag and tent and headed past Syracuse to Fair Haven Beach State Park on Lake Ontario. It felt like a long and pretty grueling ride from Ithaca, with numerous hills and a major thunderstorm. From there, I headed along the shores of Lake Ontario, past Watertown and Alexandria Bay to Ogdensburg. Then I turned around and rode back, this time taking a somewhat more inland route. By my later standards, it was a relatively short trip. But it was a start at bicycle touring and also the first time I rode along the shores of Ontario. At that point, I never imagined that I would someday ride around all five lakes, but I do remember the thrill of seeing the lake and then the St. Lawrence River come into view at the various points where the road touched up against the shore. I still have vivid memories of the deep-blue water against a blue sky as I rode north through the Thousand Islands.

Fast forward to 2003: I had just moved my spouse into an apartment in Montpelier, Vermont, but I would be commuting back and forth from Ithaca while she served as a judicial clerk for the Vermont Supreme Court. I drove a U-Haul truck. She drove her car. I had decided that when I returned, I would do so by bicycle. On a warm day in early August 2003, I hopped on my bike in Montpelier and headed to the New York border, and then cycled along the northern shore of Ontario, around through Buffalo, then back east to Batavia, and home across Highway 20, which traverses west to east through the central part of the state. The last leg was around 120 miles on a warm summer day and was to that point the longest, most difficult ride I'd experienced. It took everything I had to make the last thirty miles through the hilly Finger Lakes region.

Given the two previous trips, when I embarked on this one, I had already ridden much of Ontario. Still, I'd never done the complete circle, so this felt like a bit of unfinished business.

I drove with my bike from Ithaca to Rochester and dropped my car off at a downtown garage. Rochester is like so many of the cities that I've ridden through with its history of industrial development and postindustrial decline, but of course it has its own individual history as well. The area was originally settled by the Seneca people, one of the five nations of the Haudenosaunee, who were forced out after the colonists' victory in the American Revolution. The city is located about ten miles from Lake Ontario, on the Genesee River, which provided water power for the flour mills that originally spurred the city's growth.

But mostly Rochester has been defined by its connection to the Eastman Kodak Company. The company was founded by George Eastman in 1888, based on a strategy of selling cheap cameras and making healthy profits on film, photographic paper, and processing chemicals. Eastman brought the formerly arcane practice of photography to ordinary people. As a result, Kodak achieved near monopoly control over the consumer camera and film business and held it until the 1970s. But competition from Japanese rival Fuji, and eventually the displacement of film by digital photography, a realm that Kodak entered late—and about the time that cell phone photography began to displace digital cameras— significantly undermined Kodak's profitability. As a result, in 2012 the company filed for bankruptcy and was saved from insolvency only by selling many of its highly valued patents, for which it received about a half-billion dollars.[1]

Kodak did many good things for Rochester, employing thousands of workers and providing the economic foundation upon which the once very prosperous city rested. George Eastman was a generous philanthropist who supported education, helping to turn the Rochester Institute of Technology into a world-class institution of higher education. The George Eastman Museum houses invaluable film and photographic archives and provides the community with an ongoing stream of first-rate cultural events. But Kodak also left a toxic chemical legacy. Kodak Park (now known as the Eastman Business Park), a 1,200-acre parcel at the northeast corner of the city, where the company's main production facilities were located during most of the twentieth century, is riddled with a bewildering variety of toxic chemicals. In the 1990s, Kodak paid out over $7 million in fines to state and federal environmental authorities. Low-level radioactive waste, the residue of optical lens manufacturing, was buried in a disposal pit at one end of the property. New York State and the federal Environmental Protection Agency have more recently filed claims against the company for toxic silver that it dumped into the Genesee River.

While the company has spent millions of dollars to clean up what is a designated Superfund site, the levels of contamination are so great that it will be a very long time before restoration will be fully completed, if ever. In its bid to discharge itself from bankruptcy, the company set up a $49 million trust fund to continue restoration efforts. When objections were raised by citizens and public officials, including the EPA, as to whether the fund would be sufficient, the company reached an agreement with the state that the Department of Environmental Conservation would pay for cleanup costs between $49 million and $99 million, and that the company and the state would split any costs over that. New York State taxpayers could thus be stuck with a fairly large liability. With this and other legacy liabilities (such as bond commitments and pension agreements) resolved, the company emerged from bankruptcy in 2013 with a new name, Kodak Alaris, and a focus on digital imaging technologies.

In the meantime, health effects attributable to Kodak's history of contaminating Rochester persist. Residents and former workers suffer from high cancer rates, asthma, and other medical problems. The company has shown little interest in embracing liabilities for the health impacts of its various operations.[2] Two hundred thousand square feet of the business park have recently been leased to Columbia Care LLC to establish a medical marijuana growing operation.[3] Ironically, one of the primary applications for medical marijuana is treatment of nausea from cancer chemotherapy treatments.

I pulled my bike out of the car, attached the panniers, tent, and sleeping bag and traveled northward from the city center, on Lake Avenue, which runs along the Genesee River. Along the way, I had the opportunity to observe some of the city's northern neighborhoods, many of which seemed to be experiencing significant challenges. It was taking me longer than I had anticipated, so at one point I stopped to ask, just to be sure I was on the right track. "Just keep going," the man I asked told me. As long as I was headed north, I figured there was no way I could miss Ontario.

When I arrived at the shoreline, the lake appeared, big and blue and beautiful, stretching off to the horizon. The sun was shining. With temperatures in the seventies, it was an ideal day to start a bicycle tour. It's pleasant riding westward from Rochester. While Lake Ontario State Parkway is a four-lane highway with moderate traffic close to the city, it's also very bicycle friendly, with paths winding through the sandy marshland along the lakeshore. They run close to the water, so I experienced bountiful views of the lake, sky, and clouds as they intermingled in the distance. Lots of people were out enjoying the fine weather, on the beach, riding bikes, or simply walking.

For this trip, I had refurbished an old steel-frame Trek730 hybrid cycle. I'd had it for more than twenty years and thought it might make a nice change from the Gary Fisher mountain bike I'd been using. It definitely had a different feel. With its shorter top tube, I felt a little scrunched up, but I was sure that I'd get used to it without too much trouble.

The farther I traveled on the parkway, the more the traffic thinned, until there didn't seem to be any at all. There are no towns abutting the shore, so after Hamlin Beach State Park, apparently there isn't much reason to travel here. In fact, after passing the park, the road starts to seriously deteriorate, with large cracks in the concrete and grass growing up through them. Since it's still a four-lane divided highway, with literally zero traffic, it seemed a bit strange, if not downright surreal. Apparently the state decided at some point that hordes of people would travel along this route on the way to . . . well, where? I guess that's the question. Other than farmland and a wooded shoreline, there doesn't seem much to draw anyone. At some point, then, the state seems simply to have stopped maintaining the road. That was, of course, all fine with me, because it made for great bicycling, with one side of a four-lane highway all to myself. The cracks, while prominent, could be easily avoided.

At Lakeside State Park, the parkway ends, requiring a turn onto Highway 18, a much more typical state highway. It was still a nice flat ride through fruit farms and small villages, but it was a little bit of a letdown to no longer have a highway completely to myself. I didn't have a goal for how far I would ride, because I wasn't completely sure, with the drive to Rochester, what time I would get on the road. But given the ideal conditions, I figured I could make it to Youngstown, which sits just below the right corner where the Niagara River empties into Ontario.

I rode around Youngstown a bit and found that the first motel I tried had a sign on the office door saying no vacancy. I then asked two guys sitting in front of an antique shop in the center of town where I might find a place. They said that there was a bed-and-breakfast, but they thought the owner was away. The only other option was the Ontario House, a somewhat sketchy-looking bar up the street on the corner. The bar owner sometimes rented rooms upstairs. But, they warned me, the place was supposed to be haunted. I couldn't resist that, so I went right over.

It was a classic old bar, in a classic old rooming house, with a classic set of patrons sitting around chatting, playing lotto, and watching TV. No doubt in the era before New York's public indoor smoking ban, the place would have been inundated. I asked the bartender about a room. He told me that only the owner could rent one out, and he was out of town. I said that this was my last hope, because there weren't any other rooms in town, but he was adamant that he couldn't do it. I asked the guys at the antique shop again, and they said it looked like I'd have to ride to Lewiston, which was probably the closest place with a room. They advised me that there was a hotel on the riverfront just on the north end of town. Just take a right-hand turn down a very steep hill. I should have no trouble finding the hotel once down at the river's shoreline.

It was still only about five o'clock, so I figured I'd have time to get there, find a place, and have something to eat before turning in. The quickest route by car is on the Robert Moses Memorial Parkway, which juts off of State Highway 18 northeast of Youngstown at Four Mile Creek State Park, skirts the eastern edge of Youngstown and then goes to Lewiston. A parkway is a limited-access highway, generally four lanes, divided by a strip of grass. The purpose of this one is not clear to me, since it's only about fifteen miles long, starting in a small park and ending in a city of less than twenty thousand people. It seems to have been another one of those state highway projects designed to accommodate the hordes of people who were supposed to flock to state parks on Ontario's shore. But it doesn't seem as though the hordes ever showed up.

It's also a little surprising that they named the highway after Robert Moses. Moses, as head of New York City's Triborough Bridge Authority, transformed the metropolitan landscape, overseeing the building of highways, often against fierce local resistance, to transport commuters from sprouting suburban communities into the urban core. Moses favored automobiles over subways, trains, and buses (and no doubt bicycles). The Long Island Expressway, once known as the "longest parking lot in the world," is a testament to his urban planning philosophy. It's not clear exactly why Moses's name shows up on a parkway on this end of the state, but he did have a hand in promoting New York's extensive parkway system. Perhaps the name was less well known and less controversial here. Part of the Moses Parkway has now, unsurprisingly, been removed due to low usage.[*]

Luckily for me, State Highway 18F hugs the shoreline of the Niagara River, with very little traffic and a bicycle path running along much of it. It turned out to be a great ride, along the bluff that leads down to the wide and fast-running river below. The river's power is palpable. At this point it is somewhat less than half a mile wide, running through the narrow gorge that confines it as it rushes toward its exit into Ontario. The Niagara, thirty-seven miles in total length, begins in Buffalo and drains the water from the four other Great Lakes at a rate of 212,000 cubic feet per second. Having done so for the past twelve thousand years (hardly an eyeblink in geological time), it has eroded away the Niagara Escarpment, over which run the famous falls, moving them upstream a distance of about seven miles, in the process also carving out the gorge, along the edge of which runs the bicycle path.

The river, like much of the Great Lakes watershed, faces various ecological threats, primarily chemical contamination from one of the once most heavily industrialized parts of the United States. I have driven the ten-mile stretch of road that runs from the city of Niagara Falls to Buffalo, and it is lined with industrial facilities of one kind or another virtually the entire way. The infamous Love Canal was an unfinished channel, carved out in the early part of the twentieth century, eventually to become a disposal site for Hooker Chemical Company wastes. At one time, more than seven hundred industrial facilities located on the river dumped 750 million gallons of waste into it every day. Sewer overflows from the cities of Buffalo and Niagara Falls also drain into the river during heavy rainstorms. And even though the hydro power generated from the Niagara Falls facility significantly lowers New York State's greenhouse gas emissions, it results in a 50 to 75 percent loss in water falling over the falls itself, significantly diminishing its intensity. Things have improved over the past thirty years, as both the United States and Canada have taken steps to mitigate the worst forms of chemical dumping, but the legacy of past practices still affects the river's ecological health.

In spite of the problems, the river is still a natural wonder, not only because of its majestic power but due to the more than eighty species of fish that have been identified in its waters. The river corridor has been designated as a globally significant Important Bird Area by Birdlife International. Thirty species of endangered birds are known to either inhabit the corridor or visit it on migratory journeys, including bald eagles and peregrine falcons. The area is also habitat for numerous species of amphibians, mammals, plants, and insects designated as endangered or threatened by the State of New York.[5]

Just north of Lewiston, I took the turn suggested to me by the two antique shop guys. It was a pretty steep descent to the river but a beautiful setting once there. The Barton Hotel and Spa stands near the water's edge. The place looked a little steep for me in terms of price, but I thought I'd at least ask. I walked through French doors, across a large, tastefully appointed lobby, and asked the clerk about a single room. He informed me that there were none, but he had a suite available for $350 dollars. The place was nice but not $350-a-night nice. The ride back up the hill was steep and long enough that I couldn't quite make it, even with all the gears on my bike, so I ended up walking partway. I hate having to do that.

In Lewiston, I asked around a little about a place to stay and was directed to the southwestern edge of town. There I found what looked to be a reasonably clean, family-run strip motel. But a sign on the door said that the clerk would not return until seven thirty, which gave me a little over an hour to kill. I found an Italian Greek restaurant nearby and had a fish fry, sitting in my now pretty skunky bicycle clothes. No one seemed to care much. Afterwards, I rode down Lewiston's main street, Center Street, which features many small shops and restaurants. In fact, Lewiston is known for its restaurants, with over thirty locally owned. It's also been listed by USA *Today,* as one of the "10 Best Small Towns in America." Previously, I had associated Lewiston only with its bridge, one of three over the Niagara River between the United States and Canada. And the one I have taken on many occasions. It was a pleasant surprise to see the city up close.

Of course, given the history of industrialization, it's not surprising to learn that a seven-hundred-acre hazardous waste dump is close by. It's the only active one left in the northeastern United States and contains, among other items, a desk once used by NBC news anchor Tom Brokaw, placed there after it was contaminated with anthrax. Residents have sought relief, and the state legislature has ordered the Department of Environmental Conservation to find ways to distribute toxic substances more evenly throughout New York. But the likelihood of finding another community willing to share in the burden is small, and attempts to impose one would no doubt be met with political resistance and legal battles. In fact, Chemical Waste Management, which owns the facility, wants to expand the site, since it's running out of room. The Model City complex, a name given with perhaps no irony intended, is not the only toxic site in the area. Love Canal is ten miles south, and radioactive wastes from the Manhattan Project are stored at a facility just a stone's throw from Model City.[6]

Lewiston Village, once called simply The Landing, is one of the earliest settlements in western New York, founded in 1720. Previous to that, the area was occupied by the Haudenosaunee, whose roots can be traced back at least five thousand years. The Tuscarora still occupy a small reservation in the town of Lewiston, on the northeastern side of the village. They represent the Sixth Nation of the Haudenosaunee, who were discovered to be linguistic relatives of the larger nation when it expanded its territory southward into what are now the Carolinas in the early 1700s. The Tuscarora had been defeated in a bloody conflict with European settlers in North Carolina that occurred from 1711 to 1715 and were looking for a new territory for settlement.[7] Upon recognizing their historic connections, the Haudenosaunee welcomed them to western New York. During the American Revolution, unlike other Haudenosaunee, such as the Seneca, they sided with the colonists, and after peace was restored, they stayed on this side of the Niagara River. They even defended American fighters during the battle of Lewiston during the War of 1812.[8]

In 1960, the Tuscarora were rewarded for their loyalty to the United States when Robert Moses attempted to seize 1,300 acres of their land—nearly 25 percent of the entire reservation—to create a reservoir for a massive hydroelectric project. The Tuscarora resisted, taking their case to the U.S. Supreme Court, which, in the case of *Federal Power Authority v. Tuscarora Indian Nation,*[9] agreed to grant the government 550 acres of Tuscarora land at $1,500 an acre to create what is now known as the Robert Moses Niagara Hydroelectric Power Station.[10] This may also solve the mystery of how the Moses Parkway got its name.

After a brief tour of Lewiston's downtown, I headed back to the motel I had scouted out. A young woman was behind the desk. The office had hot air blowing into it and seemed to be about 110 degrees. I procured a room and asked about the heat. She said that the air conditioning exhaust was somehow being directed into the office. I didn't quite understand how that all worked, but I was glad to make my payment, grab my key, and finally head to the room. I had had a long day. The room was passable but just barely so. Still, it saved me from having to sleep out on the ground, for which I was grateful.

June 23, 2014

The next morning I found a bakery on Lewiston's tree-lined main drag, which offered excellent homemade pastries and gourmet coffee. Then, on a beautiful and cool sunlit morning, I rode to the Lewiston-Queenston Bridge. Never fond of riding over large bridges, I was somewhat apprehensive. But while there was plenty of traffic, a decent bicycle lane makes for a relatively safe and easy ride over. Once across, there's a steep climb up the Niagara

Escarpment, one of the most prominent geological features of the eastern Great Lakes region. The 550-mile Bruce Trail, reputedly the oldest footpath in Canada, which runs along the escarpment from here to the northern tip of Lake Huron's Bruce Peninsula, begins here. The ride up the hill was grueling, a 240-foot vertical climb, over 1,300 horizontal feet, but the view at the top is absolutely spectacular. The deep river valley cuts through the landscape, and Niagara Falls can be seen clearly a few miles in the distance, with water tumbling down its 190-foot precipice, for the final leg of its journey to the Atlantic Ocean, at which point some of it will eventually return to the St. Louis River, on the western edge of Superior, by the forces of evaporation, wind, and rain, to begin the cycle over again.

The Niagara Parkway borders the river on the Canadian side. The river's edge is tree covered with a bike path from Queenston to Niagara-on-the-Lake, ten miles north. It's a great ride. Along the way, breaks in the trees allow for a view of the distant falls. As you move farther and farther from Niagara Falls and Buffalo, with its industrial infrastructure less visible, it's almost possible to imagine what this area was like before all the development occurred. Of course, without the development, I wouldn't have the advantage of a bridge to get across, much less a bicycle to ride over it.

Niagara-on-the-Lake is on the left-hand corner where the Niagara River empties into Ontario. It's almost directly across from Youngstown, New York, where I was unable to find a reasonably priced motel. The contrast couldn't be greater. Youngstown is much smaller, for one thing, with only about two thousand residents, compared to Niagara-on-the-Lake's fifteen thousand. But that's only part of the difference. Youngstown seems like a pretty typical upstate New York community on the middle to lower end of the economic ladder. Niagara-on-the-Lake is a model of historic preservation and restoration. It is full of beautiful houses, public buildings, museums, and churches. The historic district of Old Town was designated a National Historic Site of Canada in 2003.[11] It's also, understandably, a tourist magnet.

The War of 1812 divided the Canadian communities of Queenston and Niagara-on-the-Lake from their American counterparts across the river, with several battles being fought between them. But they found common ground after that, as both communities became important landing sites for the Underground Railroad. Escaped slaves had to fear slave catchers in the early nineteenth century, individuals who acted as bounty hunters for Southern slave owners. But up until 1850, it was possible for slaves escaping bondage to evade capture in northern nonslave states that resisted their return. With the passage of the Fugitive Slave Act, in 1850, federal law required that slaves be returned to their owners. In response, freed slaves in the North and those fleeing slavery in the South had to make their way to Canada to prevent reenslavement. The Underground Railroad went into full swing.

Given its proximity to eastern slave states and its relatively short width, the Niagara River became a preferred crossing point. Many took the suspension bridge that once ran from Buffalo to Fort Erie, but others crossed via boat, generally on the southern end of the river, where the calmer waters made for safer passage. Escapees fanned out across southern Ontario, mainly settling in metropolitan areas but also disappearing into the Canadian wilderness. Niagara-on-the-Lake was both a transit point and a place for permanent settlement. A small number of African Canadians still reside here, but otherwise the only real evidence of the Railroad's history is the Negro Burial Ground, all that remains of the Calvinist Baptist Church, which from 1849 to 1853 transitioned from being an entirely white congregation to an entirely black one.[12]

After spending some time touring around Niagara-on-the Lake, checking out the historical homes and buildings, including St. Mark's Church (built in 1791), the Old Court House (now a theater), and the McFarland House (the oldest surviving house in the city), I found a park on the northeastern edge of town, at the confluence of the river and the lake. As I sat and drank some juice and ate a muffin, on the left I could see the western shore of Ontario fading off into the distance and marking the path forward.

Highway 87 from Niagara-on-the Lake to St. Catherines cuts

through farmland and vineyards, along the northern edge of the Niagara Peninsula (which is actually an isthmus, that is, a narrow strip of land joining two larger land masses). The waters of Erie and Ontario moderate the climate here, making it one of the best places in southern Ontario for agriculture, especially for fruit. The highway could have used some work, with a very narrow shoulder and broken pavement along the edges, but it's not an unpleasant ride. By taking this path, I avoided the higher-trafficked roads to the south. While the area to east and west of St. Catherines is rural, this end of the lake is densely populated. The so-called Golden Horseshoe begins at Fort Erie (directly across the river from Buffalo) and then stretches through Niagara Falls and St. Catherines. At Hamilton it curves back around through Mississauga and then on to Toronto. The region, while highly agricultural, was also once an industrial hub for both the United States and Canada.

I caught the northern edge of St. Catherines and stopped there for some pizza as it started to cloud up. After that, it was back into farm country, through the little town of Grimbsy. Next is Stoney Creek, which is at the southern edge of Hamilton. Eleven years previously, when I was making my way around the northern shore of Ontario from the other direction, I rode through the city's downtown and the heavily industrialized area that abuts it. The scene struck me as postapocalyptic. The flat highway, with no painted lane markings, was six lanes wide. Traffic was light but consisted entirely of very large trucks, rumbling along with unimaginably heavy payloads. Otherwise, the landscape appeared devoid of most recognizable life-forms. Off to the west, a large operating steel mill spewed smoke, with a large flame shooting up near the smokestack. I've tried to reconstruct my path, with a retrospective look at a map, but I haven't been able to do so in a way that makes the pieces fit. It feels a little like a dream, so maybe it was one. The truth is that I remember enjoying the ride quite a bit. It was so incongruous to be riding a bicycle through such terrain. And I've always been a fan of postapocalyptic cinemas, from *Blade Runner* to *Mad Max*.

This trip through Hamilton was an entirely different experience. I'm not sure whether I missed it before or it simply wasn't there, but an excellent recreation trail runs along the lake east of the city center. The Hamilton area is still highly industrialized, but you wouldn't know it from riding the trail. Given the warm weather, many folks were out walking, in-line skating, cycling, and skateboarding. While you cannot avoid some awareness of the city itself, which is only a mile or two away, it does feel like a protected space, a testament to smart urban planning and wise waterfront usage. Off to the northeast, as the shoreline curves back around, you can see the urban spaces that crowd the edge of the lake, with Toronto's central core farthest up in the distance.

Crossing Hamilton Harbour, though, did present a bit of a problem. The harbor is enclosed by two strips of land, which protect it from storms kicking up in Burlington Bay, but a small canal—the Burlington Bay Canal—connects the two. While the lift bridge over the canal is only about 150 feet long and easy enough to get over, it's getting up to it that's the problem. To get from the trail, which is at the water's level, up to the bridge, requires climbing a fairly long, narrow staircase. There was no way I could carry my fully loaded bike up the stairs, so I had to pull everything off of it. It took three trips to get it all to the top. On the last one, my handlebar light became detached and fell down to the bottom of the hill, so I had to climb back down to get it.

From the deck of the bridge, however, is a terrific view of Hamilton Harbour, which is now surrounded by a bird sanctuary, which gives the impression that it is a protected area, with an insulating buffer between the economic activity in the city and the waters that flow into the lake. But despite the appearance, the harbor is one of the most polluted parts of the entire Great Lakes ecosystem.

In geological terms, it is a relatively recent formation. During the last ice age, glaciers slowly moved southward and scrubbed out and deepened the Ontarian River valley, which is believed to have the same outflow orientation as the current Great Lakes drainage basin. As the ice advanced, it cut off the water's exit through the current St. Lawrence outlet, forcing the water into the Mississippi River valley. As the melting ice retreated, it remained trapped in the Ontario Basin, creating a much larger lake, known as Lake Iroquois, which drained through the Mohawk River near Syracuse, into the Hudson, and then to the Atlantic Ocean. Eventually, the ice retreated enough to create an opening through the St. Lawrence River valley. The weight of the massive 6,500-foot ice sheets, had, however, depressed the earth's crust to the point that water now flowed westward, turning the lake into an Atlantic Ocean bay. The bedrock slowly rebounded, starting in the southwest, moving toward the northeast, following the same path as the ice's retreat. The southern shore has now mostly rebounded, but the northern shore of the lake, especially the northeastern tip, is still undergoing this process. As it has done so, at a rate of about one foot per century, water levels have risen on the southern and western lakeshores. The formation of Hamilton Harbour has been part of this process, filling with water as the northeastern end of the lake has returned to its preglacial elevations.[13]

Since the harbor doesn't have a major river to flush its waters out into the lake, the high levels of pollution that have been discharged into it have tended to collect there. When the ship canal was dredged, however, it widened the waterway between the harbor and Lake Ontario, allowing a greater rate of inflow and thus a greater flushing rate. Of course, that has meant a greater pollution load in the lake as a whole, and Hamilton Harbour itself still remains heavily polluted.[14]

Once over the bridge, the waterfront trail continues and becomes a path that takes you through Burlington and Oakville, Hamilton's well-kept northern suburbs. Lakeshore Road is flat and well maintained, with a wide bike path marked on the side of the road. I considered stopping for the night in Oakville but decided to push on through.

At one point, Lakeshore Road turns right and briefly disappears into Southdown Road, as the forward path is blocked by an oil refinery. This seems to mark a kind of boundary between the leafy suburbs to the south and the edge of Mississauga, a large industrial city that lies on the southern end of Toronto. As I rode through one intersection, I was cut off by a large truck pulling right to negotiate a left-hand turn. Did I run a red light without realizing it? Did he not see me? I wasn't sure, but it was a close call. He pushed me into the curb. I hit my rim pretty hard, but the damage appeared to be minimal.

Mississauga, is the sixth largest city in Canada. While most of its growth is attributable to its proximity to Toronto, it also has its own identity, with a well-defined city center. But I stuck to the Lakeshore Road, which cuts south of the downtown and is a long, not particularly attractive commercial strip. The road there is a four-lane highway with no shoulder. I wasn't that far from Toronto, but it was getting a little late, so I looked for a place to stay. I found a passable strip motel on the highway. It certainly wasn't fancy, but it was clean. The owner was very formal but also very accommodating. After checking in and showering, I went out for food and ended up in a sports bar. The people next to me were drinking heavily and talking quite loudly. The place was chock-full of large, flat-screen TVs. The scene reminded me why I am not particularly a fan of sports bars. I ordered the free-range chicken burger, which wasn't very tasty. After that, I went back to my room and soon fell asleep. It had been a long day. I'd ridden from just north of Niagara Falls nearly to Toronto. While it was easy riding on a flat road with little wind, it was only my second day of riding, and my body hadn't entirely adjusted to eight to ten hours on a bike.

June 24, 2014

I was up early for the ride through Toronto. I didn't see much reason to spend a day there. I've been to Toronto several times, and it's a wonderful Canadian city: prosperous, modern, sophisticated, multicultural. But given my familiarity with it, it didn't seem necessary to spend time there this trip. However, riding through it was unavoidable. Out of Mississauga and closing in on Toronto, there's signage for a cycle trail, but it was difficult to tell whether it was a roadside path or whether there was one along the lakefront. A couple of times I rode down to the lake, looking for a dedicated bike path, only to be disappointed. Still, the ride was tolerable at street level, and a few miles south of the city there's a clearly marked path that is away from the main road. It is a little difficult to follow, sometimes traversing the streets of suburban neighborhoods and sometimes through grasslands that border the lake. At one point, I took a wrong turn and ended up in a sandy area known as Humber Bay Park, which spills into the lake as a sandy delta of Mimico Creek. I ended up at a dead end on the water's edge, but while it was a mistake, it turned out to be a propitious one, in that it gave a great lakeside view of Toronto's city center just a couple of miles to the north.

A little bit farther along, the path split off into different sections again in a way that I found confusing. I stopped to check my map, and as I did so, another cyclist stopped to help with directions. At this point, the city looms up ahead as you approach the border of downtown, passing near a three-hundred-foot wind turbine, the first in North America to be sited within a major urban center. Owned by the WindShare Cooperative, it was also the first community-owned wind turbine in Ontario. After rounding the turbine, the lakefront curves around, allowing a panoramic view of the city as it spreads out along the lake.

As I was taking in the view, the same cyclist who had given me directions previously, who introduced himself as Jake, came up alongside. He said that the city center was all torn up because they were extending the trail system through it. Eventually there would be nice new bike path, but in the meantime it was a nightmare. He said that if I stuck with him, he could guide me through the city. That sounded wonderful. As we were riding, a woman, Emily, came up alongside, and she joined us as we made our journey through midtown Toronto, across construction sites, along sidewalks, following the signs that were the bike path's detour. It was quite the maze and fairly bumpy in places. Jake said it literally destroyed his other bike.

As we rode past the capital complex, Emily peeled off to get to her office. When were almost at the end of the detour, Jake, a true good Samaritan, said he had to get to work and took off back the other direction, at which point he had led me through the entire downtown. Now I was back on an open highway, which had plenty of room for bikes. There I was able to pick up another bike path that took me along the lake, past Asbridges Bay, where ice was once collected for Toronto residents, until the water became too polluted to use it, and then on the boardwalk, along tree-lined Woodbine Beach, and into the residential neighborhoods that reach out to the eastern edge of the city proper.

Once past the city's edge, the path leads through Toronto's eastern suburbs. These continue for about thirty miles and are far from bicycle friendly. It gets hillier, and it started to look like some serious rain might be on the way, but that was not the main problem. The problem was that the area is, well, suburbia: Ajax, Pickering, Whitby, and Oshawa are indistinguishable from one another, at least as they appear from Highway 2, the main drag. While I am sure that there are nice residential areas away from the highway, populated by interesting people, living meaningful lives, from the perspective of a casual observer on a bike, the area is defined by fast-food joints and strip malls. The curbed street, with no bicycle path, forces a cyclist into traffic. The contrast to the older suburbs in the south that I had ridden through is enormous. While they are often intermixed with industrial facilities of various kinds, they are much more attractive and strike a casual observer as more livable. But from the looks of things, the eastern side of the city is where all the growth and development is headed.

When I rode the northern shore of Ontario ten years ago, I went from east to west. About twenty or thirty miles east of Oshawa, I went into a store to grab some water and noticed that the lights were out. I didn't think too much of it, because it was quite a hot day and I thought the owner might be trying to save money on electricity or just make it seem cooler. As I approached the city, I realized that I'd need some cash, so I went to an ATM in one of the little towns, probably Belleville, although I don't have a clear recollection at this point of exactly where I was. What I do remember is that the lights were out in the machine, and it wasn't working. At that point, it dawned on me that there was no electrical power, and we might be experiencing some kind of blackout. A woman was standing on the sidewalk as I left the bank. I mentioned to her the problem with the ATM, and she said that there was a power outage through a large area of southern Ontario and the northeastern United States.

Then she answered the question that had immediately leaped to mind, given the two short years since 9/11: "It's not terrorism," she said. I have to admit I was somewhat relieved to hear that, but that did not solve the problem of what to do, given that there was no power and I was running out of money, with little chance of getting any more until the lights came back on. I didn't have much choice except to keep riding. I noticed Darlington Provincial Park on the map, and I thought it might be best to head there. I stopped at a gas station/convenience store to ask for directions. The three or four people there were very chatty, given that everyone wanted to talk about the blackout. No one had any real information about it, but they did give what turned out to be accurate directions to the park.

When I arrived, I was told that it would be no problem pitching a tent, but the showers weren't working, because they relied on electricity. I paid my last twenty bucks and found a place near the water's edge, with a clear view of Toronto about twenty miles to the west, curving around along the shore. I took some soap and swam out into the very warm water to wash the sweat off. As the sun went down, I could see the shadow of the darkened city under the moonlight. It was quite something to see a major North American city without electricity, fading in the darkness, off in the distance. It's a scene I have never forgotten.

The next day, I rode through downtown Toronto from east to west. For three blocks the stoplights would be on, and they would be off for the next three, in a checkerboard pattern that repeated itself into the city's center. Cars were lined up at gas stations that had power. By late morning, everything seemed to be restored. I was happy to have been on the road during the outage. Not only was it a bit of an adventure, but I didn't have to sit around my house, waiting in the darkness for the electricity to come back on, worrying about such mundane matters as opening the refrigerator too many times

The 2003 Northeastern blackout was the second most widespread in history. Eight eastern and midwestern states were affected in some way—Michigan, Ohio, New York, Pennsylvania, Massachusetts, Delaware, Rhode Island, and New Jersey— plus the entire province of Ontario. Fifty-five million people in the United States and Canada lost power. Hard to imagine as it may be, the whole problem began when an overloaded power line rubbed against a tree branch, causing what's called a "flashover." The ensuing power surge would usually cause only a localized blackout, but the software system designed to alert operators to the problem failed to function, so they didn't attempt to bring the system back into balance. When that occurs, the system becomes destabilized and starts to shut down. In the end, Ohio's FirstEnergy was found at fault for failing to keep trees near its transmission lines properly pruned and for failing to diagnose the problem as it ricocheted through the system.

This time around, I had intended to stop at Darlington Provincial Park again. But it was about twenty miles out of the way to the south, so I thought I'd keep going, even though the sky was threatening rain. A mile or two after Oshawa, traffic thinned, and I was back in farmland. It felt great to be away from the suburbs. Highway 2 has a decent shoulder here, and there was very little traffic. The moderate hills lead to hilltops that allow great views of open landscapes. I kept thinking that I would stop, but I felt good so decided to continue on to Port Hope.

A few miles outside of the small village, a car stopped in front and signaled to me. The driver offered to let me rest up and have a drink at his bed-and-breakfast. I was out in the middle of nowhere and didn't have any intention of stopping, but I appreciated the gesture, although I got the distinct impression that he was trying to pick me up. As I chatted with him, I realized that about a dozen mosquitos had landed on my arms and legs. "Gotta go," I told him, which allowed for a quick and amicable departure.

As I approached Port Hope, the clouds were thickening, and I heard thunder. I tried to hurry, but I was also tired after a fairly grueling day. The village runs from the top of a hill downward toward the lake. I had no idea about accommodations, so I asked someone on the street about a place to stay. He seemed a little strange and somehow not entirely in touch with things, but he advised me that there was a bed-and-breakfast along the street and a hotel with lions on the front if I turned right at the bottom of the hill. I decided to go for the lions.

The lions were out in front of the Carlyle Inn Hotel and Bistro. It's a beautifully restored nineteenth-century hotel. I walked through the entrance just as it started to pour, so one way or another I was committed if a room was available. I was a little worried about the price, given that this was Canada and given my experience in Lewiston, when I was offered a $350 room. I talked to Kate, the waitress, working behind the bar. She said I could go look at the rooms, as the owner was out for the moment. I went to the third floor and opened the door to find a beautifully restored and very tastefully decorated room. The place was amazing and about as different from my usual accommodations as I could imagine. Kate told me that a single room would cost $120 Canadian, which I thought was a very fair price, considering. I waited at the bar until the owner, Dave, came back from wherever he was. He told me to bring my bike around to the back door, where they put it in the kitchen. He then helped me take the gear off and carry it into the large first-floor room that he had available. It would certainly be difficult to complain about the service.

Dave said he'd taken over the place in 1989. The building was originally constructed as a bank in 1857, was converted to a residence and doctor's office in 1882, and then became a residence and dairy in 1927. It was turned into the Carlyle restaurant in 1986, at which point Dave and his wife, Jeanne, bought it and began the restoration that eventually created the Inn Hotel and Bistro.

After I cleaned up, I went back to the bar/restaurant for what turned out to be a four-course gourmet dinner, which I ate while chatting with Kate. I was the only one in the bar area, although there were other people scattered in different rooms. I didn't mind flirting with Kate as I drank craft beer and ate dinner. She had grown up in Port Hope and lived just a couple of blocks away from the hotel. She said that the inn was a huge draw for people from Toronto on the weekends. While it was quiet on a Tuesday night, it would be packed starting on Thursday night through the weekend. Lucky for me, I showed up on a weeknight. Kate said that there was an excellent local theater in town and plenty of other tourist activities in the area. I felt like I'd hit the jackpot: beautiful hotel, great dinner, and pleasant conversation.

The next morning, as I watched the local news, I saw that a tornado had been spotted in a Toronto suburb the day before. While I'd experienced a little rain, I'd avoided heavy weather, another bit of good luck. I'm not completely sure what to do if you are caught in a tornado while riding a bicycle. The Bicycle Bis website recommends heading toward a ditch and covering up your head, since flying debris, falling power lines, and lightning are the biggest threats, and hoping that the gully you are lying in doesn't fill up with water.

I bicycled through central Mexico during the rainy season once. Huge cloudbursts would open up in the afternoons, during which I would try to find shelter, not always successfully. I noticed motorcyclists would simply get off their bikes and stand up straight in their rain gear until the storm had passed, a practice that probably made as much sense as anything. City streets would fill up with four or five inches of water, due to poor drainage. Not wanting to wait until the water cleared, I would ride through, hoping like hell that I wouldn't hit something that would wreck one of my rims. One thing about touring around on a bicycle, you learn that while inclement weather might be a nuisance and result in some discomfort, it's very unlikely to endanger or kill you. It adds to the challenge and, if approached with the right attitude, to the fun of the experience.

June 25, 2014

I decided the next day to try to make it to Kingston, which would be a one-hundred-mile ride over moderately hilly terrain. It was overcast when I started, but it wasn't raining, and there was no rain in the forecast. Once away from Toronto, this side of the lake is sparsely populated and rural, not unlike the northern shore of Lake Erie. Highway 2 cuts through the small towns of Cobourg, Colborne, and Smithfield.

Cobourg sprang to life in 1867 when the Cobourg Peterborough railway was constructed. It became known for its production of ore tipping cars, which could be tilted upward on one side to slide iron and copper ore from the train cars onto awaiting barges for transportation to the many steel mills that were sprouting up along the lake's shorelines. The highway moves away from the lakeshore at this point, as it makes its way through Brighton, the starting point for the Murray Canal, which opened in 1889, allowing ship traffic to avoid the longer journey around Prince Edward Peninsula.

Next is Trenton, which is at the confluence of the Trent River and the Bay of Quinte. The bay constitutes a jagged strip of water that separates Prince Edward Peninsula from the Ontario mainland. I crossed a bridge at the center of town over the Trent River, which is the starting point for the Trent-Severn Waterway. The waterway runs from here to Georgian Bay, making it possible to travel via water from the southeastern end of Lake Huron to Lake Ontario, covering a distance of about two hundred miles. The only alternative route is to travel west through Georgian Bay, from there south through Huron to Detroit, across Lake Erie from west to east, up through the Welland Canal near Buffalo, into Lake Ontario's westernmost end, finally traversing from there to points east. In other words, the waterway cuts out more than a thousand miles of otherwise necessary travel. That being said, it's not exactly a straight path as it snakes around through several lakes and rivers, which have been connected with a series of canals, many of which have locks. Moreover, the waterway was never wide or deep enough to accommodate the larger Great Lakes freight carriers. As a result, by the time of its completion in 1920, it had become irrelevant to the industrial-scale shipping that began to mark Great Lakes commerce. It is now used mostly by motorboaters, canoeists, and kayakers.[15]

Near the village of Shannonville, I was a little confused at an intersection, unsure which road was Highway 2. As I stopped to check my map, a man stopped his car and asked if I was OK. "Sure," I said, "just wondering which direction to go." He gave me several options, all of which would keep me moving eastward, and informed me that his passion was cycling. "I retired fifteen years ago," he said, "and cycling is my life now." He knew every road in the area, had biked all of them, and provided incredible detail about each. Highway 2 was fine with me, though, so I decided to just stick with it.

A few miles later, my forward progress was stopped at a train crossing. With a bicycle it's of course possible to pull up to the tracks to get a good look at the train. This was a long one, and I waited some time as oil tanker car after oil tanker car rolled slowly by. Likely this was oil that had been fracked out of the Bakken oil fields in North Dakota. And it was a train probably not much different from the one that derailed in Lac-Mégantic, Quebec, killing forty-two people and destroying half the downtown. Bakken oil is the world's most combustible, primarily because it contains more volatile gases than other kinds of crude. According to the most widely used vapor index, Bakken oil is about 30 percent more volatile than North Sea oil, which is next highest on the list, and 50 percent more volatile than Saudi oil. Given the risks involved, serious questions have been raised about transporting this kind of oil via tanker car, but there's really no other way to move it. The oil companies would no doubt favor a pipeline, but opposition to pipelines has become increasingly fierce. The protests at Standing Rock, initiated by Sioux water protectors and supported by a large coalition of activists, including military veterans, brought international attention to pipeline safety issues. Pipelines are susceptible to leakages and sometimes explosions. The impact of Canadian firm Enbridge's 2010 pipeline rupture in the Kalamazoo River required a billion-dollar cleanup, and the environmental havoc it created is still being felt.[16] In truth, there probably is no completely safe way to control or transport such highly combustible materials. At the very least, communities along its transportation pathways should be alerted to the potential disasters to which they might be subjected, tracks should be properly maintained, and conductors should obey safe driving practices.[17] But that still may not be enough.

By the time I reached Napanee, a small city at the mouth of the Bay of Quinte, originally settled in the late eighteenth century by British loyalists, I was really starting to feel the ride. But I was determined to make the additional twenty miles to Kingston. It was a tough slog though, one of many long days on the bike on this trip. As I got closer to Kingston, I starting to perk up in anticipation of resting up a little, until I noticed a long and quite steep hill leading into the outskirts of the city. Well, at this point I had no choice but to ride up it. Encountering a long, steep, and unexpected hill at the end of a long day's ride tends to happen more often than you might expect, although I have never been able to figure out why.

After yesterday's luxury accommodations, I decided to opt for a cheap strip motel on the outskirts of the city. I figured I could ride, walk, or take the bus into the center. The place I chose seemed to be providing housing for some construction workers. Several were coming and going in and out of their rooms in work clothes. An affable woman at the desk gave me a good price at fifty dollars. "Cyclists' discount," she informed me.

As I walked my bike toward the room, one of the workers walked up and said he wanted to take a look at it. He asked about my trip. He said he was from L.A. and used to mountain bike with famous people, L.A.-level famous. He loved mountain biking, even though he was a big guy. He said he had a big bike. He remarked that my bike must be very expensive, which made me just a little nervous for some reason. And the truth is that it is not an expensive bike. I explained that it was almost twenty years old and moderately priced when I bought it new. He noted that even though it was a hybrid, it might work for mountain biking. I said that might be true, but I didn't use it for that. "No," he said, "Man, you're a *road* rider," and the way he said it struck me as quite funny. At that point, any trepidation that I harbored about him completely evaporated.

I had ridden through Kingston ten years earlier but hadn't stopped, so I wanted to check out the town. I asked the woman at the motel's front desk about buses. She didn't seem to know much about the schedule but directed me to a bus stop up the street. After I showered, I walked to it and asked a young man there, apparently waiting for a bus, who had to remove his earbuds to hear me, if he knew anything about how the buses ran. I assumed there was one that would take me downtown. He was helpful and explained which number was for the express. It was about seven kilometers, a little farther than I had anticipated, and farther than I wanted to walk at this point. It was $1.75 for a one-way ride. I had enough change because, of course, Canadian lower-denomination dollars are coins. I was ready. It seemed like a long wait.

I started chatting with an older guy at the stop, who explained to me where to get off the bus at the city center. Kingston was seeming to be a pretty friendly place. When the bus finally showed up, I got on but was having trouble with the readout for the ticketing machine. It had a number for the amount inserted and also for the amount owed, but it was confusing. I was sure I had enough money when I got on the bus, but the readout wasn't showing what I'd put in. The bus driver said, "Don't worry about it. Just give me what you've got." I said, "I'm from out of town. I was pretty sure I put in enough money." The driver said, "You probably did. I trust you." Nice bus driver.

When I sat down, the older guy began to talk about football, both the Canadian and American versions. He was a huge fan. He went on to tell me about a number of great American football players that started out in the Canadian league. I wasn't even sure there still was a Canadian league, but he assured me that there was and went into some detail regarding who was good nowadays.

He was extremely friendly and showed me where the restaurants were in the center of town and also where to catch the bus back to the motel, which would not be the same place as I was dropped off. He had moved to Kingston from Toronto a number of years ago, and he obviously loved his adopted city.

I had an excellent dinner at a Cambodian/Thai restaurant and then headed to the bus stop, stopping in between at a little bar for a beer. Sitting there, I began chatting with the person next to me, Albert, a rather large man, who began extolling the difference between Canada Day, which was coming up, and Saint-Jean-Baptiste Day in Quebec. Saint-Jean-Baptiste Day, he said, was kind of a finger in the eye to Anglo Canada. A key difference was that Canada Day was a family day, with picnics and barbeques, whereas Saint-Jean-Baptiste Day was primarily about getting drunk. He, as it turned out, was French Canadian but had been in Kingston for a while. He'd also lived in Milwaukee, while he was in college, for a summer job that involved selling security systems. It was a scam, he explained, because potential customers were told that the system was free if they put a sign in their yard, but once they agreed, it turned out there were monthly surcharges that added up to about forty dollars. He still managed to sell a fair number but felt somewhat guilty about it in retrospect.

When he went out to take a cell phone call, I started chatting with his friend, Jonathan. It turned out that they had been in the Canadian military together and that there was a base in Kingston. The second guy worked for the Canadian military intelligence service. His large friend was a geophysicist who worked for a company that analyzed fracking-related data. They would compile the information and then sell it to the gas companies or to regulators. Since they were independent of each, their information was considered solid and unbiased. This led to a broader conversation about fracking.

New York, at this point, the result of actions of Governor Andrew Cuomo, had put fracking on hold while health studies were being compiled about its impacts. I supported a ban and told Jonathan the reasons why. Primarily, I didn't want to see the industrialization of the upstate New York landscape. Jonathan, while pretty supportive of the process, agreed that what I alluded to would happen. He said in Texas they had made a huge mess, with trash everywhere.

When I got home, I did a little research on Saint-Jean-Baptiste Day and learned that Albert had been essentially correct. Celebrations of Jean Baptiste (or John the Baptist) in France were common in prerevolutionary France, and in Canada can be traced back to the seventeenth century. But in 1834, a French Canadian nationalist and newspaper publisher, Ludger Duvernay, along with some colleagues, attended a celebration of St. Patrick's Day in Montreal. From this germinated the idea that the French, like the Irish, should have a patriotic celebration of their national heritage. Duvernay took it as his mission to turn Saint-Jean-Baptiste Day into that celebration and worked tirelessly to do so. French Canadians embraced it, organizing parades, lighting bonfires, and setting off fireworks in celebration. Pope Pius X even designated Saint-Jean-Baptiste as the patron saint of French Canadians in 1908. And in 1977, it became a recognized statutory holiday in Quebec.[18] My research did not reveal any references to high levels of alcohol consumption, but neither did it rule it out, so I will have to take Albert's word on that one.

June 26, 2014

I was up early for the ride through Kingston. I wanted to catch the eight thirty ferry to Wolfe Island, and then to the United States. I had the choice of the ferry or riding to the Thousand Islands Bridge, just south of Alexandria Bay. I'd been over the bridge before, when I went across in 2003. And I'd ridden to Alexandria Bay on my first solo bicycle tour in the early 1900s. I didn't feel the need to experience it again. On the other hand, I'd never been across on the ferry, so while I suppose it was technically cheating to miss the very eastern end of the lake on a circumnavigation, I didn't feel particularly guilty about it.

It was about a four-mile ride into town, downhill most of the way, on a beautiful, sunny morning as Kingston was waking up.

I couldn't find anyone at the ferry terminal, so I rode up to a guy sitting in his car to find out where to buy tickets. "It's free," he said. "Great," I responded. "Is this the line?" "If you're on a bike, you just ride up to the front over there." I had about forty minutes to kill, so I went to a nearby Tim Hortons and had my usual bagels, orange juice, and coffee.

It was a quick ride to Wolfe Island, with Kingston receding in the background. The island is named after British general James Wolfe and is included as one of, in fact the largest, of the Thousand Islands, an archipelago scattering downward from the St. Lawrence into Lake Ontario. Some of the islands are quite small. In fact, to be counted, one needs to have an area of only a square foot. Nearly two thousand have met the criterion. Wolfe Island was originally called Ganounkouesnot, or Long Island Standing Up, by the indigenous Mohawks who once inhabited the area.

After I landed, I wondered if the ferry leaving from the other side traveling to the United States would be timed so as to catch the cars that were exiting from this side. I'm not sure why I thought this, but it made sense to me at the moment. So I decided I would have to book as fast as I could to catch it. The distance sign on the road leading from the terminal said "10." I figured that I could do it in forty-five or fifty minutes if it wasn't too hilly. The ride turned out to be mostly flat through deserted farmland. There was no traffic on the road at all. Nice riding on a warm sunny day. Sooner than expected, I saw what looked to be water. I was a little confused. Had my speed increased that much, given the shape I'm in from my daily treks? But there was no way, really, I could have ridden ten miles so fast. Then it occurred to me, I was still in Canada, and it was only ten kilometers.

I could see the ferry about halfway across as I arrived, so I thought I'd timed things pretty well, although probably completely by accident. When the ferry arrived, though, the captain got off, jumped on his bike, and said he'd be back at ten fifteen, forty-five minutes later. So I had some waiting to do. I sat on the dock in the sun and ate some trail mix, as I watched the ferry captain ride his bike to a nearby house, hop on a riding lawn mower, and proceed to mow his lawn. Nice work if you can get it. While waiting, I thought I would use the portable potty, but it was so full of disgusting bugs I decided to wait. At ten fifteen, my bike and three cars were loaded onto a ferry that was quite a bit smaller than the first one. The charge this time was two dollars. Welcome to the United States of America.

Back in the United States, I rode out of the village of Cape Vincent, a picturesque town of about twelve hundred people. From there I rode through the hilly farmland of Ontario's eastern tip to Dexter. The coastline here looks as though it's been shredded, so as to create the numerous bays and inlets and the innumerable islands, large and small. Small streams and some rivers—the Chaumont, the Perch—cut through the hilly landscape, emptying into the lake before it in turn flows into the mouth of the St. Lawrence River. The area constitutes the counterpoint to Duluth, which I had previously ridden through, twelve hundred miles west, which sits on the western tip of Lake Superior. Here, as in so much of the Great Lakes region, French, British, Native American, and American histories intermingle in astonishingly complex ways. Champlain landed just across the lake in Kingston. And the French missionaries Father Chaumonoit and Father Dablon were in the area in 1655, attempting to convert the Onondaga people, one of the then five nations of the Haudenosaunee Confederacy.

The British gained control after the French and Indian Wars, which began in the late seventeenth century and ran into the mideighteenth century. The conflict began in Europe as a response to the growing power of Prussia, but it evolved into an early version of a world war as European powers, primarily the British and French, battled for control of colonial empires across the globe. The impacts of these wars cannot be overstated. The British gained control of North America but at a staggering cost that led to a fiscal crisis. The crown responded by raising taxes, taxes seen as onerous and unfair in the American colonies, creating resentments and setting the stage for future rebellion. During the course of the war, the British expelled the French Acadians from what are now Canada's Maritime Provinces, and many of them eventually settled in Louisiana.

At Dexter, the road drops due south along the lake's southeastern edge and runs near Sackets Harbor, an important site for a later war, the War of 1812. Because it was at a protected location on the southern edge of Black River Bay, it became the major shipyard for the American Navy during the war. The British attacked it twice. The first battle, which was the first engagement between American and British forces, was fought in 1812 on the lake. American forces successful repelled the British warship *Royal George*. In 1813, the British landed an invasion force, joined by Native American fighters, which successfully attacked the village of Henderson Bay. But the Americans reorganized and prevented the British from overtaking Sackets Harbor, and they eventually withdrew on naval vessels.

The village continued to prosper as a center for shipbuilding through much of the nineteenth century, and the first Great Lakes steamer was constructed there. The stately and well-preserved nineteenth-century homes that line the streets are a testament to the prosperity that once marked what for a brief period of time was the third largest population center in New York State.

The road became hillier and hillier as I skirted the edge of the Tug Hill region, on the southwestern side of the Adirondack Mountains. This is snowbelt country. Western winds that blow across Ontario have plenty of opportunity to capture moisture before dropping it over the colder land mass on the eastern side. Watertown, a moderate-sized city just east of here, gets about a hundred inches a year. Up on Tug Hill, it's even heavier, given the colder temperatures that kick in at the higher elevations. There snowfall averages are as high as two hundred inches a year.

The ride on Highway 3 south along the eastern rim of Ontario runs through an unpopulated part of New York State, one of the least populated lakeshores on the American side. There are few villages, and much of the lakefront is turned over to wildlife refuges and state parks. It's an ideal area to cycle, with New York's wide shoulders and very little traffic. The hills can be a little challenging, as this is also the hilliest part of the Ontario shoreline, but they also yield the benefit of great views of the rolling landscape. At Port Ontario, the road crosses the Salmon River. The view is spectacular; the river splits and widens to about a hundred yards before its entrance into the lake. True to its name, the Salmon is one of the great recreational fishing rivers in the Ontario region, with plentiful salmon and trout. The native Atlantic salmon, a landlocked variety, were an important food source for the Haudenosaunee who originally inhabited the area. These were completely fished out by the white settlers from both the river and Lake Ontario by the late nineteenth century. Nowadays, the Salmon River is stocked with nonnative Chinook and Coho salmon, originally imported from the Northwest.[19]

I continued on what turned out to be about an eighty-mile ride south and then west to Oswego, following the southeastern elbow of the lake. At Oswego, I booked a motel room at the top of the hill on the eastern edge of the city. As in Kingston, the rooms seemed to be mostly occupied by construction workers. They had all left their boots in the hall in front of their rooms. I showered and then walked down the rather pedestrian-unfriendly shopping strip and grabbed a completely forgettable dinner at a nameless restaurant chain. I was tired and dead asleep by nine thirty.

June 27, 2014

This was a quick trip around Ontario, something that I had intended, given that I'd ridden much of it at least once before, and some of it twice before. Plus, it's a flat ride for the most part, and I had optimal conditions for much of it. Mostly it was warm and sunny, and the wind, even as I traveled westward, was quite tolerable. Given that, today would be the last day of my Great Lakes riding experience. I had only about seventy-five miles to go to get back to Rochester, and I knew that the terrain eventually flattened from here. The weather continued to be accommodating, but the prediction was for things to heat up into the eighties or nineties by later in the day.

Most of the ride was on 104, a major highway with moderate traffic and a good shoulder. Leaving Oswego, I passed by the entrance to Oswego University, once known as the State University of New York at Oswego. I spent a week there in junior high school at a debater's camp. At the time, the campus was practically brand-new. Nelson Rockefeller, a legendary Republican governor of New York, launched a building spree in which he expanded campuses of existing state schools and built new ones. His vision was to provide an affordable college education to everyone in New York State who qualified, and to make campuses geographically accessible in the more rural parts of the state. The satellite schools had been upgraded from teachers colleges to liberal arts institutions with a wider array of programs. Rockefeller even took an interest in designing new campus buildings, which were modernist, sometimes successfully so, sometimes not. I. M. Pei was hired to design many of the buildings on the Fredonia University campus. Albany's campus is sometimes derided for its ugliness. Owego's campus, on the shore of Ontario, integrated older buildings with newer ones in tasteful ways.

But what I most remember about my week in Oswego was not the campus but all the dead fish that had washed up on the shoreline. One night a group of us went down to the water to build a bonfire and sing folk songs, but the stench was so great that we had to end the event early. Those were in the dark days for the Great Lakes. As a kid, l lived about twenty miles from Erie, which I was told never to swim in because of the sewage. And here what I encountered were piles and piles of dead fish. The fish kills resulted from algae blooms, in turn caused by industrial pollution and municipal waste. Sometimes the algae was so thick that it affected wave action, further compounding the problem of oxygen depletion. One author named Ontario the "algal bowl."[20] These experiences soured my relationship to the lakes themselves for years afterward. I thought of them as toxic cesspools.

In a way, these tours around the lakes have reestablished a connection that could have been made long ago. In college I hitchhiked to California, taking the Trans-Canada for the first part of the trip. When one driver dropped me off in what seemed to be the middle of nowhere on the north shore of Superior, I told him I had food but was a little worried about water. He said that wouldn't be a problem. I could just drink the water from the lake. I found this concept to be astounding. Drink the water from one of the Great Lakes? I couldn't imagine it. But when I made my way to the shore, the water was as clear as a bell, so I drank it and suffered no ill effects.

My guess is that those who grew up, even in the 1960s and 1970s, on or near Superior or northern Lake Michigan had an entirely different conception of the Great Lakes than I did. But such is the vastness of the waters and the region, that on one end you could drink the waters, and at the other, algae blooms were so thick that the waves couldn't break. And, of course, the general flow is eastward, so contaminants are picked up along the way. And there were (and still are) many large industrial cities between here and the northwestern edge of Lake Superior. Things have improved in Ontario since the bad old days of huge fish die-offs. By the mid-1990s, phosphorus and nitrogen levels, important indicators of ecological stress and key causes of man-made eutrophication, a form of early lake death, had dropped significantly. The clarity of the lake's waters had improved, and native species had begun to return.[21] Partly this is due to water pollution control regulations and the construction and upgrading of municipal waste treatment plants. Many of these policy improvements were the result of the Great Lakes Water Quality Agreement, signed by the United States and Canada in 1972, with the promise of improving the ecological health of all the lakes. But improvements in Ontario are also due to the decline of industrial production in the cities that line the eastern end of the lake.

In spite of these positive developments, there are still numerous threats to the lake. The Great Lakes Environmental Assessment and Mapping Project has published a map featuring each of the Great Lakes, with cumulative environmental stress levels marked in colors from red to green to blue, red being the most stressed and blue being the least. Superior is almost entirely blue, with a couple of small red patches near Duluth and Thunder Bay.

Huron is also mostly blue but a somewhat lighter shade, indicating somewhat higher overall stress levels. Michigan is red all along its edges but mostly light green, indicating moderately high stress levels. Erie is about 40 percent red, the rest being mostly orange, with a few light-green patches in the middle. Ontario is about 75 percent red, with a few orange patches in the middle. In other words, it remains the most ecologically stressed of all the lakes.

Chemical contamination of Ontario continues to be a problem due largely to the persistence of toxins, such as PCBs and dioxin, in any ecosystem. Over 150 invasive species of various kinds, both flora and fauna, threaten the lake. But Atlantic salmon now have a toehold in the lake, and under the commonly accepted measures of swimming, fishing, and drinking, things are looking up. Most beaches are safe most of the time. Many cities on the lake use it as a source of drinking water. And it's OK to eat the fish, as long as you don't make it your main source of protein and are reasonably careful about which fish you consume.[22] Such is the state of "the beautiful lake," the English translation of "ontario," the name attributed to the lake by the Haudenosaunee people, who arrived at its pristine shorelines some five thousand years ago.

There is a series of short, sharp hills coming out of Oswego. I remembered these from the first solo bike trip that I did in the early 1990s. At that time, I rode from Ithaca to Fair Haven Beach State Park and camped. It seemed like such a grueling ride, but it was only about sixty-five miles, which wouldn't phase me these days, even though I am twenty-five years older. At that time, I was riding in the other direction, but I still remember these hills.

About thirty miles outside of Oswego, things really do start to flatten. At one point, I stopped to check the map because I was thinking about cutting up along the water for the last part of the ride into Rochester. As I was doing so, someone came up behind me on a bicycle and startled me. It turned out to be Matt. He asked if I was OK, and I said yes, that I appreciated the concern, but I was just doing a map check. He said he'd just finished an incredibly grueling trip from Toronto across Vermont and New Hampshire to the coast of Maine, and now he was on his way back. He looked to be about my age, maybe a little older. I found something about his manner to be a little off-putting, as though we were engaged in some kind of competition. If we were, he had clearly won, because riding east to west across Maine, New Hampshire, and Vermont takes you through some of the most mountainous areas on the East Coast.

He was on his way back to Toronto, now on a path that I had taken just a few days ago. We chatted a bit longer, discussing the relative merits of staying on the main highway or cutting up along the lakefront. He was going to stay on 104, because he wanted to get back. I wasn't in that much of a hurry and told him I'd likely take the scenic route. And then he took off at very quick pace, and before long he was over the horizon.

A little bit later, another cyclist pulled up. This time it was Mark, who was on a high-end Trek carbon-fiber road bike. I liked Mark better. He asked some questions and then told me that the Lake Road bridge across Irondequoit Bay was out, so I'd be better off going south to catch the Erie Canal bicycle trail to Rochester. He asked me if I knew the other cyclist, and I said I'd just met him. I thanked him for his advice, and then he took off. I got the impression he wanted to tell Matt the same thing.

I skipped the obvious turnoff north based upon Mark's advice, but after a few more miles, I checked the map and saw that his suggestion would lead me a number of miles out of my way. Too many. I thought I'd just stay on the main highway until near the city limits and then take an alternative path cutting south of the bay, thus missing the Highway 104 bridge. I stopped for a drink, because it was really starting to heat up.

As I guzzled the first of two generic sports drinks I'd bought, Matt pulled up. I didn't quite understand how he'd ended up behind me, but I didn't ask. We again discussed which route to take, and I told him my plan. This time we chatted for longer, and I warmed up to him. He turned out to be an ultramarathoner, which explained his competitive streak. He said that he felt like he was running too much, so he decided to start biking long distances. But now he was worried that the biking would mess up his running. He was considering kayaking as a potential alternative. I realized that he wasn't trying to impress me. These questions were clearly a central defining feature of his life. After a few minutes, I took off, and I assumed he would try to catch me. But before long was my turnoff, and soon thereafter I was approaching greater Rochester and into the land of malls and narrow shoulders.

About twenty miles east of Rochester, Highway 104 becomes a major four-lane arterial. Fortunately, 404 splits off, running on a parallel path south and eventually cuts southward around the bay. The first suburb I encountered was the town of Webster. Daniel Webster spoke to members of the Whig Party there in 1837. The Whigs grew in opposition to Andrew Jackson, favoring more economic centralization, protectionism, and industrial development. They also objected to Jackson's policies of forcing Native people off their eastern lands and exiling them to the west. The most infamous of these removals was the Trail of Tears, which involved the forced relocation of the Cherokee from Georgia to Oklahoma and defied a Supreme Court ruling. On the day that Webster spoke in this area, he apparently focused on economic policy. The audience was so impressed that they decided to name their town after him.

From Webster onward, it's suburban sprawl until the city limits. At one point, however, the road touches up against the southern tip of Irondequoit Bay, which offers a nice view to the north. Unfortunately, the heavy traffic on a busy highway tends to detract from the experience. The bay is an artifact of the last ice age, when the Genesee River was rerouted a few miles to the east. Glaciers scoured out what had been the river's mouth and left a four-mile-long gash through what are now Rochester's eastern suburbs.

East Rochester is clearly one of the more distressed parts of a distressed city. I noticed empty lots where there had once been houses, cordoned off by pieces of wood sticking up out of the ground. Apparently, this was how the city responded to the vacant spaces once the houses were torn down. At one point, as I was riding by a bus stop, a young man yelled, "Hey, you're about to get hit by a bus." He startled me, and the bus did, in fact, get pretty close as it cut me off on its way to a bus stop. Then the guy yelled, "No, man, they can't hit *you*." He was kidding around in a friendly way, but I can imagine I seemed a little strange riding through the neighborhood in bicycle clothes with loaded panniers and camping gear bungeed on to my back rack.

I arrived at the end of the street that I was on, Ridge Road, At that point, the Genesee River blocks the path forward. I wasn't exactly sure which way to turn. As two guys in a car rounded the corner, I pointed left and yelled out, "Downtown?" "Yes," they both yelled back and nodded vociferously. As I turned to look more carefully, I could see the buildings of Rochester's downtown center.

I cruised into town while trying to get my bearings. I knew that my parking garage was in the center of the city but wasn't exactly sure where. I should have mapped it out better. As I continued riding south, another guy on a bike pulled up and told me that he really liked my back rack. "Very sturdy," he said. I told him that it was a standard rack and pretty cheap to buy. His was attached to the seat post and seemed a bit wobbly. I explained that he'd need eyelets to install one like I had. When we stopped at a stoplight, I quickly checked to see if he had them. He did. I told him it wouldn't be a problem for him.

Soon enough I was in the city center, where there are a number of public parking garages located. I had remembered that mine was designated for the public library. I found a garage that listed the library along with some other offices and the Marriott Hotel. I went into it, looking for my car. It didn't look familiar at all. The cars were parked on the inside of the lane, whereas I distinctly remembered my car being near the street side. It was also much larger than the one I had remembered. I rode around for a while and saw nothing that looked familiar. I was starting to get a little worried. I spent about ten minutes doing this, when I spotted a garage attendant and thought I'd tell him I couldn't find my car. He told me that I couldn't bring a bike into the garage, and there were signs saying so. He was really angry, angrier, I'd argue, than the circumstances warranted. I can see why they wouldn't want to have kids riding their bikes around in a parking garage, but I thought that if someone just pulled one from their car and rode out with it, that couldn't cause much harm or danger.

I tried to deflect his anger by getting his sympathy about my plight. "I'm completely lost and not sure what to do." But it wasn't working. In the meantime, a second attendant came over to see what was up. He was much more helpful and said that the garage was huge and that it would help if I knew which entrance I had parked near. I said all I remembered was something about the library. He said, "Maybe it's the library garage on Court Street." Court Street, which sounded familiar. He told me to go out and down the block and I'd see it. "Once you get there, just ride right in," he told me, as the other attendant looked on pretty unhappily. In any event, I took off down the street, found the garage, did, in fact, ride right into it, found my car, packed up, hooked in my iPod, and drove home.

Conclusion

Future Prospects

Finishing my circling of the Great Lakes generated a sense of accomplishment and satisfaction, but I also felt something of a letdown. Where to now? My immediate impulse was to start over again. Because, really, what else would provide a comparable experience? After some consideration, I decided that I should give it some time before I repeat the journey. Twenty years from now, when I turn eighty, seems about right. By then, as a retiree and Social Security recipient, I should have the luxury of time to do all the lakes in one fell swoop, rather than breaking them up over a series of summers. Of course, much can happen between now and then that could interrupt such a plan, such as, for example, physical infirmity or death. Barring that, if I survive and am physically intact enough to repeat this venture, I can't help but wonder what the region that I encounter will be like.

The geological foundations of the Great Lakes region will have shifted, if at all, only minutely, as wind and weather slowly wear away at soft sedimentary rock, with virtually no impact on the ancient exposed outcroppings of the Canadian shield. The earth's crust at the far eastern end of Ontario will continue its slow rebound to the elevation that it had reached before the advent of the last ice age, and will have risen two or three inches, ever so slightly pushing the lake's water westward into Hamilton Harbour. The Niagara Escarpment will still stretch from Lake Ontario's shoreline up through the Bruce Peninsula, although a few inches may be shaved off, nudging it eastward, at Niagara Falls. Unlike the West Coast, which can lurch several inches along a fault line in a few short seconds, with potentially tragic consequences, the underlying structures of the Great Lakes region are quite stable, at least from a human perspective. There's a certain comfort in that.

At the human level, change is likely to occur. What about the cities in this region? Will they continue to wither, or will their prospects improve? Chicago will, of course, still be Chicago, an economically and racially divided city, hopefully with diminished violence, but with the wealthy still working in the Loop's skyscrapers and living along the North Shore and in leafy suburbs that ban bicycle traffic. The manufacturing centers in the south, from Gary through East Chicago, will be unlikely to return to their former glory. The middle classes and poor will be scattered through various parts of the city, struggling to hold onto what they have, trying to keep a toehold in an increasingly globalized and digitalized postindustrial economy. Chicago is a city whose connections to the larger national and international economies are so large and diverse that, while it will probably experience ups and downs, it is unlikely to experience an extended period of complete collapse.

As for Detroit, Cleveland, Buffalo, and other long-suffering industrial hubs? In 2013, New York governor Andrew Cuomo announced a plan to invest one billion dollars in the Buffalo–Niagara Falls region. A large chunk of the investment involved subsidizing a solar panel production facility for investor Elon Musk's firm Solar City. But the Buffalo Billion, as it was called, became mired in charges of political favoritism for providing sweetheart contracts to Cuomo campaign contributors. And Solar City looked increasingly to be a shaky investment. Still, the wide-ranging nature of the one-billion-dollar program did benefit some sectors, especially health care and the University at Buffalo, and it evidenced a renewed interest in a part of the state long neglected by Albany.[1] Given this, perhaps on my next ride through the area, I will see more wind turbines on Lake Erie, along with banks of solar arrays. I'll have pedaled through a revitalized downtown, stopping at a farmers market, where growers will display produce from urban gardening, and will stop for lunch at one of the new restaurants started by a members of the city's increasingly diverse population.

Detroit declared bankruptcy in 2013. With the city on the verge of complete default, Governor Rick Snyder appointed an emergency manager, Kevyn Orr, giving him responsibility for finding revenue sources and negotiating with creditors. At one point, Orr floated a plan to sell off the art collection in the Detroit Institute of Arts as a way to raise funds. The city and museum officials balked but eventually agreed to turn the institute over to a nonprofit corporation, in return for funding from several foundations to the tune of $800 million. Judge Steven Rhodes eventually gave the bankruptcy court's blessing to the deal. Detroit is now able to pay its daily bills and is attempting to deal with its crumbling infrastructure. Some economists believe that collapse can provide the basis for true revival, as happened in Europe and Japan after World War II. The cleared ground provides for a fresh start. In Detroit, the ground has not been completely cleared, since long-term debt obligations for public employee pensions will haunt the city's finances for years, but, as with Buffalo, there is some evidence that Detroit is on the rebound, as it tries to re-create itself as America's first "post-post-apocalyptic" city.[2] Quicken Loans founder Dan Gilbert, a native of Detroit, is committed to investing in the downtown area. JP Morgan Chase has offered $200 million in investment. The Michigan Central Station has new windows, as part of a major restoration project, and, well, the streetlights are starting to come back on.

As of this writing, in the summer of 2016, Cleveland was preparing to host the Republican National Convention with the hopes of bringing attention to a steady revitalization that has been occurring in this other historic rust-belt community. Of the cities that I encountered in my travels, it seemed to be the most vibrant, having turned its economy to culture, sports, education, tourism, and health care. Unfortunately, given the fracturing nature of the Republican Party, the ensuing publicity may do little to bolster the city's image. Too much attention to Donald Trump, perhaps, and not enough to the Rock and Roll Hall of Fame. LeBron James returned to his old team in 2014 and helped to improve it. In 2016 they staged a spectacular comeback against the Golden State Warriors to win the NBA championship, the first time a Cleveland team had won a major sports championship since 1964. And that same summer, the Cleveland Indians made it into the World Series, although they ultimately lost to the Chicago Cubs three games to four.

Likely, when I travel through these parts in twenty years, the cities will look pretty similar to what they are now, perhaps with some improvements, but with the same nineteenth- and early-twentieth-century buildings and city centers dominating the downtown areas, and acres of single-family houses stretching off into suburban housing developments, in ways that have defined them since the mid-twentieth century.

Apart from the people and their economic prospects, the biggest problems that this region and the lakes themselves will face are ecological. No doubt, the legacies of chemical contamination will still be present, in spite of efforts to clean up at least some of them. Chemical residues are mired in the lakebeds and ensconced in innumerable landfills throughout the entire region, and they will continue to slowly leach their contents in the lakes' watersheds. But the unlikelihood of a resurgence of an industrial economy bodes well for lessening the contamination load in the long run. Cross-national attempts to protect and rehabilitate the lakes may also lead to various, at this point unforeseeable, improvements. With some luck and a consistent commitment to restoration efforts, indigenous salmon, lake trout, and sturgeon may continue to increase their numbers.

The biggest threat to continuing environmental improvements in the Great Lakes is climate change. Milder winters are already having an effect on annual ice coverage. Lake Superior may experience virtually ice-free winters two decades from now, with shorter periods of ice cover on the other lakes as well. Less ice means more evaporation, and in turn shallower lakes. Lake Erie could drop as much as four or five feet due to climate change. Lower levels and warmer waters exacerbate existing problems, intensifying the impacts of high phosphorus levels, fostering algae blooms, and providing more hospitable conditions for invasive species, such as zebra mussels. Warm-water fish species, such as smallmouth bass and yellow perch, may thrive, but cold-water species, such as lake trout, will be stressed by these changes. Some bird species, such as yellow-headed blackbirds, will go into decline.[3]

The politics between the United States and Canada will hopefully not deteriorate in any significant way in the next twenty years. It's difficult to imagine something that would change them. In a worst-case scenario, climate refugees will start to move into southern Canada as parts of the United States become less habitable, straining relations between the two countries. Crossing the borders on a bicycle will hopefully still be a relatively easy operation.

Bicycles will still be bicycles. Perhaps some new innovations will be introduced, something along the order of disc brakes or carbon-fiber frames, but the basic design is unlikely to be significantly altered. I may be riding a recumbent at that point, as a concession to age, but only if I can master the one that I've got by then, for which there is no guarantee.

With some luck, some of the people that I encountered will still be out there riding, walking, or driving around. Mike will likely still be in Alpena. Maybe he did get that job at the NOAA Museum, and he'll have two or three new bicycles and a brood of cats, and will have read them the complete works of William Shakespeare, Charles Dickens, and James Baldwin. "One *n*" Denis, the engineer from Sault Ste. Marie, will be well into his nineties, but I imagine that he will be making maps for the local bike club and tooling around on Sunday morning while his wife is at church, with a zillion gizmos attached to his latest bicycle purchase. Maybe I'll run into barber Ron-Da-Man standing in front of a completely refurbished Michigan Central Station. Or maybe I'll see him inside, where I will buy him a latte at the Detroit Coffee Company's newest location. I'll be looking forward to seeing all of them and meeting many others along the way.

Notes

Introduction

1 Thomas Stevens, *Around the World on a Bicycle* (Charleston, SC: Nabu Books, 2010).

2 David Herlihy, *The Lost Cyclist: The Epic Tale of an American Adventurer and His Mysterious Disappearance* (New York: Houghton Mifflin, 2010).

3 Anne Mustoe, *A Bike Ride: 12,000 Miles around the World* (London: Virgin Books, 2010); Frosty Wooldridge, *Bicycling around the World: Tire Tracks for Your Imagination* (Bloomington, IN: AuthorHouse, 2004); Barbara Savage, *Miles from Nowhere: A Round-the-World Bicycle Adventure* (Seattle: Mountaineers Books, 1985).

4 Josie Dew, *Long Cloud Ride: A Cycling Adventure across New Zealand* (New York: Little, Brown, 2008); Dew, *A Ride in the Neon Sun: A Gaijin in Japan* (New York: Hatchet Group, 2012); Dew, *Slow Coast Home: A 5,000-Mile Cycle Journey around the Shores of England and Wales* (New York: Little, Brown, 2003); Dew, *The Wind in My Wheels: Travel Tales from the Saddle* (New York: Little, Brown, 1993).

5 Erika Warmbrunn, *Where the Pavement Ends: One Woman's Bicycle Trip through Mongolia, China and Vietnam* (Seattle: Mountaineers Books, 2006).

6 Mark Jenkins, *Off the Map: Bicycling across Siberia* (Emmaus, PA: Modern Times Books, 2008).

7 Andrew X. Pham, *Catfish and Mandala: A Two-Wheeled Voyage through the Landscape and Memory of Vietnam* (New York: Picador, 2000).

8 Dervla Murphy, *Full Tilt: Ireland to India with a Bicycle* (London: Eland Publishing, 1965). Murphy's adventures did not end with this tour. In fact, she has written twenty titles on her travels to Tibet, Cuba, Ethiopia, and Palestine, among other places. Now in her eighties, she continues traveling and writing much as she always has.

9 John Seigel Boettner, *Hey Mom, Can I Ride My Bike across America?: Five Kids Meet Their Country* (Houston, TX: Sbf Productions, 1990).

10 T. E. Trimbath, *Just Keep Pedaling: A Corner-to-Corner Bike Ride across America* (Bloomington, IN: iUniverse, 2002).

11 Bicycle Touring, http://bicycletouringpro.com/blog/books-about-bike -touring/. Accessed June 10, 2014.

12   See, for example, Tom Ambrose, *The History of Cycling in Fifty Bikes: From the Velocipede to the Pinarello: The Bicycles That Have Shaped the World* (Emmaus, PA: Rodale Books); David V. Herlihy, *Bicycle: The History* (New Haven, CT: Yale University Press, 2006); James Witherell, *Bicycle History: A Chronological Cycling History of People, Races, and Technology* (Cherokee Village, AR: McGann Publishing, 2010).

13   Jerry Dennis, *The Living Great Lakes: Searching for the Heart of the Inland Seas* (New York: St. Martin's Press, 2004).

14   Mike Link and Kate Crowley, *Going Full Circle: A 1,555-Mile Walk around the World's Largest Lake* (Duluth, MN: Lake Superior Port Cities, 2012).

15   Harvey Botzman, *'Round Lake Erie: A Bicyclist's Tour Guide* (Rochester, NY: Cyclotour Guide Books, 2004); Botzman, *'Round Lake Ontario: A Bicyclist's Tour Guide* (Rochester, NY: Cyclotour Guide Books, 2010); Botzman, *'Round Lake Huron: A Bicyclist's Tour Guide* (Rochester, NY: Cyclotour Guide Books, n.d.); Botzman, *'Round Lake Michigan: A Bicyclist's Tour Guide* (Rochester, NY: Cyclotour Guide Books, n.d.); Botzman, *'Round Lake Superior: A Bicyclist's Tour Guide* (Rochester, NY: Cyclotour Guide Books, n.d.).

16   Wayne Grady, *The Great Lakes: The Natural History of a Changing Region* (Vancouver, BC: Greystone Books, 2007).

17   Helen Hornbeck Tanner, ed., and Miklos Pinther, cartographer, *Atlas of Great Lakes Indian History* (Norman: Oklahoma University Press, 1986).

18   Donald R. Hickey, *The War of 1812: A Forgotten Conflict* (Champagne-Urbana: University of Illinois Press, 2012); Alan Taylor, *The Civil War of 1812: American Citizens, British Subjects, Irish Rebels, and Indian Allies* (New York: Vintage Books, 2011); Richard Buel, *America on the Brink: How the Political Struggle over the War of 1812 Almost Destroyed the Young Republic* (New York: Palgrave Macmillan, 2004); Hugh Howard, *Mr. and Mrs. Madison's War: America's First Couple and the Second War of Independence* (New York: Bloomsbury Press, 2012).

19   Race Across America, http://www.raceacrossamerica.org/raam/raam2.php?N_webcat_id=22.

20   Jack Kerouac, *On the Road* (New York: Penguin, 1999); William Least Heat-Moon, *Blue Highways: A Journey into America* (Boston: Little, Brown, 1999).

21   Robert M. Pirsig, *Zen and the Art of Motorcycle Maintenance: An Inquiry into Values* (New York: Bantam Books, 1985).

Lake Huron

1   Elaine McDonald and Sarah Rang, *Exposing Canada's Chemical Valley: An Investigation of Cumulative Air Pollution Emission in the Sarnia, Ontario Area* (Toronto: Ecojustice, 2007), http://www.ecojustice.ca/publications/

reports/report-exposing-canadas-chemical-valley/attachment. Accessed January 5, 2015.

2   U.S. Environmental Protection Agency, "What Are the Major Threats Impacting the St. Clair–Detroit River Ecosystem?" *State of the Great Lakes 2005,* http://www.epa.gov/solec/indicator_sheets/st_clair_ecosystem.pdf. Accessed August 15, 2014.

3   Olde Town Historic District, http://www.oldetownporthuron.com/.

4   "Lake Huron," *Wikipedia,* http://en.wikipedia.org/wiki/Lake_Huron. Accessed August 17, 2014.

5   Wayne Grady, *The Great Lakes: The Natural History of a Changing Region* (Toronto: Greystone Books), 21–25; "Lake Huron Facts and Figures," Great Lakes Information Network, http://www.great-lakes.net/lakes/ref/huronfact .html. Accessed August 21, 2014.

6   323 U.S. 214 (1944).

7   Donald I. Dickmann, "Forests and Forestry from an Historical Perspective," in *Michigan Geography and Geology,* ed. Randall Schaetzl, Joe Darden, and Danita Brandt (New York: Custom Publishing Co., 2009), 614–25.

8   Ibid.

9   Shaetzkm, Darden, and Brandt, *Michigan Geography and Geology,* Appendix B, 658–71.

10 "Race Across America," *Wikipedia,* http://en.wikipedia.org/wiki/Race_ Across_America#Records. Accessed August 21, 2014.

11 Michael Schumacher, *November's Fury: The Deadly Great Lakes Hurricane of 1913* (Minneapolis: University of Minnesota Press, 2013).

12 Mackinac Bridge Authority, The Mackinac Bridge, http://www.mackinac-bridge.org/.

13 Donald R. Hickey, *The War of 1812: A Forgotten Conflict* (Champagne-Urbana: University of Illinois Press, 2012); Alan Taylor, *The Civil War of 1812: American Citizens, British Subjects, Irish Rebels, and Indian Allies* (New York: Vintage Books, 2011); Richard Buel, *America on the Brink: How the Political Struggle over the War of 1812 Almost Destroyed the Young Republic* (New York: Palgrave Macmillan, 2004); Hugh Howards, *Mr. and Mrs. Madison's War: America's First Couple and the Second War of Independence* (New York: Bloomsbury Press, 2012).

14 Grady, *The Great Lakes,* 117–32.

15 Phil Bellfy, *Three Fires Unity: The Anishnaabeg of the Lake Huron Borderlands* (Lincoln: University of Nebraska Press, 2011), 131–36.

16 Ibid.

17 Sault Ste. Marie, Ontario, *Wikipedia,* http://en.wikipedia.org/wiki/ Sault_Ste._Marie,_Ontario#Economy.

18 Basil Johnston, *Ojibway Heritage* (Lincoln: University of Nebraska Press, 1976), 28–29.

19   Thomas E. Lee, "The First Sheguiandah Expedition, Manitoulin Island, Ontario," *American Antiquity* 20 (October 1954): 101–11.

20   Robin Brownlie, *A Fatherly Eye: Indian Agents, Government Power, and Aboriginal Resistance in Ontario, 1918–1939* (Toronto: University of Toronto Press, 2003), 4–8.

21   C. F. M. Lewis, "Late Quaternary Events on Manitoulin Island," in *The Geology of Manitoulin Island*, ed. Bruce A. Liberty and Frank D. Sheldin (Michigan Basin Geological Society, 1968), 60–70.

22   Walter M. Tovell, "The Entrance to Georgian Bay (The Drowned Portion of the Niagara Escarpment)," in *The Geology of Manitoulin Island*, ed. Liberty and Sheldin, 71–76.

23   Peter E. Kelly and Douglas W. Larson, *The Last Stand: A Journey through the Ancient Cliff-Face Forest of the Niagara Escarpment* (Toronto: Natural Heritage Books, 2007), 9–15.

24   Ibid., 31–40, 41–51, 53–66, 17.

25   Bruce Trail Conservancy, http://brucetrail.org/. Accessed June 12, 2105.

26   John Spears, "Wind Turbines Churn Rural Voters," *thestar.com*, http://www .thestar.com/business/article/1051515—wind-turbines-churn-rural-votes.

Lake Erie

1   Herbert F. Hern, *The Portage Trail: A Historic Indian Portage from Lake Erie to Lake Chautauqua*, http://www.prendergastlibrary.org/?page_id=5328. Accessed May 21, 2015.

2   Helen Hornbeck Tanner, ed., and Miklos Pinther, cartographer, *Atlas of Great Lakes Indian History* (Norman: University of Oklahoma Press, 1987), 54–56.

3   Edward Wellejus, *Erie: Chronicle of a Great Lakes City* (Woodland Hills, CA: Windsor Publications, 1980), 19–27.

4   David Frew, *Shipwrecks of the Great Lakes* (Charleston, SC: History Press, 2014), 43–48.

5   Harvey Botzman, *'Round Lake Erie* (Rochester, NY: Cyclotour Guide Books, 2004).

6   "22 Most Segregated Cities in America," *Business Insider*, http://www .businessinsider.com/most-segregated-cities-in-america-2011-3?comments_ page=2&=#5-cleveland-ohio-has-a-726-white-black-dissimilarity-score-18.

7   Maumee River, *Wikipedia*, http://en.wikipedia.org/wiki/Maumee_River. Accessed May 22, 2015.

8   Ibid.

9   Continuous casting involves creating large slabs of metal that can then be rolled for use in finished products. It replaced the ingot system, which generates small bars of metal.

10   Jonathan Haeber, "Exploring a Defunct Detroit Steel Factory," Bearings, http://www.terrastories.com/bearings/. Accessed January 13, 2013.

11   Charlie LeDuff, *Detroit: An American Autopsy* (New York: Penguin Books, 2013), 40.

12   Scott Martelle, *Detroit: A Biography* (Chicago: Chicago Review Press, 2012), 232.

13   W. R. Ferrand, *The Glacial Lakes around Michigan* (Lansing: Michigan Department of Natural Resources, 1967).

14   Wayne Grady, *The Great Lakes: The Natural History of a Changing Region* (Vancouver, B.C.: Greystone Books, 2007), 23–24.

15   Ibid., 235–36.

16   "Water Quality," Lake Erie Water Keeper, http://www.lakeeriewaterkeeper.org/lake-erie/water-quality/. Accessed May 25, 2015.

17   Tanner and Pinther, *Atlas of Great Lakes Indian History,* 30.

18   "'Here's Johnny!': The Shining Scene Is Scariest in Movie History, Claims Study," theguardian.com, October 31, 2013, http://www.theguardian.com/film/2013/oct/31/the-shining-heres-johnny-scariest-movie-scene-jack-nicholson. Accessed May 25, 2015.

19   "Niagara Movement (1905–1909)," BlackPast.org, http://www.blackpast.org/aah/niagara-movement-1905-1909. Accessed June 26, 2015.

20   Danny Hakim, "The Peace Bridge (What Else?) Sets Off a Cuomo-Canada War," *New York Times,* May 27, 2013, http://www.nytimes.com/2013/05/28/nyregion/cuomo-and-canadians-in-verbal-war-over-peace-bridge.html?pagewanted=all.

Lake Michigan

1   Port Washington, Wisconsin, http://www.visitportwashington.com/. Accessed May 26, 2015.

2   Carl Ziller, *History of Sheboygan County, Wisconsin, Past and Present,* vol. 1 (Sheboygan, WI: S. J. Clark Publishing Company, 1912), 70.

3   "European Revolutions of 1848," Immigration in America, November 11, 2011, http://immigrationinamerica.org/487-european-revolutions-of-1848.html. Accessed June 3, 2015.

4   Robert L. Kaiser, "After Twenty-Five Years in the U.S., Hmong Still Feel Isolated," *Chicago Tribune,* December 27, 1999, http://articles.chicagotribune.com/1999-12-27/news/9912270079_1_hmong-impact-of-welfare-reform-barriers. Accessed May 27, 2015. Richard Straka, "The Violence of Hmong Gangs and the Crime of Rape," *Crime and Justice International* 76, 19 (September/October 2003), http://www.cjimagazine.com/archives/cji5c60.html?id=690. Accessed May 27, 2015.

5   "Hmong in Wisconsin," *Wikipedia*, https://en.wikipedia.org/wiki/Hmong_
     in_Wisconsin. Accessed February 14, 2017. Jeremy Hein, *Ethnic Origins:
     The Adaptation of Cambodian and Hmong Refugees in Four American Cities*
     (New York: Russell Sage Foundation, 2006).

6   "Sputnik Crashed Here," RoadsideAmerica.com, http://www.roadsideamerica
     .com/story/12959. Accessed May 28, 2015. "Sputnikfest," Rahr-West Art
     Museum, http://www.manitowoc.org/index.aspx?nid=1109.

7   Hjalmar R. Holand, *Old Peninsula Days* (Minocqua, WI: Northland Press,
     1959), 135–37.

8   Allan F. Schneider, "Geomorphology and Quaternary Geology of Wisconsin's
     Door Peninsula," in *Wisconsin's Door Peninsula: A Natural History*, ed. John C.
     Palmquist (Appleton, WI: Perin Press, 1989), 32–48.

9   "Door Peninsula," *Wikipedia*, http://en.wikipedia.org/wiki/Door_Peninsula.
     Accessed June 4, 2015.

10   Holand, *Old Peninsula Days*, 73.

11   Carol I. Mason, "Historic Indians of the Door Peninsula," in *Wisconsin's Door
     Peninsula*, ed. Palmquist, 134–46.

12   Wisconsin Initiative on Climate Change Impacts Working Group, *Potential
     Climate Change Impacts on the Bay of Green Bay—An Assessment Report*,
     July 2010. http://www.seagrant.wisc.edu/home/Portals/0/Files/Habitats%20
     and%20Ecosystems/GreenBayAssessmentReport_WICCI_.pdf. Accessed
     June 4, 2015.

13   John Hughes, "When Green Bay Was a Valley: The Au Train-Whitefish-Green
     Bay Spillway," in *Wisconsin's Door Peninsula*, ed. Palmquist, 49–65.

14   Kevin Kincare and Grahame J. Larson, "Evolution of the Great Lakes," in
     Michigan Geography and Geology, ed. Randall Schaetzl et al. (New York:
     Custom Publishing, 2009), 174–90.

15   Alexander Winchell, *The Grand Traverse Region* (Ann Arbor, MI: Dr. Chase's
     Steam Printing House, 1866), 5.

16   Alan F. Arbogast, "Sand Dunes," in *Michigan Geography and Geology*, ed.
     Schaetzl et al., 274–84.

17   These boundaries are, of course, somewhat fungible. Schaetzl et al., "Introduc-
     tion: Defining the State of Michigan," in *Michigan Geography and Geology*,
     1–10.

18   David J. Meltzer, *First Peoples in a New World: Colonizing Ice Age America*
     (Berkeley: University of California Press, 2009), 41–48.

19   William Lovis, "Between the Glaciers and Europeans: People from 12,000
     to 400 Years Ago," in *Michigan Geography and Geology*, ed. Schaetzl et al.,
     389–99.

20   George L. Cornell, "Native Americans," in *Michigan Geography and Geology*,
     ed. Schaetzl et al., 402–11.

21   Jeff Alexander, "Grand River Series: Waterway's History Is One of Ruin
     and Recovery," *Muskegon Chronicle*, July 11, 2010, http://www.mlive.com/

outdoors/index.ssf/2010/07/grand_river_series_waterways_h.html. Accessed June 10, 2015.

22   "Stuart Padnos Finds Beauty in Odd Shapes with His Metal Sculptures," *hollandsentinel.com*, October 8, 2008, http://www.hollandsentinel.com/article/20081022/NEWS/310229853. Accessed June 29, 2015.

23   Mick Dumke, "Benton Harbor: After the Fire," *Colorlines Magazine*, March 22, 2005, http://www.thefreelibrary.com/Benton+Harbor%3A+after+the fire%3B+A+small+riot+in+the+Midwesth+caught...-a0129814339. Accessed June 11, 2015.

24   John C. Hudson, *Chicago: A Geography of the City and Its Region* (Chicago: University of Chicago Press, 2006), 53–55.

25   City of East Chicago, http://www.eastchicago.com/. Accessed June 19, 2015.

26   Hudson, *Chicago*, 151.

27   Ibid., 237.

Lake Superior

1   Steel Plants of North America, https://www.steel.org/~/media/Files/AISI/Public%20Policy/Member%20Map/NorthAmerica-Map2013/SteelPlant_NorthAmerica_AISI_version_June252013.pdf. Accessed May 3, 2016.

2   "History of the Pasty," http://www.hu.mtu.edu/vup/pasty/history.htm. Accessed December 28, 2015.

3   Loriene Roy, "Countries and Their Cultures: Ojibwa," UNICEF USA Official Site, http://www.everyculture.com/multi/Le-Pa/Ojibwa.html. Accessed December 28, 2015.

4   Lon L. Emerick, *The Superior Peninsula* (Skandia, MI: North Country Publishing, 1996), 21–23.

5   Ibid., 77.

6   National Working Waterfront Network, "Transforming Marquette, Michigan's Waterfront with Form-Based Code," http://www2.vims.edu/bridge/water access/case_study.cfm?ID=43. Accessed June 22, 2015.

7   "Lower Harbor Ore Dock History and Inspection Report," Marquette, Michigan, http://www.mqtcty.org/oredock.php. Accessed May 11, 2016.

8   Michigan Tech, http://www.mtu.edu/. Accessed June 30, 2015.

9   Steve Lehto, *Death's Door: The Truth behind the Italian Hall Disaster and the Strike of 1913* (Royal Oak, MI: Momentum Books, 2013), 5–12.

10   Ibid., 13–31.

11   Ibid., 167–80.

12   Duluth, Minnesota, *Wikipedia*, https://en.wikipedia.org/wiki/Duluth,_Minnesota#cite_note-14. Accessed May 11, 2016.

13   Richard Hudelson and Carl Ross, *By the Ore Docks: A Working People's His-*

tory of Duluth (Minneapolis: University of Minnesota Press, 2006), 3–5, 112–18, 271–72.

14   Anita Zanger, *Duluth: Gem of the Freshwater Sea* (Cambridge, MN: Adventure Publications, 2004), 33–39.

15   "Ore Dock," *Wikipedia*, https://en.wikipedia.org/wiki/Ore_dock. Accessed July 1, 2015.

16   Jessica Marshall, "Geology: North America's Broken Heart," *Nature*, December 4, 2013, http://www.nature.com/news/geology-north-america-s-broken-heart-1.14281. Accessed May 10, 2016.

17   "Grand Marais," Visit Cook County Minnesota. http://www.visitcookcounty.com/communities/grand-marais/. Accessed December 30, 2015.

18   Fort William First Nation, http://fwfn.com/. Accessed December 30, 2015.

19   "Our Famous Canadian Goose," Wawa: A Place to Live, http://www.wawa.cc/living-in-wawa/about-wawa/our-famous-canada-goose/. Accessed May 10, 2016.

20   Barbara Chisholm and Andrea Gutsche, *Superior: Under the Shadow of the Gods* (Toronto: Lynx Images, 2001), 90–92.

21   Ibid., 48–62.

Lake Ontario

1   "Kodak," *Wikipedia*, https://en.wikipedia.org/wiki/Kodak. Accessed January 7, 2016.

2   Matthew Daneman, "Kodak Bankruptcy Officially Ends," *USA Today*, September 3, 2013, http://www.usatoday.com/story/money/business/2013/09/03/kodak-bankruptcy-ends/2759965/. Accessed May 18, 2016; Michael I. Niman, "Kodak's Toxic Moments," *Alternet*, May 28, 2003, http://www.alternet.org/story/16030/kodak's_toxic_moments; Steve Orr, "Kodak Taking Steps to Handoff Environmental Concerns," *USA Today*, May 30, 2013, http://www.usatoday.com/story/money/business/2013/05/30/kodak-taking-steps-to-hand-off-environmental-concerns-/2372503/; Department of Justice, U.S. Attorney's Office, Southern District of New York, Manhattan, "U.S. Attorney and EPA Announce Agreement with Eastman Kodak Company for Clean Up of Rochester, New York, Business Park and the Genesee River," March 12, 2014, https://www.justice.gov/usao-sdny/pr/manhattan-us-attorney-and-epa-announce-agreement-eastman-kodak-company-clean-rochester. Accessed May 19, 2016.

3   Nathan J. Lichtenstein, "A Relic of Rochester Industry Reborn," *Reporter Magazine*, December 29, 2015, http://reporter.rit.edu/features/relic-rochester-industry-reborn. Accessed May 19, 2016.

4   "Robert Moses State Parkway," *Wikipedia,* https://en.wikipedia.org/wiki/
     Robert_Moses_State_Parkway. Accessed January 7, 2016.

5   "Niagara River," Buffalo Niagara RiverKeeper, http://bnriverkeeper.org/
     places/niagara-river/. Accessed May 19, 2016; "The Niagara River Corridor
     'Globally Significant' Important Bird Area," The Friends of Times Beach
     Nature Preserve, http://www.friendsoftimesbeachnp.org/niagara-river
     -corridor-globally-significant-important-bird-area.html. Accessed May 19,
     2016. Andrew Reeves, "Cleaning Up the Niagara River," *Alternatives Journal,*
     December 13, 2012, http://www.alternativesjournal.ca/community/blogs/
     current-events/cleaning-niagara-river. Accessed May 19, 2016.

6   Anthony Depalma, "A Toxic Waste Capital Looks to Spread It Around; Upstate
     Dump Is the Last in the Northeast," *New York Times,* March 10, 2004, http://
     www.nytimes.com/2004/03/10/nyregion/toxic-waste-capital-looks-spread
     -it-around-upstate-dump-last-northeast.html. Accessed January 8, 2016.

7   "Tuscarora War," *Wikipedia,* https://en.wikipedia.org/wiki/Tuscarora_War.
     Accessed January 8, 2016.

8   "Tuscarora People," *Wikipedia,* https://en.wikipedia.org/wiki/Tuscarora_
     people. Accessed January 8, 2016.

9   FPC *v. Tuscarora Indian Nation,* 362 U.S. 99 (1960).

10   "Tuscarora Reservation," *Wikipedia,* https://en.wikipedia.org/wiki/Tuscarora_
     Reservation. Accessed January 8, 2016.

11   "Niagara-on-the-Lake," *Wikipedia,* https://en.wikipedia.org/wiki/Niagara
     -on-the-Lake. Accessed January 8, 2016.

12   Underground Railroad Tour, Greater Niagara, USA, http://www.greaterniagara
     .com/driving_tours/underground_railroad_tour.html. Accessed May 19,
     2016.

13   "Lake Ontario," *Wikipedia,* https://en.wikipedia.org/wiki/Lake_Ontario#
     Geology. Accessed May 24, 2016.

14   B. B. Wolfe, T. W. D. Edwards, and H. C. Dutie, "A 6000-Year Record of
     Interaction between Hamilton Harbour and Lake Ontario," *Aquatic Ecosys-
     tem Health and Management* 3 (2000): 47–54, https://sciborg.uwaterloo
     .ca/~twdedwar/reprints-pdf/2000-aehm-wolfe-et-al.pdf. Accessed May 20,
     2016.

15   "Trent-Severn Waterway: The Waterway," *Canadian Geographic,* March 2010,
     http://www.canadiangeographic.ca/travel/travel_magazine/mar10/national_
     historic_sites2.asp. Accessed May 25, 2016.

16   David Hasemyer, "Enbridge's Kalamazoo Spill Saga Ends in $177 Million
     Settlement," *Inside Climate News,* July 20, 2016, https://insideclimatenews
     .org/news/20072016/enbridge-saga-end-department-justice-fine-epa
     -kalamazoo-river-michigan-dilbit-spill. Accessed February 14, 2017.

17   Russell Gold, "Bakken Shale Oil Carries High Combustion Risk," *Wall Street
     Journal,* February 23, 2014, http://www.wsj.com/articles/SB1000142405270
     2304834704579401353579548592. Accessed May 23, 2016.

18   "Saint Jean Baptiste," *Wikipedia,* https://en.wikipedia.org/wiki/Saint-Jean
      -Baptiste_Day. Accessed May 26, 2016.

19   "Salmon River," *Wikipedia,* https://en.wikipedia.org/wiki/Salmon_River_
      %28New_York%29. Accessed May 25, 2016.

20   J. R. Vallentyne, "The Algal Bowl: Lakes and Man," Miscellaneous Special
      Publication No. 22 (Ottawa: Department of the Environment, Fisheries and
      Marine Service, 1974).

21   "Ecosystem Watch: The Status of the Lake Ontario Ecosystem," Great Lakes
      Fisheries Commission, https://www.google.com/#q=current+ecology+
      of+lake+ontario+. Accessed May 26, 2016.

22   EPA Canada, "State of the Great Lakes, 2011 Highlights, An Overview of
      Status and Trends in the Great Lakes Ecosystem," https://www.ec.gc.ca/
      grandslacs-greatlakes/DEA99937-E0B6–4F10–8F0A-993661A2F9CC/
      Highlights%20Report%20E%20130827%20FINAL.pdf. Accessed May 26,
      2016.

Conclusion

1   Jesse McKinley and Vivian Yee, "One Billion Went to Buffalo: Cuomo
     Donors Benefitted," *The New York Times,* May 24, 2016, http://www.nytimes
     .com/2016/05/25/nyregion/a-tangle-of-interests-behind-cuomos-1-billion
     -boon-for-buffalo.html?_r=0. Accessed June 13, 2016.

2   Ben Austin, "Post-Post-Apocalyptic Detroit," *The New York Times,* Jul 11, 2014,
     http://www.nytimes.com/2014/07/13/magazine/the-post-post-apocalyptic
     -detroit.html. Accessed June 9, 2016.

3   Global Warming and the Great Lakes, National Wildlife Federation, https://
     www.nwf.org/Wildlife/Threats-to-Wildlife/Global-Warming/Effects-on
     -Wildlife-and-Habitat/Great-Lakes.aspx. Accessed June 13, 2016.